Lucinda Hancock | Yokuts | 1903

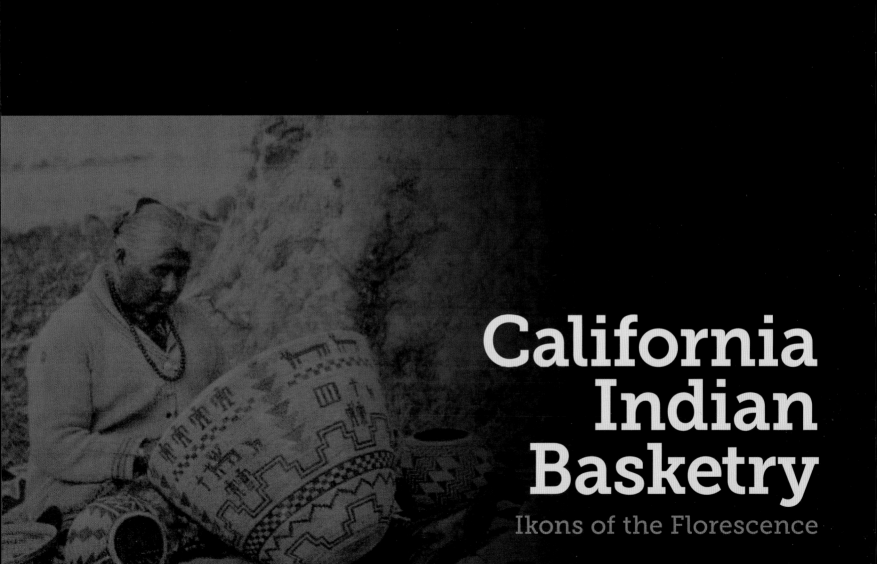

California Indian Basketry

Ikons of the Florescence

California Indian Basketry

Ikons of the Florescence

Wayne A. Thompson
Eugene S. Meieran
Edited by Alan P. Garfinkel

SUNBELT PUBLICATIONS, INC.

San Diego, CA

California Indian Basketry: Ikons of the Florescence

Sunbelt Publications, Inc.

Edited by Alan P. Garfinkel, PhD
Project management by Lorna Johnson
Cover and book design by Kathleen Wise
Production management by Deborah Young
Printed in China

Sunbelt Publications, Inc.
P.O. Box 191126
San Diego, CA 92159-1126
(619) 258-4911, fax: (619) 258-4916
www.sunbeltpublications.com

24 23 22 21   4 3 2 1

Library of Congress Cataloging-in-Publication Data

Names: Thompson, Wayne A., author. | Meieran, Eugene S., author. | Garfinkel, Alan P., editor.

Title: California Indian basketry : ikons of the florescence / Wayne A. Thompson, Eugene S. Meieran, ScD, 2021 ;
  edited by Alan P. Garfinkel, PhD.

Description: First edition. | San Diego, California : Sunbelt Publications, Inc., 2021. |
  Includes bibliographical references and index.

Identifiers: LCCN 2019020126| ISBN 9781941384510 (hardcover : alk. paper) |
  ISBN 9781941384527 (softcover : alk. paper) | ISBN 9781941384589 (deluxe : alk. paper)

Subjects: LCSH: Indian baskets--California. | Indians of North America--Material culture--California. |
  Indian basket makers--California--Biography.

Classification: LCC E98.B3 T49 2021 | DDC 746.41/208997--dc23 LC record available at https://lccn.loc.gov/2019020126

Dedication

There was once a brief moment in time when tiny groups of Native American artists living in what is now California and western Nevada, desperate survivors of events of devastating proportions, blazed like a bright star in the night and created the finest woven baskets in the history of human artistic achievement.

This book is dedicated to those great artists and to the scholars, photographers, collectors, dealers, and descendants who have kept their memory from slipping away unnoticed into the darkness of unrecorded and forgotten history.

Table of Contents

Preface

I believe antique Native American triple-rod and grass-bundled coiled basketry from California's 1890s through the 1940s—a period known as the Florescence (Flowering)—is unsurpassed in beauty and quality by any other basketry ever made. Unfortunately, it is also highly unappreciated by a large percentage of the art-world population! As an aspiring collector searching for knowledge about this highly evolved art form, I was disheartened by the limited amount of information available about these great masterpieces: their history, provenance, and the artists who created them.

There are a small number of informative books on the Florescence Period of California Native basketry, but they either cover a single tribal group in great detail or they lightly cover a wide spectrum of artists and baskets distributed over both time and location. They are filled with a wealth of information derived from exhaustive research and often contain vintage photographs of the weavers—some with their baskets—and there are also some pictures of the masterpiece baskets, but usually they only show low-resolution images in black and white, or if in color, show small images. While such pictures are of high value, they do not contain the rich information that more modern photographic technology can bring to them. Books such as those by Craig Bates, Marvin Cohodas, Frank Latta, Christopher Moser, Pat Kurtz, Eva Slater, Justin Farmer, Brian Bibby, and others were an inspiration for this book, but left many gaps in what I wanted to understand.

This book tries to bridge those gaps. This is not a book on weaving technique—that is very well covered elsewhere—by Ralph Shanks, John Kania, Justin Farmer, and others. Nor is it simply a book of nice photographs. This book was written with the intention of fulfilling three main objectives:

First is to document and show as many of the great Florescence baskets as possible, using modern color photographic methods. Indeed, this was the initial aim of the book, before its scope and impact took hold of us and led to including the next two objectives.

The second objective was to document the finest artists responsible for the Florescence: their tribal affiliations and artistic history. Other books are usually focused on specific localities and tribes and do not cover the full extent of the Florescence.

The third is to give provenance and history to the great pieces by relating specific baskets to the artists using historical records and vintage photographs—often unpublished—in the hands of private collectors and dealers. This desire led to visiting many museum collections and libraries across the country, as well as to private collections and dealer inventories, to gather information.

To that end, here are some statistics. There are 46 major artists whose baskets and history are shown in some detail. There are an additional 15 weavers mentioned but for whom we have not included personal details, but 10 are seen in vintage photographs. There are 15 other weavers known to be exceptional artists, but for whom we have no great basket images. And, because there were many weavers' photographs taken, but without any identification other than their tribal identity, we decided to include a number of unknown weavers' photographs as a tribute to these forgotten artists. Finally, since unlike Pueblo pottery from that same time period, which was often signed by the potter—baskets do not contain signatures, and provenance is only established by historical or photographic records combined with expert analyses. We have included 33 beautiful Florescence baskets, which, unfortunately, have little provenance and cannot be attributed to specific weavers. But these are masterpieces and need to be recognized as such.

We have included 409 basket photographs in color, a number of which we had to have personal photographers go and take pictures because the original photographs were only in black and white or were of extremely poor quality. We show 228 vintage black and white photographs; 77 of the baskets appear in 72 of the vintage photographs, and 31 of the 55 artists are shown with baskets seen in this book. An additional 35 baskets are seen in vintage photographs of historical collections. Of the 46 featured artists, all but nine (Mary Wrinkle, Tootsie Dick, Magdalena Augustine, Lupe Alberras, Mary Smith Hill, Lillie Frank James, Juanna Sands, Ellen Amos, and Mrs. Elizabeth Graham) are seen in the vintage photographs. In all we visited over 50 museums, private collections, libraries, tribal reservations, historical societies, and dealers. There are many basket images included which do not seem to be in any published book or journal; for example, a seventh Lucinda Hancock olla was discovered during writing of this book (Fig. 449)—until then historical documents only listed six of her major ollas.

Time was not our ally. Even though the last of the featured artists passed away nearly a half century before we started the book back in 2007, there are still living descendants as well as friends and acquaintances of many of the artists with personal knowledge and interactions with them. For example, Bob Adams and Jerry Collings were personal friends with a number of artists discussed here. But even so, several collection experts (including Bob who passed away after this

book was started), basket dealer Sandra Horn, Lou Sancari of the National Anthropological Archives of the Smithsonian, basket collector Eddie Basha, and most recently Pat Kurtz, have passed away, thus significantly reducing the number of people with personal knowledge of this great era. Ten years from now, much of this information might not be available outside of the work presented in this book!

As a mineral collector, I wrote a book titled *Ikons, Classics and Contemporary Masterpieces of Mineralogy* (2007) intended as a reference source for collectors aspiring to build great mineral collections. As a collector of fine Pueblo pottery, I also was introduced into the world of Native American art. But when I looked at Florescence baskets and saw the tremendous amount of effort required to weave a masterpiece basket (months and years versus days or weeks to make a fine pottery olla), I decided that this art form had to be documented before it was too late. Thus, this book.

There is one important caveat to explain. As a collector in fine mineral specimens, I had to be extremely careful in making sure that the mineral specimens I collected were legally "pure"—neither stolen or taken from forbidden areas—and did not have with them associations such as the "blood diamonds" acquired. And it is the same in basketry: collectors and dealers must be very careful when dealing with ethnic and tribal objects regarded as valuable and collectible art. As a result, we have largely stayed away from items including the beautiful Pomo feathered baskets which may contain banned materials such as eagle feathers, and are now usually only seen in museums. Collecting baskets containing eagle and other specific feathers is strictly forbidden, and so we avoided illustrating them here.

–Wayne A. Thompson
May 1, 2020

* * *

Wayne Thompson and I approached this book from two different perspectives; Wayne as a self-employed and self-taught expert on historic Pueblo pottery and subsequently on specific aspects of Native American basketry, and an acclaimed collector of mineral classics (as exemplified in his book, *Ikons, Classics and Contemporary Masterpieces of Mineralogy*, published in 2007). In contrast, I am a materials scientist, who worked for a large computer technology company my entire professional life. I am untrained in the nuances of Native American basketry, although my wife and I have collected Pueblo pottery for over 40 years. Wayne

brings an extensive knowledge of the period covered in this book, a result of reading (and remembering and assimilating) important details about the weavers and their masterpiece baskets. I brought an ability to search the Internet, museums, and libraries of the world for specific instances of basket history and imagery. These searches pertained to the specific images and the historical and personal background relating to the baskets' history and the weavers who created them.

The result of our collaboration is this book. The process of assembling the data, photographs, and background information, and putting it all together in this book took us over ten years. To complete the project, we collaborated with nearly a hundred dealers, collectors, museum curators, anthropological experts, authors, and soul-mates, without whom this book would never have been completed.

Wayne created the framework for the book: the selection of masterpiece weavers, what baskets were to be illustrated, the sequence of weavers' biographies in the book, and the format for the illustrations. I provided the final images, created the image layout according to Wayne's vision, dealt with the bureaucratic details necessary to bring the book to professional standards, and the details of getting the book published. Many museums, dealers, and collectors generously allowed us to use their pictures and helped check on the accuracy of our work. During this process, two people were extensively engaged in book preparation: Alan Garfinkel, a PhD anthropologist with extensive credentials in the domain of Native American art, and Lorna Johnson, with a great background in working with authors of books on Native American basketry. Debi Young, Sunbelt Publication's savvy production manager, and Kathleen Wise, book designer par excellence, completed this collaboration.

If this were a scientific textbook, dealing largely with factual evidence and perhaps occasional speculative but justifiable evidence, this book might have been written quite differently. But this is a book about Native American art, supported by whatever evidence we could glean, and not a scientific textbook using nice pictures to make a case. In the art world, the conditions are different, especially when it comes to the art forms illustrated in this book. We only "know" if a particular weaver made a specific basket if there is uncontested photographic evidence, or a historical record such as a sales slip with a description, or a verifiable story (e.g., "I was with my wife when she bought this Lucy Telles basket directly from her," but even that kind of statement is possibly only anecdotal). Otherwise, it is all conjecture and subject to controversy.

Hence, there is a great deal of material in the book— both intentionally as well as inadvertently (for which we apologize)—that can be reasonably questioned. For example, many Indian names have been Anglicized, and the exact spelling is indeterminate (Scees Possack Bryant vs Cees Possack Bryant, for example). Since baskets were unsigned, baskets were attributed by experts to specific weavers based on design,

or weaving technique, or material used, and were then disputed by other experts. Basket dimensions were either missing or varied depending on who made the measurement and exactly where the measurement was made. Even "factual" evidence such as birth or death dates were not always accurate; the birth date found in literature for even the most famous of all weavers, Dat So La Lee, or Dat So La Li (aka Louisa Keyser) ranges from around 1825 to 1850! Tribal identities were occasionally given differently by different authors and anthropologists.

Of particular importance is the "real" color of the baskets. Photographs varied in time from the early 1900s to recent times, from daguerreotypes to tintypes to film to color film to solid-state imaging. Lighting varied from outdoor sunny to outdoor cloudy to indoor fluorescent to indoor incandescent to indoor room lighting to LED lighting, from a warm lighting spectrum to a cold lighting spectrum, from direct light to diffused light, from amateur to professional, from low resolution to high resolution photography. Hence, while every attempt has been made to show the "correct" color of the basket (e.g., the basket's owner would say the image color is pretty good), all basket colors are but approximations to reality.

Finally, although we did identify inconsistencies and correct the historical records in a few instances, in the absence of any other documentation or supporting evidence we relied upon the words of image and basket owners and from the world of reputable collectors and dealers, without any interpretation or correction on our part. If a collector told us their basket was made by a particular weaver in a particular year, and was of a particular size, having no other evidence to the contrary, we accepted their word as accurate.

As such, there are bound to be factual errors in this book, errors of judgement, and errors of provenance. What we have done is the best we can under the circumstances. Where there are many variables and a lot of unknowns, we have tried to present accuracy in pictures and text. Our chosen subject was the weavers and masterpiece Native American Indian Baskets (the Ikons, to use Wayne's term from his book on mineral classics) of the Florescent Period from California and western Nevada. We encourage readers to notify us of errors, additions, or corrections to photographs, historical records, and opinions expressed in this book. Such supplemental information and revisions can only help make the historical record more accurate.

–Gene Meieran
May 1, 2020

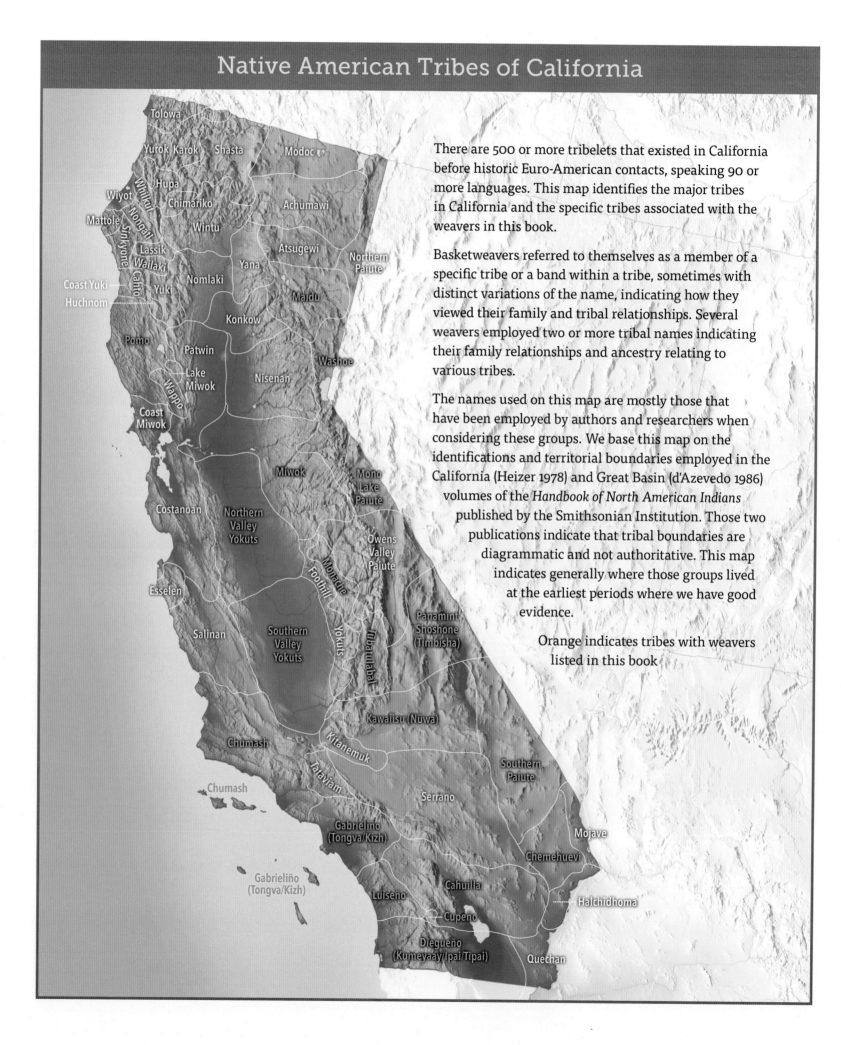

Native American Tribes of California

There are 500 or more tribelets that existed in California before historic Euro-American contacts, speaking 90 or more languages. This map identifies the major tribes in California and the specific tribes associated with the weavers in this book.

Basketweavers referred to themselves as a member of a specific tribe or a band within a tribe, sometimes with distinct variations of the name, indicating how they viewed their family and tribal relationships. Several weavers employed two or more tribal names indicating their family relationships and ancestry relating to various tribes.

The names used on this map are mostly those that have been employed by authors and researchers when considering these groups. We base this map on the identifications and territorial boundaries employed in the California (Heizer 1978) and Great Basin (d'Azevedo 1986) volumes of the *Handbook of North American Indians* published by the Smithsonian Institution. Those two publications indicate that tribal boundaries are diagrammatic and not authoritative. This map indicates generally where those groups lived at the earliest periods where we have good evidence.

Orange indicates tribes with weavers listed in this book

Tolowa
Yurok Karok Shasta Modoc
Hupa
Wiyot Whilkut Chimariko Achumawi
Mattole Nongatl Wintu
Sinkyone Lassik Atsugewi Northern Paiute
Wailaki Yana
Caltto Nomlaki
Coast Yuki Yuki Maidu
Huchnom
Konkow
Pomo Patwin
Lake Miwok Nisenan Washoe
Wappo
Coast Miwok
Miwok Mono Lake Paiute
Costanoan Northern Valley Yokuts
Owens Valley Paiute
Monache
Esselen Foothill Yokuts
Panamint Shoshone (Timbisha)
Salinan Southern Valley Yokuts Tubatulabal
Kawaiisu (Nüwa)
Chumash Kitanemuk
Tataviam Southern Paiute
Chumash Serrano
Gabrielino (Tongva/Kizh) Mojave
Chemehuevi
Gabrielino (Tongva/Kizh) Cahuilla
Luiseño Halchidhoma
Cupeño
Diegueño (Kumeyaay/Ipai/Tipai) Quechan

Introduction

For thousands of years, California has been home to numerous Native American cultures each with their own language, tradition, and cultural heritage. One of their artistic heritages was that of basketmaking, an essential skill for all of these groups. Food gathering, preparation, and storage required use of a variety of baskets, as did religious practices, recreational activities, and even the care and transportation of babies. Baskets were used for trade and given as gifts, and a family's wealth was often measured in part by the number and quality of baskets they owned. A woman's value to her family was sometimes based, in part, on her basketry skills.

The different California Native groups used a range of weaving techniques and materials, creating different basket shapes tailored for specific functions. As was the case for baskets made all over the world at the time, California Indian baskets were made from native plants by the weavers using somewhat similar basketmaking techniques. However, the baskets California Native peoples produced were aesthetically equal to and often better than any similar objects produced by other indigenous cultures throughout the globe.

Spanish explorers made landfall and visited California in the sixteenth century when Cabrillo's ships made contact in 1542. The Spanish established their first mission in Alta California in San Diego in 1769. During the nineteenth century, the attractive Indian baskets really caught the attention of both the Spaniards and the Russian traders as they gathered many of them to be taken back to their homelands. Indeed, the largest collection of pre-1850 baskets still resides in a Russian museum—the State Hermitage Museum in Saint Petersburg.

Fig. i1. Petra Pico, Ventureño Chumash, ca. 1890 Ventura County Historical Museum and Society, item #4661.

During that time, the Spanish established a series of missions along the California coast from south of the present Mexican/California border to Sonoma, north of San Francisco. One of these missions was within the homeland of the Chumash and was located near the present-day city of Santa Barbara.

Chumash weavers had been creating exceptional baskets for generations before the arrival of the Spanish, and indeed continued to weave baskets during the Spanish occupation. In 1902, Petra Pico (Fig. i1)—the last of the great Chumash artists—passed away, effectively ending the period of Chumash weaving just as the Basketry Florescence Period was beginning. Fortunately, there now seems to be a revival of weaving by new Chumash artists.

The impact of these missions and their related activities almost destroyed all elements of the coastal native cultures that they encountered, with similar results in Central and South America during the same period. So rapid and thorough was this process that much of the local history and material artifacts have been lost. However, the Spanish colonization fortunately had somewhat less of an effect on Native tribes living in the interior of California.

In 1848, the United States defeated Mexico in the Mexican-American War, and California became a United States possession. Gold was discovered in the Sierra Nevada in 1848, and the resulting Gold Rush brought tens of thousands of Anglo-Americans into direct contact (and often conflict) with the indigenous Native American cultures. In little more than a single generation, many of these Indian cultures were nearly obliterated. Populations were reduced by 80 to 90 percent due to diseases; some tribes became extinct and even those Indians who did survive found that their traditional way of life was now nearly impossible. Ancestral hunting and fishing areas were taken from them and as a result their continued survival depended on adapting to an ever-increasing and encroaching Euro-American civilization.

Indian males worked on ranches, farms, or in mines, while the women became cooks, maids, nannies, or laundry workers. Fortunately, some continued to weave baskets that they used for family needs, applying techniques handed down from their ancestors. Indians often took the names of the white families for whom they worked and survived under their employer's protection.

By the late 1880s, glass and metal containers had become readily available to the Indians, and survival no longer depended on the production of functional baskets woven from native materials. At the same time, Anglo-Americans began to visit scenic areas of California such as Yosemite and Lake Tahoe and purchased old woven Indian baskets as souvenirs. Indian women, highly skilled at basketmaking, no longer needing to weave baskets for domestic use, and were consequently able to respond to this new market by weaving artistic baskets expressly for sale to an ever-increasing number of tourists.

Two very important factors influenced what these weavers now produced. First, the new freedom from the cultural demands and taboos that had governed basket production for many generations encouraged individual experimentation and artistic expression by the weavers. Second, the basketmakers were exposed to Anglo-American cultural influences and the design preferences of their new customers. These new buyers wanted to buy baskets with human and animal figures, floral designs, messages, and eye-dazzling geometric patterns. With the dramatic changes in the circumstances of Native Californians and the resulting new economic opportunities, the beginning of a new stage of basketmaking was inaugurated which led to the introduction of new basket shapes, colors, and designs. In addition, baskets that were being fashioned anew were no longer simply utilitarian ethnographic artifacts; they became beautiful art objects exhibiting a wide array of different sizes, shapes, and colors. The resultant explosion of creativity was the beginning of the golden age of baskets, now known as the "florescence" (flowering) of California Indian basketry, a term first attributed to Marvin Cohodas in 1979, designating a period from about 1895 to about 1940 (Cohodas 1979a). This book is about the basketmakers of that period, and the marvelous baskets they created.

A number of Florescence baskets have survived the ravages of time, and now grace many museums and private collections. Coincidentally—and very fortunately—the art and science of photography was "flowering" at the same time as the Florescence period and many photographers ventured into the then still "Wild West" to take pictures of an emerging new tradition. Basket collectors and art historians owe a great debt of gratitude to these photographers—for without them, there would be no record of the artists who created these beautiful baskets. This book is about these artists and their baskets, but it is also a tribute to these tireless photographers of the past whose photographic skills captured a time in history now long gone.

The Florescence

ca. 1895 to ca. 1940

The beginning of the Florescence Period of California Indian Basketry in the mid-1890s was stimulated by several key factors. Although baskets had long been used as functional objects in Natives' homes, various subsistence activities, or as trade objects, for the first time in Indian experience, baskets had commercial artistic value beyond their functional or cultural purposes. This new freedom allowed weavers to produce baskets for sale, free of traditional constraints that formerly dictated size, shape, style, and pattern. The purpose of basketweaving was completely transformed.

One of the major influences in California Indian basket-weaving arose from the relationship developed between merchants Abraham and Amy Cohn and a Washoe Indian basketweaver named Dabuda, probably born around 1835. The Cohns owned a clothing store called "The Emporium" in Carson City, Nevada, and Amy had a strong interest in Indian artifacts. Dabuda had married Charley (aka Charlie) Keyser and she took the name Louisa Keyser. Dabuda (Louisa Keyser) in the year 1895 was working as one of the maids in the Cohn household. During that time, when the Cohns recognized how incredibly skilled Dabuda was at creating basketry they became her "patrons." Acting as her patrons, they supplied Dabuda and her husband with a house, food, and clothing, effectively releasing her from the chores of daily life. In return, Louisa worked full-time, exclusively for the Cohns, producing numerous baskets for sale. She also changed her weaving name to Dat So La Lee, probably in honor of the first white man to admire and collect her baskets, Dr. S. L. Lee.

Dat So La Lee was an extremely talented, innovative, and gifted weaver. Perhaps her most significant innovation was to adapt a traditional basket form characteristic of the Native Californian Pomo and Maidu tribes to produce a basket form shape called the *degikup*. To promote Dat So La Lee and her work, Amy Cohn fabricated stories about the importance of the degikup style to the Washoe Indians and about Dat So La Lee's life, enhancing (and embellishing) her reputation as a true artist. Her creations were numbered and catalogued by Amy Cohn with an "LK" number, and a certificate of authenticity was supplied for each basket that was sold. Dat So La Lee ultimately created about 120 superb baskets beginning in 1895, although her lifetime output may have been closer to 300 baskets ranging in size from perhaps 4 inches in diameter to over 25 inches in diameter.

Two well-known authors, just after the turn of the century, further stimulated public interest in California Indian basketry. George Wharton James (1858–1923), a prolific lecturer, journalist, and Methodist minister, published more than 40 books, numerous pamphlets, and magazine articles on California and the American Southwest. His 1901 article "Basket Makers" appeared in *Sunset Magazine* (James 1901b), and his two-volume book entitled *Indian Basketry and How to Make Baskets* (James 1901a) was particularly influential.

American ethnologist and Smithsonian curator Otis Tufton Mason (1838–1908) published his exhaustive two-volume work in 1901, *Indian Basketry*, which remains in print to this day (under the title of *American Indian Basketry*).

Other more recent books include *Indian Baskets* by Sarah Peabody Turnbaugh and William A. Turnbaugh (1986), and *The Fine Art of California Indian Basketry* by Brian Bibby (1996). In addition, there were many books, pamphlets and articles about specific tribal basketmaking (cf. Barrett 1908; Kroeber 1909, 1925; Merrill 1923; O'Neale 1932; Shanks 2015).

The fame created around Dat So La Lee and her baskets made The Emporium a popular destination for visitors. In 1914, Gottlieb Adam Steiner purchased one of her works—basket LK42—from the Cohns for the then fantastic price of $1,400. Adjusted for inflation in the value of consumer products and wages, this would be equivalent to between $90,000 and $180,000 today! The tremendous success of Dat So La Lee's baskets influenced many other Washoe weavers, inspiring them to increase their production and, in turn, boosting basket production by neighboring Native cultures such as Mono Lake Paiute (Kuzedika), Maidu, and even more distant Pomo tribes.

Another very important development was the spread of the Arts and Crafts Movement throughout Europe and America. As the world was in the grip of the Industrial Revolution, there was then (as now) a longing to return to simpler times and to acquire objects that had not been mass-produced. In California it became fashionable for the socially conscious to have an "Indian room" in their homes. The growth of numerous private and public collections increased the demand for baskets, which led to the rise of the great basket dealers of the time. Grace Nicholson, the Fred Harvey Company, and many other entrepreneurs were trying to buy quantities of baskets even faster than the weavers could produce them, thus encouraging the development of new weavers in tribes from all over California. A weaver could often make as much money producing baskets as she could have made doing domestic work, and still be her own boss. If her work was good, she was generally assured of a sale even before the basket was completed.

In 1916, one of the most important events of the Florescence occurred: the creation by the United States Government National Park Service (NPS) as an independent governmental agency of the United States. The NPS and several private concerns collaborated to stage cultural events with a Native theme. One of these was to become known as Yosemite Indian Field Days, a two-day event held in late summer: part rodeo, part Indian powwow, and part country fair. By 1920, one of the major elements of the event was an Indian basketry competition with cash awards for the winners. Those artisans and their baskets, which were selected as winners in the competition were assured of sales, particularly for their highly acclaimed, prize-winning baskets.

Fig. i2 Carrie Bethel, Mono Lake Paiute. Braun Research Library Collection. Autry Museum, Los Angeles. Item number N.30966.

Such competition encouraged several of the best weavers to produce many of the finest baskets ever made. Yosemite Indian Field Days lasted until 1929, and it inspired other similar events, such as June Lake Field Days and the Bishop Harvest Days—and even a contemporary event akin to these earlier expressions known as the Indian Basket Day, held each June. But one of the most significant byproducts of the Yosemite Indian Field Days was the patron-artist relationship that developed between Carrie Bethel (Fig. i2)—possibly the finest artist of the Florescence—and James Schwabacher, one of the great basket collectors of his day. Schwabacher purchased almost every basket produced by Carrie Bethel, who in turn was able to further develop her talent.

While working with Schwabacher, Bethel created several extraordinary baskets; however, such efforts were enormously time-consuming (indeed, one of her baskets took four years to complete!). Unfortunately, making these masterpieces took so long that Carrie's folio contains fewer than a dozen great works, with only six pieces over 20 inches in diameter.

As mentioned in the Introduction, the Florescence began during a time of catastrophic change for the Native Californian people. In a sense, the decline of Native Californians both in number and in their ability to preserve their traditional pre-contact culture were the catalysts that ignited the Florescence. However, just as quickly as the Florescence began, it also abruptly terminated. The devastating economic effects of the Great Depression of 1929—especially on acquiring luxury items such as artistic works—brought the Florescence to a quick and abrupt close.

With a greatly reduced market, most of the old Native weavers simply stopped producing baskets, and in the absence of demand, few new weavers took their places. Consequently, as the great weavers began to decline, much of the knowledge and skill they had inherited or acquired from their mothers and grandmothers, and their prolific basketmaking knowledge

concerning how and where to gather the best materials and how to prepare these materials, ceased to be transmitted. While a few of the great artists continued to produce work through the 1930s and 1940s and even into the 1950s, by the 1960s production of these fine baskets had almost completely ceased. In 1974, Carrie Bethel—the last of the great Florescence weavers—died, and what many researchers and scholars have identified as the golden age of California Indian basketry slipped into history.

Short biographies and much factual data about the weavers of the Florescence cited in this book can be found in Gregory Schaaf's highly useful book *American Indian Baskets I* (2006).

Fig. i3. Chumash tray.
15" diameter.
Wayne and Stevia Thompson Collection.
Jeff Scovil photographer.

Attributes of Masterpiece Baskets

As with most art, the value of the work ultimately depends on the appeal it makes to a prospective owner and is therefore highly subjective. On the other hand, over a period of time, some artists and their artistic works endure and thrive and are dearly sought after. Others simply fade away. The surviving art pieces, deemed as works of a great artist, are quickly snapped up and reside in private estates and museum collections, and only occasionally show up in art sales and in important auctions. Somehow, these pieces of art acquire an acknowledged "greatness"—hard to define but nonetheless recognizable by experts in the field—and are highly desired by avid and knowledgeable collectors.

Most of the qualities of a "great" basket have to do with its overall visual appeal or aesthetics. Several factors contribute to a basket's aesthetics, which, of course, vary in relative importance according to each collector's personal taste. Regardless, most knowledgeable collectors tend to agree on which basket may be fairly called a masterpiece.

There are, of course, many weaving and coiling techniques used throughout the world, and each technique, whether it be twining, single-rod or triple-rod, or some other technique, has its own association with what might be termed masterpiece baskets. In this book, the focus is on one specific method of weaving baskets: triple-rod coiled basketry. While there are many tribes that weave baskets using this technique, we feature triple-rod baskets created by weavers who resided predominantly from near the westernmost edge of California's Great Basin to the eastern edge of Lake Tahoe, Nevada. These tribes fashioned their most prized creations during the Florescence period, dating from circa 1895 through about 1940.

This specific type of basketry technique, group of artists, and time period was chosen because many experts believe these types of baskets represent the very best of the basketmaking artists. Additionally, based on technique, skill, artistic expression and consistency of quality perspectives, these are the artists and their artistic expressions that are specifically showcased in this volume.

Furthermore, from a simple logistic perspective, a volume of this size and form dictated selecting a small group of baskets rather than a large group. Specifically, this volume tries to present the best basketmakers from one of the best regions in the world. This was the authors' focus and of course could be handled in a book of reasonable size. However, the basket attributes discussed below can be applied to all baskets wherever they are made and by whatever technique the basketweaver employed. Here then are some of the characteristics often used to denote "greatness" in woven baskets.

Basketry Types and Ornamental Designs

Considering the textile arts of Native Californians, basketry reigns supreme. California Indian basketry is considered to represent the highest quality of any in North America. Coiled basketry was preferred by all of the Native groups in southern California. In northwestern California some ethnolinguistic groups only employed twined wares. Along with coiled baskets, twining was part of the basketry assemblage for all of southern California. Only with the Pomo did men weave baskets, otherwise this was womens' work.

A great variety of types and usages are characteristic. Carrying or seed-gathering baskets often were fitted with a carrying strap. Acorns and small or large seeds were contained in these vessels. Hoppers were employed with stone mortars; asphaltum or pine pitch was used to attach the bottomless basket for milling seeds or berries. Trays, seeds, and beaters were other forms. The trays were the bases for gambling games; they were also used as shakers, sifters, or parching trays. Special purpose baskets were the most elegant and were frequently adorned with feathers or beads and were used for dedicatory ceremonials. Yokuts and Monache created necked jars for the rattlesnake ceremonies and such baskets were used by the Tübatulabal and Kawaiisu as "treasure" baskets. Food bowls and boilers were made for eating and cooking food. Basket hats were worn to protect the head from the tumpline attached to carrying or burden baskets. Water bottles were crafted by twining and covered with pitch or asphaltum for containing the liquid—smaller ones provided individual canteens.

Close-coiled over a triple-rod foundation produced bowl-shaped incurving baskets known as degikup style during the historic period.

Design elements on basketry are often named. The names denote animals or parts of the human body. Names include: arrowheads, butterflies, turtle necks, quail plumes, ants, deerback crossings, pine trees, dragonflies, eyes, and going sideways. Historic designs include: rattlesnakes, flowers, birds, eight-pointed stars, serrated diamonds, crosses, deer, bighorn sheep, and human figures (men, women, and even children).

Design or Pattern

Basket beauty is determined in part by its layout or design. Eye-dazzling geometric patterns combined with human, animal, insect, and floral designs are always desirable, and when these patterns are well balanced and seem to flow across the surface of the basket, the result is art in one of its most beautiful forms. Some weavers also used lighter-colored, undecorated backgrounds to create negative patterns. The ability to weave two-dimensional designs in a three-dimensional space with real effectiveness and eye-catching appeal was achieved by only a few of these magnificent artists.

Of significant interest is the degree by which the basket represents traditional Native American designs and motifs. In addition to designs created to satisfy the new tourist customers, many beautiful baskets were created to tell a story through their design.

Basket Shape

A flowing and well-balanced shape is critical to the visual appeal of a basket. The artist must have the ability to control curves and angles to achieve grace and balance. Degikups, bottleneck ollas, trays, and flaring bowls, when well executed, are simply very pleasing to the eye. Less conventional shapes, while they can be interesting to specific people, most often fail to achieve a high aesthetic level of appeal to the larger community.

Baskets have many shapes which appeal to collectors: trays, bowls, jars, and degikups (a term generally applied to specific shapes made by Washoe weavers, but used in this book as a general term for a flat-based spherical basket which curves in toward a small opening at the top).

Color

The use of color is very important in making a basket attractive. Early baskets were commonly monochromatic or simply employed a dark color—usually very dark brown or black—on a lighter natural tan background. Soon after, "fancy" baskets became polychromatic: the addition of yellow, bright red, and orange patterns greatly enhanced the appeal of these later baskets. Some artists mastered the use of color to achieve very bold, sometimes intricate, interactions, creating visual delights for the viewer. In many cases, such techniques became the artistic signatures of particular weavers, who would use variations of a specific motif or theme in many of their works.

Technical Execution

Technical execution is the foundation upon which the beauty of a basket is based and serves to distinguish a merely good weaver from a true master. There are many factors by which technical excellence is judged.

First, there is the knowledge of which plant materials should be used, when they should be harvested, and where they grow their best. The most commonly used materials were sedge grass, bracken fern root, redbud, willow shoots, and juncus (Bibby 1996). For some of these plant materials, there was a very limited growing season—perhaps only a few weeks. During this limited period was when the plants could be collected to maximize their color, size, and strength of fiber. Indeed, sometimes the quality or beauty of a particular raw material might depend upon which side of a creek or canyon it grew, receiving just the right amount of light, shade, and moisture. Alternatively, a particular sandy riverbank might have been discovered where the plants grew long, straight roots; in such a case it was common for a weaver to work hard to clear an area of rock and debris to create a good patch of ground so that the harvest in later years would be successful. For many years these cleared "fields" were passed down from mother to daughter.

Once the best materials had been gathered, often over a period of weeks or months, they had to be painstakingly prepared. Typically, they were washed and trimmed, coiled, and then either stored in darkness or left out in the light to achieve the desired results. Bracken fern root had to be buried in swampy mud, sometimes for a year, to absorb iron and become darkened to an even blackness. In later years, the use of nails in a bucket of water replaced this practice for a number of weaving materials and produced the same result.

Willow shoots, juncus, and other materials used for the coiled foundation remained whole, but had to be trimmed to a uniform diameter; the wefts were split, usually into three equal pieces. This meant pre-slicing two sides, then holding the center slice firmly between the front teeth and pulling evenly on the two other parts to peel them apart. Anything other than perfect precision in this process would produce uneven/unusable strands. The pieces then had to be sized. In earlier times, they were shaved with an obsidian blade. Later, a tin can lid with holes of graduated sizes was used by many tribes throughout the state—including the Mono Lake Paiute—for willow shoots and other materials such as juncus (Craig Bates personal communication 2017). Each strand was pulled in succession through several holes of decreasing diameter until the strands themselves were uniformly of the desired width. This process was used for the stitching materials, and again, anything less than absolute perfection would lead to an obvious flawed and visually imperfect basket. The resulting uneven areas in a basket generally disqualified it from being judged a masterpiece. Tin can lids were not used for sedge or redbud.

When weaving the basket, the artist had to be a patient and talented technician as well as a perfectionist. Whatever the weaving style (overlapping stitching, split stitching, etc.), the execution had to be perfect—anything less would detract from the beauty of the finished basket. In earlier times, a bone awl was used to puncture holes in the coils to tie the stitching together. In later years, when metal tools had become available, a steel shaft sharpened to a fine point was used. This simple tool of a nail affixed to a wooden cabinet knob enhanced the artist's ability to produce a great basket; it also lasted much longer than the bone awl and almost never broke—and because it stayed sharp longer it was less likely to split the coils.

Size and Technique

The role of a basket's size in determining its quality is often debated. Clearly, while sheer size alone is not a criterion of quality, it almost always has a profound effect on the estimation of a basket's value and collectability. Generally speaking, smaller baskets were easier and less time-consuming to make and consequently baskets of smaller stature usually sold faster and for considerably lower prices. Simple economics therefore dictated the production of far more smaller baskets than larger baskets. Weaving larger baskets was a much rarer expression. However, in many cases a masterpiece small basket might be technically and artistically superior to a larger one and take even longer to weave and may command a commensurately high price.

Dat So La Lee—considered by many to have been one of the finest weavers of all time—achieved stitch counts of 32 or 33 per inch on her larger degikups (up to 17 inches). Some small Panamint baskets have stitch counts nearing 60 per inch, but to achieve 30+ per inch on a larger piece was an incredible feat.

Another consideration concerning size is that many weavers were either incapable of producing larger pieces or unwilling to do so. Carrie Bethel and Lucy Parker Telles each took approximately four years to make their largest basket. Several other weavers—e.g., Minnie Mike (Carrie Bethel's sister) and Alice James Wilson (Lucy Parker Telles' sister)—began larger baskets, but for various reasons failed to complete them. Hence, large high-quality, artistic, and well-shaped baskets, made by but a few artists, are very rare and among the most valuable of collectible baskets. On the other side of the coin, Pomo weavers created fantastically large baskets, several feet in diameter. But they also created extremely small baskets, some less than 1/4 inch in diameter! While these extremes of woven baskets are technical marvels, illustrating both patience as well as incredible skill in basketmaking, their very extreme size on both ends of the spectrum often prevents many of them from being recognized as artistic masterpieces.

Extensive discussions on the characteristic weaving techniques for specific tribal groups both in California and the Great Basin can be found in the works of Albert Elsasser (1978) and Catherine Fowler and Lawrence E. Dawson (1986).

Provenance

The "provenance" of a basket refers to its history or specifically its genealogy. Unlike ceramic pottery that was created at about the same period, baskets do not commonly come with either signature or documentation, although from a present-day perspective it is highly desirable that they do. Hence, circumstantial information pieced together by experts much later in a basket's history is regarded as very important, while not as tangible as more direct documentation.

Given this lack of documentary evidence, a photograph of the basket with its maker is the pinnacle of provenance information. However, other valuable tangible kinds of documentation include photographs in famous old collections, or in books and publications such as auction catalogues, and representations in postcards or paintings. Old written collection ledgers with accurate descriptions and information on dates of purchase or purchase prices add to the stature of a great piece.

More recent photographs of a piece published in *American Indian Art*, *Arizona Highways*, or any of the current books on basketry all contribute to provenance information. All facts about a great basket should be recorded. While great provenance may not make an average basket great, it will always make a great basket more desirable.

Finally, one may have to only rely on an expert's opinion, formed after many years of experience of comparing designs, styles, coloring, and other "fingerprints" of the basketmaker: such provenance is usually referred to as "attribution." Even so, in several cases where baskets have been attributed to a particular weaver, re-examination of the basket or finding new historical records of baskets in out-of-date publications have led to "re-attribution." In this book we have tried to use the most current information available to give proper provenance to each basket, and to employ the basket owner's attribution as being the most accurate. We apologize for any errors that may be found.

Rarity

In judging the value and collectability of a great basket, its rarity is always evaluated in relation to its beauty. An unattractive but rare old basket, while historically important, may have little value to all but the most specialized collectors. On the other hand, a very beautiful but common basket, while holding a good value, may be limited in desirability by the fact that many other similar baskets are routinely available. But a very rare and very beautiful basket will have a greater value which will most probably escalate over time beyond rational expectations; this will be a piece that every collector dreams of owning.

Age and Condition

Baskets of the Florescence do not vary much in age, most falling within the 45-year time span between 1895 and 1940, and 90 percent of these were made between 1900 and 1930. Many great baskets, of course, however, were made before

the Florescence; these earliest examples are extremely valuable and many are very beautiful. Nearly all are virtually unobtainable, as they reside in museum and university collections. Only rarely do they appear on the open market. And given their age and material used, it is very important that the baskets be clean and exhibit little wear and tear.

Quality

Often regarded as subjective, basket quality has a strong influence on monetary value. By quality, one is referring to specific attributes such as damage, repair, and restoration, loss of color, wear and tear, breaks and damage, lack of symmetry, etc., all of which may not be noticeable when simply seeing a basket from a distance or in a photograph. Since the current value of a fine basket was not often appreciated when the basket was purchased, it may have been mishandled, used for utilitarian purposes for which it was not designed, may have been buried and subjected to water damage, etc., or the basket might be an earlier creation by the weaver and simply not have the beautiful symmetrical shape now desired by serious basket collectors, or the design might be off-center. Small details such as these might have an enormous impact on a basket's value; a few even well-hidden poor stitches can impact a basket's value, compared to a "perfect" example.

Note that the terms "quality" and "value" are not synonymous; an inexpensive basket may be of high quality, and a truly expensive basket may be of poor quality. But given equivalence in size, technique, design, rarity, etc., a higher quality basket always commands more value than a lower quality one.

Authenticity and Attribution

Unlike paintings and other fine arts, baskets are rarely signed, and hence—unless credible evidence is provided—the *authenticity* of a particular basket (e.g., absolute positive identification of the weaver) is often questioned. Credible evidence includes photographs of a basket in the hands of the weaver (as seen in many of the photographs in this book), detailed descriptions of baskets in ledgers (such as the ledger created by Abe and Amy Cohn for Dat So La Lee, now in the Nevada Historical Society), reliable sales receipts with basket descriptions, basket identification by the weaver, etc. Otherwise, baskets are mostly *attributed* to a particular weaver, using circumstantial evidence such as basket design and weaving technique, photos related to a weaver but not showing the weaver and basket in the same picture, and educated guesses by experts in the field. Even so, experts are occasionally in error, and upon studying the baskets in more detail they may re-attribute baskets to a different weaver than originally thought.

In this book, we rely mostly on the photos of weavers holding their own baskets as proof of authenticity. Some master weavers such as Dat So La Lee, Carrie Bethel, Mrs. Dick Francisco, Lucy Parker Telles, and others, have such idiosyncratic techniques and designs that make their creations unmistakable. Otherwise, we have relied on the authentication or attribution as supplied with the basket image by the basket owner. We do not represent ourselves as academic scholars, and hence apologize for any errors found in the book, but we believe that the extensive photographic evidence illustrated here provides a basis for attributing baskets to particular weavers. Indeed, one of the goals of this book is to help identify masterpiece weavers from old photos and attribute wonderful baskets to known weavers. Any comments or critiques about the authenticity or attribution of baskets in this book are certainly welcome.

About Basket Images

The vintage photographs and basket images illustrated in this book come from a number of sources: old photographs taken with poor-quality lenses and developed with obsolete technology, photographs by family members using whatever camera they had available at the time, professional photographs by well-known photographers, museum photographs used originally for archival purposes, and photographs taken at museums under less than optimal conditions, etc.

Since different films, lighting conditions (bright light, dim light, colored light, filtered light, outdoor natural light, etc.), developing procedures, reproduction procedures, photographic editing, and printing processes, etc. were used, the actual quality of the photographs used here varies considerably—from superb photographs to some of considerably lesser quality. Since the authors were unable to personally view every basket shown and had to rely on the quality of the photographs released for publication, it is expected that some of the basket colors do not fully represent the actual basket colors as may be seen if they were seen in either bright sunlight or under "white" light using incandescent or fluorescent lighting conditions. We can only say we did the best we could, under severe photographic constraints and limited access, to photograph the baskets ourselves. (We employed a professional photographer to take as many basket images as we could).

In addition, the baskets shown here vary in size from fairly small (a few inches in diameter) to very large, perhaps 32 inches in diameter. Learning from experience in the book *Ikons*, showing images of mineral specimens of various sizes, it was decided to show baskets in sizes "relative" to one another as much as possible. Tiny mineral specimens, often less than a few millimeters across, are commonly shown in pictures as the same size as cabinet specimens 60 centimeters across, in order to show specimen details. Many collectors were disappointed on seeing the actual specimen since they expected to see a large specimen rather than the barely visible piece. To avoid this problem in basket-size perception, perhaps 95% of the baskets shown here are in relative proportion, as defined by the table below.

Finally, we have added a Figure Notes Appendix to the book, to draw special attention to some of the images—either due to some interesting historical fact, some image quality issue, or to simply point out an interesting feature of the picture. It should be noted that many of the baskets illustrated here are seen in both black and white images and in color photographs in the references cited. More information on specific baskets may also be found there.

Guide to Sizing of Baskets Throughout Book

ACTUAL BASKET SIZE	APPROXIMATE SIZE SHOWN IN BOOK
1 to 5 inches	2 inches
6 to 9 inches	3 inches
10 to 15 inches	4 inches
16 to 20 inches	6 inches
21 to 24 inches	8 inches
> 25 inches	9 inches

Highlights of Triple-Rod and Grass-Bundled Coiled Techniques

We chose triple-rod coil baskets from specific Native American tribes in California and western Nevada during a specific time interval, the Florescence (ca. 1895– ca. 1940) as the focus of this book because we believe they represent the best of the art of basketweaving. The specific baskets shown represent the best of those coiled baskets, as selected by us in concert with a number of recognized basket experts and professionals. We intentionally avoided paying much attention to equally exquisite feathered or beaded baskets from the same time period and geographical area and by the same weavers, to focus specifically on a particular type of basketry and avoid creating too large a book.

These triple-rod and grass-bundled coiled baskets exhibit both the tightest weave of the possible basketmaking techniques while providing a large scope of design capabilities (Allen 2013). Many of the weavers featured have also woven baskets using twining techniques as well as single-rod coiling and grass foundation coiling; these techniques are briefly illustrated on this page.

As can be seen, twined baskets have a fundamental difference in appearance from coiled baskets. In addition, even coiled triple-rod baskets may have different appearances due to stitching characteristics. The finer the stitches, the greater the difficulty in weaving, often resulting in higher basket value.

There are many fine descriptions of these different weaving techniques in the literature and online. Readers interested in learning more about weaving technique are encouraged to visit these sources of basketweaving technology: Allen 2013; Cohodas 1984; Dalrymple 2000a, 2000b; Farmer 2004; Kania and Blaugrund 2014; Shanks 2006, 2010. Of particular value is the book by Otis Tufton Mason, republished in 2012 (originally published in 1901). These sources provide a wealth of information on different basketweaving techniques, along with numerous descriptive images.

For excellent information on basket quality and collecting, see *American Indian Baskets: Building and Caring for a Collection* by William and Sarah Peabody Turnbaugh (Turnbaugh and Turnbaugh 2013).

Twined

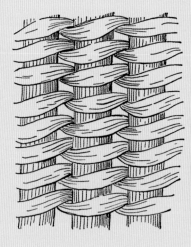
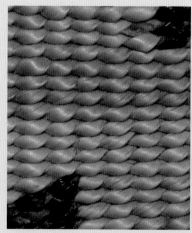

Coiled

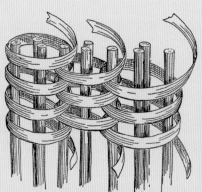

©2004–2019 Florida Center for Instructional Technology.

Fine Weave

Coarse Weave

Mary Knight Benson baskets. See Figs. 118 and 119.

Important Events in the History of California Indian Basket Collecting

1895–1925	Abraham and Amy Cohn are the patrons of Dat So La Lee.
1900–1930	Emergence of great dealers like Grace Nicholson and the Fred Harvey Company.
1901	Otis Tufton Mason (1901) and George Wharton James (1901) publish books on California Indian basketry.
1916–1929	Yosemite Indian Field Days.
1920s–1958	Carrie Bethel/James Schwabacher artist/patron relationship.
1929	The Great Depression signals an end to the California Indian Basketry Florescence.
1940–1945	World War II prevents a re-emergence in California Indian basket collecting.
1971	The Green Collection Sale at Sotheby's (Parke Bernet Galleries) brings shockingly high prices for great baskets.
1975	*American Indian Art* magazine begins publication; it will go on to become an authoritative publication for collectors until it ceased publication in 2016.
July 1975	*Arizona Highways* (Stacey 1975) publishes a basket issue.
Late 1970s–1990s	Numerous new collectors emerge. The value and collectability of baskets escalates while availability decreases. Several scholars, with the help of numerous collectors and dealers, begin to piece together the history of the great artists of the California Indian Basketry Florescence.
1990	California Indian Basketweavers Association (CIBA) formed.
2000–2008	Great baskets attain prices comparable to those of great paintings. Several pieces by Carrie Bethel and Dat So La Lee each bring over $1,000,000.

Highlighted Basketweavers and Baskets

In the first section of this book, we highlight 46 weavers of masterpiece triple-rod coiled baskets, noting some biographical and tribal background. In the second section another 15 weavers are illustrated but in less detail, showing vintage photographs of the weavers and photographs of their baskets where available.

Even this does not do justice to the many fine weavers whose contributions to the art—for one reason or another—have received even less attention. Further, many fine baskets for which the identity of the weaver is unknown now reside in private or museum collections.

Consequently, in a third section of this book, we try to remedy this a bit by including photographs of weavers who are acknowledged as masters but for whom we did not have images of the baskets they created. We also show images of masterpiece baskets where we were unable to unambiguously identify the weaver—although the basket style and image credits allows us to identify the tribe with which the weaver was affiliated.

Of course, many important weavers and baskets still have not been included—otherwise the book would have become an unread and exceptionally ponderous table-top fixture!

Clearly, important baskets that should have been included in this book are missing, and some of the "unknown" weavers may be recognized after publication of this book. Furthermore, the identity of weavers of the "unknown" baskets shown here may in the future be identified, or the baskets themselves be attributed to a particular weaver. We welcome any corrections and additions to this book to remedy any such shortcomings; of particular value would be vintage photographs of weavers for whom we were not able to find any! Indeed, one of the purposes of this book is to help identify basketweavers and connect unknown baskets to known weavers and to correct any misrepresentations of basket or weaver provenance or historical fact.

As stated in the Preface, this book started out as a book about baskets, with only brief mention of the weavers, but as the book progressed, it turned into a book more about the weavers as well as the baskets that they so masterfully created. The book is intended as a tribute to these weavers. So we also want to share some of the observations of the descendants of these weavers, to illustrate the influence their ancestors had on the present generation. There are too few of these vignettes, but perhaps in the not-too-distant-future—while memories are still reasonably fresh—more comments can be accommodated, and a future printing of the book could contain these anecdotes along with corrections and additions to this edition.

Finally, we wish to pay tribute to the many people who contributed to helping us recognize the value and importance of this art form from the early basket collectors and dealers, to the present-day collectors, dealers, academicians, and researchers, without whom the art of California basketweaving would have been lost in the sands of time. Reading about these collectors and academics brings a sense of relief that they recognized the art for what it is. These celebrated basket makers produced the finest woven baskets in the world by combining ancient techniques with innovative designs and shapes, thus creating an emerging new world of art aimed at appreciative collectors.

One important comment: there is no specific ordering of these 46 weavers—either by tribe, prominence, or alphabetically. We intentionally randomized the order, to avoid showing individual, basket style, or tribal preference. But please note the two images of Lucinda Hancock holding her baskets, the first of a young Lucinda at the front of the book, and an older Lucinda at the back of the book, illustrate the scope of our focus: a short time span over which an entire and remarkable art form evolved and flourished.

Tina Charlie
Mono Lake Paiute (Kuzedika) | 1869–1962

Tina Charlie was born on the eastern side of the Sierra Nevada near the shores of Mono Lake, Mono County, California (Bates and Lee 1990). She spent her entire childhood around Mono Lake and the nearby community of Bodie. Her parents were Patsy Jim and Pete Jim; Pete had been a tribal headman. Tina's younger sister, Nellie Charlie (see pages 206–208) also became an important basketweaver, as did her niece Daisy Charlie (see page 197).

Following tribal custom, Tina and Nellie both married Young Charlie, a Mono Lake Paiute, according to the California Index to the Census Roll of Indians, 1928–1933. The three Charlies lived together on Rush Creek (Bates and Lee 1990). Nellie separated from Young Charlie in 1927 but continued to live near Tina and her former husband.

As documented by California basketry scholars, throughout the 1920s Tina developed into a master weaver and was a regular competitor in the public galas associated with Yosemite Indian Field Days and June Lake Field Days (Bates and Lee 1990). In 1925 she entered a fine negative degikup that was among the first ever made. Her 1929 stunning First Prize-winning grand degikup is regarded as possibly the first of the great "giant" degikups (Fig. 2). Tina certainly was a talented artist, with exceptional technical skills and an innovative approach to the art of basketweaving.

In the 1950s, Tina moved in with Nellie and Nellie's granddaughter Jesse Durant; the three of them lived near each other on the Bishop Indian reservation in the Owens Valley of eastern California. The Charlie sisters (Tina and Nellie) wove baskets every day until Tina died in 1962 (Dean et al. 2004).

Although Tina never developed an artist-patron relationship, such as that of Dat So La Lee and the Cohns, Ella Cain, a prominent collector who lived in this area of eastern California, acquired several of Tina's finest baskets in the 1920s. These baskets remained in the Cain Collection until Bonhams and Butterfields Auction House sold the collection at auction in 2005. There was an unprecedented basket collector response at the auction and the prize-winning 1929 degikup brought in $347,000, the highest price ever paid at auction at that time for an American Indian basket (Fig. 2). Sadly, these artists never saw recompense anywhere near these prices.

Without question, Tina Charlie, along with Carrie Bethel, Lucy Parker Telles, and Dat So La Lee, was one of the very finest of many California Indian basketry artists. Her baskets are exhibited in many of the most prestigious museum collections and are treasured by all serious basket collectors and scholars of the art. The Yosemite Museum in Yosemite Valley has several of her wondrous baskets.

Fig. 1 Tina Charlie holding the basket shown in Fig. 2 at Yosemite Indian Field Days in 1929. Carrie Bethel and Alice Wilson are to her left. Photograph courtesy Yosemite Museum and Research Library, National Park Service Catalogue number YOSE RL 2122.

Fig. 2* Tina Charlie degikup.
10" high by 20" diameter, 1928/1929.
Wayne and Malee Thompson Collection.
Jeff Scovil photographer.

*See Appendix 3, Figure Notes | Pg. 307

Fig. 3 Tina Charlie degikup.
10½" high by 26" diameter, ca. 1930s.
Photograph courtesy Yosemite Museum and Research Library.
National Park Service Catalogue number YOSE 37865B.

Fig. 4 Tina Charlie with basket shown in Fig. 5 in 1944. Photograph courtesy Bridgeport Museum, Mono County, California.

Fig. 5 Tina Charlie degikup. 8¾" high by 16" diameter. Photograph courtesy Gene Quintana. John Law photographer.

Fig. 6 California Governor Friend Richardson holding Tina Charlie basket (Fig. 7) at Yosemite Indian Field Days in 1925. Tina is to his left. Lucy Parker Telles and Carrie Bethel are to the immediate right of the Governor. Photograph courtesy Yosemite Museum and Research Library. National Park Service Catalogue number YOSE RL 15419.

Fig. 7* Tina Charlie degikup.
8½" high by 12½" diameter, ca. 1925.
© 2012 Bonhams & Butterfields Auctioneers Corporation. All rights reserved.
German Herrera photographer.

See Appendix 3, Figure Notes | Pg. 307

Baskets, Babies and Bead Work
Indian Field Day — June Lake

Fig. 10 Jane Jones, manager of the "Wai Pa Shone" Trading Post, holding the basket shown in Fig. 11, ca. 1939. To her right is Dorothy Amora Stanley and to her left is Irene McCauley. Photograph courtesy Yosemite Museum and Research Library. National Park Service Catalogue number YOSE RL 1423.

Fig. 11 Tina Charlie degikup. 12" high by 24" diameter, ca. 1930. Photograph courtesy Turtle Bay Exploration Park, Redding, California.

Fig. 12 Tina Charlie, ca. 1950.
Photograph courtesy Alan Blaver.

Salena Davis Jackson was born in 1874 and grew up in Coppertown, California, in the lower Genesee Valley of eastern-central Plumas County. While she was still young, Salena and her family were forced by white settlers to move to Shim Flat, lower down the valley (Kurtz 2010, 2011).

Salena learned to weave from her mother, an accomplished weaver. She married Tom Young who had been married to Salena's sister, Ina Jackson. Ina (see page 280) was also a fine weaver (Kurtz 2010:18–20, 2011).

Salena's weaving materials usually stayed in the tradition of other Maidu weavers—using big leaf maple, willow, sedge root, and redbud plant materials (Kurtz 2010, 2011). Her basket shapes and designs were usually of the old Maidu style. Her early use of the degikup form was

Fig. 14 Salena Jackson (center) with baskets shown in Figs. 15, 16, 17, 18, 21, 22, 24, and 28. Photograph courtesy Pat Kurtz.

likely due to Pomo influence from the west and may have had an effect on the nearby Washoe weavers just to the east. She mastered the use of bright red-colored redbud, outlined in black bracken fern root, creating negative patterns against lighter backgrounds.

Salena made at least five matched sets of trays and bowls (or degikup) (see Figs. 15–18, 21, 22) and some of these bowls appear to be new style baskets (Fig. 28). One tray (Fig. 31), photographed in the Cady Collection (Fig. 33), dates to about 1905, and has 16 human figures.

A vintage photograph, circa 1930, shows Salena standing behind approximately 30 of her baskets (five of which were later purchased for a distant cousin of Salena by Natalie Linn), combined with several from a portion of the Cady Collection (purchased by Bob and Carol Adams). Three are photographed in *Our Precious Legacy* (Kurtz 2010). These demonstrate Salena's exceptional technical expertise, versatility, and artistic talents.

The personal notes of Frank and Rilla Cady (who lived in Susanville, California and assembled one of the finest collections of Maidu basketry) refer to Salena as one of the most exceptional Maidu weavers. In the 1890s, Rilla traveled in a horse-drawn buggy around Plumas County, California, to visit Maidu weavers, and purchased many of their works (Bob Adams personal communication 2009). In the 1915 publication of *Illustrated History of Indian Baskets and Plates Made by California Indians and Other Tribes* by Viola M. Roseberry, Salena is named as "one of the finest basket-weavers left among the Maidu" (Roseberry 1915).

Salena was recognized as a fine weaver in her own time and is still considered to be one of the finest artists in the history of California basketry. Her baskets are highly prized in many private as well as museum collections. Only occasionally are her artistic accomplishments offered for sale at shows and important auctions.

Fig. 15 Salena Jackson tray.
19¼" diameter, ca. 1920.
Natalie Linn Collection.
Justin Tunis photographer.

Fig. 16 Salena Jackson bowl.
7¼" deep by 15½" diameter, ca. 1920.

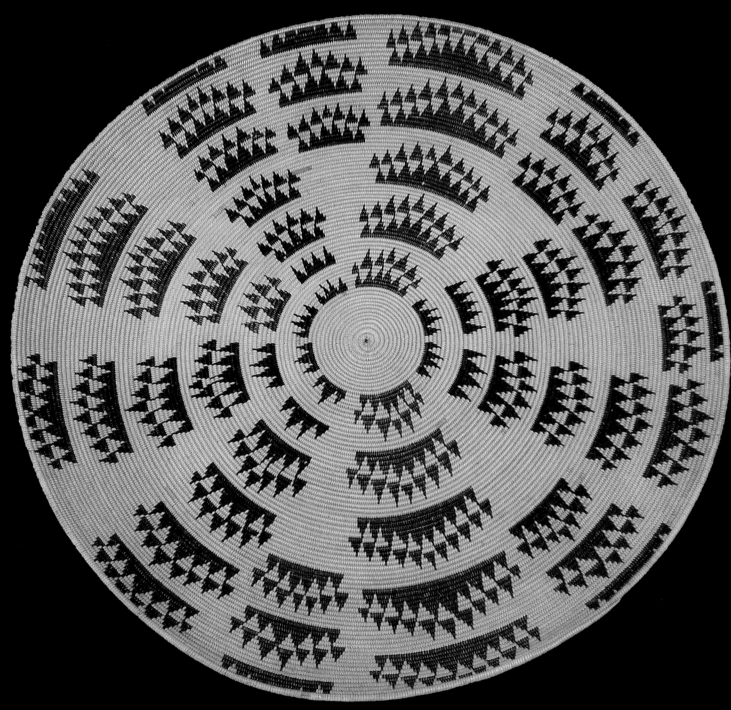

Fig. 17 Salena Jackson tray.
27½" diameter, ca. 1920.
Photograph courtesy Turtle Bay Exploration Park,
Redding, California.

Fig. 19 Salena Jackson bowl.
2¾" deep by 5½" diameter.
Mark McQuinn and Stacy Steinwand Collection.
Todd Adams photographer.

Fig. 20 Salena Jackson with baskets shown in Figs. 15, 16, 17, 18, 21, 22, 24, 28; ca. 1930. Photograph courtesy Bob and Carol Adams.

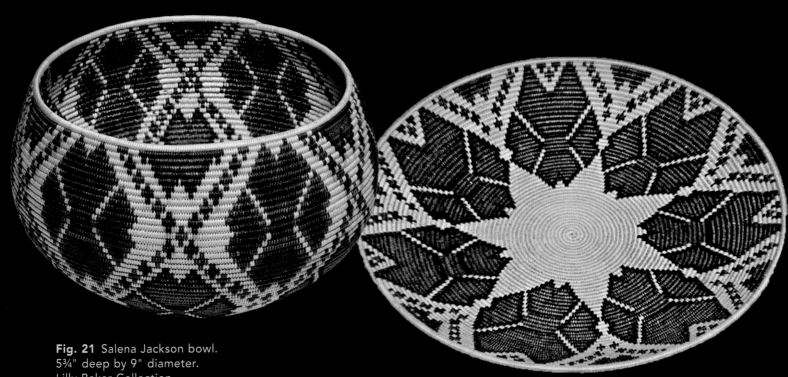

Fig. 21 Salena Jackson bowl.
5¾" deep by 9" diameter.
Lilly Baker Collection.
Photograph courtesy Pat Kurtz.
David Bozsik photographer.

Fig. 22 Salena Jackson tray.
14½" diameter.
Lilly Baker Collection.
Photograph courtesy Pat Kurtz.
David Bozsik photographer.

Fig. 23 Salena Jackson's stepson, Herb Young, ca. 1950, with a collection of Salena's baskets including those shown in Figs. 15, 16, and 24. Photograph courtesy Pat Kurtz.

Fig. 24 Salena Jackson degikup. 8" high by 14" diameter, ca. 1920. Wayne and Stevia Thompson Collection. Jeff Scovil photographer.

Fig. 25 Salena Jackson tray.
3½" high by 21¾" diameter.
Natalie Linn Collection.
Gene Meieran photographer.

Fig. 26 Salena Jackson degikup.
17" diameter, ca. 1915.
Photograph courtesy Terry DeWald.
Jeff Scovil photographer.

Fig. 27 Photograph of Salena Jackson degikup shown in Fig. 26. Photograph previously appeared in *Roseberry* (1915) as Plate 7.

Fig. 28 Salena Jackson tray.
17½" diameter, ca. 1900.
Thaw Collection, Fenimore Art Museum,
Cooperstown, New York.
Gift of Eugene V. and Claire F. Thaw.
Catalogue number T0817.
Richard Walker photographer.

Fig. 29* Salena Jackson oval bowl.
6" high by 11" wide by 13" long, ca. 1920.
Photograph courtesy Gene Quintana.
John Law photographer.

*See Appendix 3, Figure Notes | Pg. 307

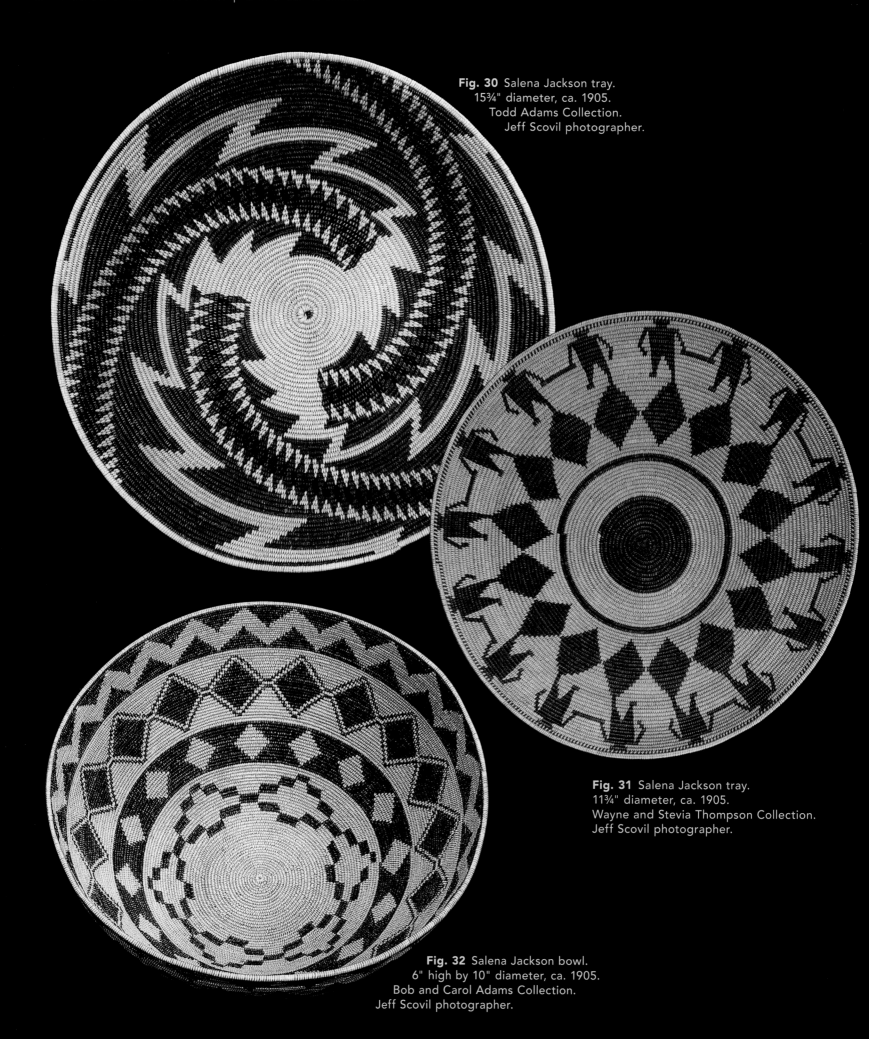

Fig. 30 Salena Jackson tray.
15¾" diameter, ca. 1905.
Todd Adams Collection.
Jeff Scovil photographer.

Fig. 31 Salena Jackson tray.
11¾" diameter, ca. 1905.
Wayne and Stevia Thompson Collection.
Jeff Scovil photographer.

Fig. 32 Salena Jackson bowl.
6" high by 10" diameter, ca. 1905.
Bob and Carol Adams Collection.
Jeff Scovil photographer.

Fig. 33 Cady Collection, ca. 1905, with Salena Jackson baskets shown in Figs. 30, 31, and 32. Photograph courtesy Bob and Carol Adams.

Fig. 34 Salena Jackson degikup. 4¾" high by 7¾" diameter. Terry DeWald Collection. Terry DeWald photographer.

Fig. 35 Salena Jackson degikup. 8½" high by 17" diameter, ca. 1920. Alex Schwed Collection. Todd Adams photographer.

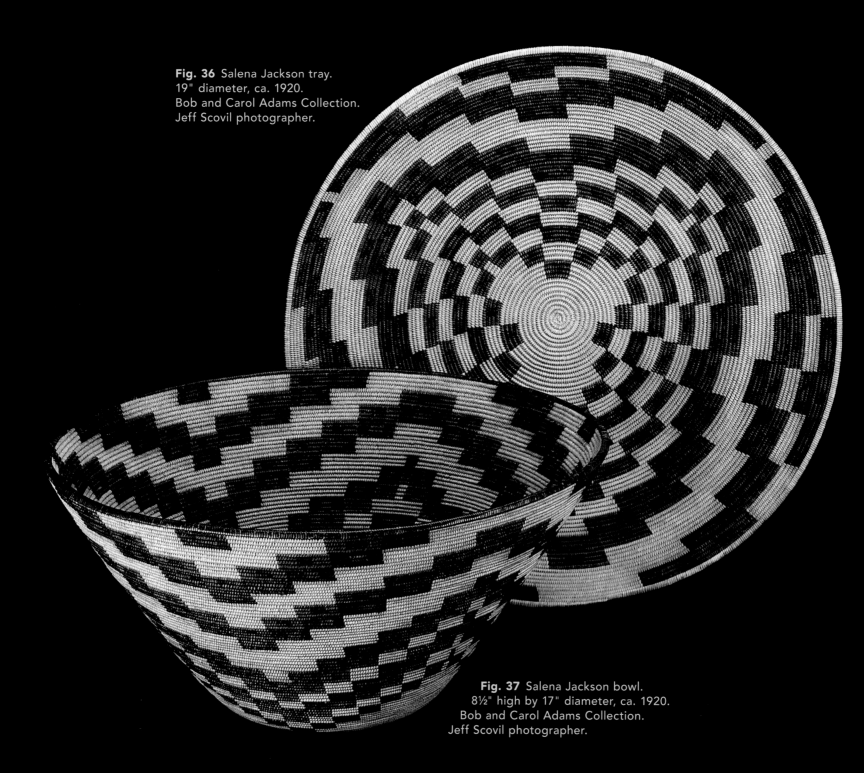

Fig. 36 Salena Jackson tray.
19" diameter, ca. 1920.
Bob and Carol Adams Collection.
Jeff Scovil photographer.

Fig. 37 Salena Jackson bowl.
8½" high by 17" diameter, ca. 1920.
Bob and Carol Adams Collection.
Jeff Scovil photographer.

Louisa (Lasyeh) Francisco
"Mrs. Dick Francisco"
Bancalache Yokuts | 1857–1953

Louisa Francisco, the Yokuts basketweaver known today as Mrs. Dick Francisco, was born in Glennville, California (Latta 1949). By the time of her death, she was the last full-blooded member of the Bancalache Yokuts, whose territory ranged from Kernville and Bodfish along the Kern River in the far southern Sierra Nevada to Porterville in the Central Valley (Latta 1949:191). Mrs. Dick Francisco, whose English name was Louisa (Indian name Lasyeh), spent most of her life on the Tule River Reservation near Porterville (Latta 1949:192).

Dick Francisco, a Koyeti Yokuts Indian who ran a farm and cattle ranch, was originally married for many years to a woman named Martha, but by 1915 he was widowed and lived alone through June 1922 (Indian Census Tule Reservation 1890, 1893, 1900, and 1915–1922).

In late 1922 or 1923[1], when he was 73 or 74 years old, he married Louisa, then 57 or 58, and already the creator of many baskets. And so, to personify her properly, she is referred to here as Louisa Francisco.

Before her marriage to Dick Francisco, Louisa was married for at least 28 years (since 1885 or before) to Leymas (Romando) Olivier[2], and thus was known as Louisa Olivier during those years. This early union produced at least three children: Mary Alfonsa (1885), Domingo (1889), and Pereneuso (1893), though only Mary lived to adulthood. Louisa and Leymas appear to have had a falling-out in the last years of marriage and lived separately from 1911 to 1913. Leymas died in 1913 or 1914[3] (Indian Census, Tule Reservation 1895, 1898–1914).

Dick Francisco, born June 22, 1849, died of pneumonia in March 1934 at the age of 84 (Indian Census, Tule Reservation, 1934), and Louisa lived on for nearly 20 years, until the age of 96. She ultimately became famous for her baskets, being identified and specifically recognized as "Mrs. Dick Francisco," even though she made many of her notable baskets before acquiring that name.

In his *Handbook of the Yokuts* published in 1949, Frank Latta used Mrs. Dick Francisco as an important source of information concerning Yokuts customs and lifestyles. She was considered by the Yokuts who knew her well to be very knowledgeable about the lives of the Yokuts, past and present (Latta 1949:198).

Louisa Francisco is known today as one of the finest and most important weavers in the history of California basketry. She created many of the best bottleneck baskets made by the Yokuts, with coil counts reaching 12 per inch and stitch counts up to 23 per inch (Bob Adams personal communication 2009).

A photograph on page 192 of Latta's book (Latta 1949:192) shows Louisa holding two of her bottleneck baskets (Fig. 41). She wove on grass-bundle foundations, using traditional Yokuts design elements such as water-skaters, flies, quail plumes, rattlesnake bands, and most notably humans, and even butterflies. Her weaving style appears to have been unaffected by some of the wider trends characterizing the Florescence—although she clearly took advantage of the newly developed markets of non-Indian buyers to expand and perfect her artistic talents.

She is most famous for her superb gambling or gaming trays, which rank with the greatest masterpieces of Native American basketry, some reaching diameters of 32 inches and requiring more than a year to make (Collings 1975:13). Eighteen of her gambling trays (numbering in total between 20 to 25) are fully illustrated in this book.

Beginning in the mid-1890s, Helen Harvey of Porterville accumulated a large collection of Native American Californian baskets including many of Mrs. Dick Francisco's finest works. Mrs. Harvey recorded many of her acquisitions in a handwritten ledger, with basketry descriptions, sizes, dates, and even the names of many of the artists. She also took a number of photographs. The ledger and photographs together provide priceless information. The latter archival materials are today in the private collection of Bob and Carol Adams (Bob Adams personal communication 2009).

The Harvey collection contained approximately 150 pieces, including possibly the largest group of Mrs. Dick Francisco's baskets ever assembled. Around 1943, Ms. Harvey began selling her collection to the Cummings, Crew, and Carr families of Porterville (Bob Adams personal communication 2009).

Fig. 38 Mrs. Dick Francisco with basket shown in Fig. 39, ca. 1905.
Photograph courtesy Bob and Carol Adams.

Fig. 39 Mrs. Dick Francisco gambling tray.
31" diameter, ca. 1900.
Thaw Collection, Fenimore Art Museum, Cooperstown, New York.
Gift of Eugene Victor Thaw Art Foundation.
Catalogue number T0797.
John Bigelow Taylor photographer.

Fig. 40 Mr. and Mrs. Dick Francisco, June 1932.
Photograph courtesy Bancroft Library, University of California,
Berkeley. Catalogue number BANC PIC 1978.90.

Fig. 41 Mrs. Dick Francisco with two bottleneck ollas, ca. 1929.
Photograph courtesy Yosemite Museum and Research Library.
National Park Service Catalogue number YOSE 04937.

Fig. 42 Mrs. Dick Francisco bottleneck olla.
8" high by 14½" diameter.
Natalie Linn Collection.
Justin Tunis photographer.

Fig. 43 Mrs. Dick Francisco bottleneck olla.
6¼" high by 11¼" diameter.
Natalie Linn Collection.
Jeff Scovil photographer.

Fig. 44 Mrs. Dick Francisco bottleneck olla.
7" high by 14" diameter.
Alex Schwed Collection.
Todd Adams photographer.

Fig. 45 Office in Cummings home, ca. 1940. Mrs. Dick Francisco baskets shown in Figs. 46, 48, 49, 50, and 60. Photograph courtesy Bob and Carol Adams.

Fig. 46* Mrs. Dick Francisco gambling tray.
28" diameter.
Private collection.
Photograph courtesy Sotheby's.
See Appendix 3, Figure Notes | Pg. 307

Fig. 47 Mrs. Dick Francisco gambling tray.
30¾" diameter.
Alex Schwed Collection.
Todd Adams photograph.

Fig. 48 Mrs. Dick Francisco gambling tray.
29½" diameter.
Robert and Bunny Jochim Collection.
Jeff Scovil photographer.

Fig. 49 Mrs. Dick Francisco gambling tray.
30" diameter.
Private collection.
Jeff Scovil photographer.

Fig. 50* Mrs. Dick Francisco gambling tray.
32" diameter.
Wayne and Stevia Thompson Collection.
Jeff Scovil photographer.
See Appendix 3, Figure Notes | Pg. 307

Fig. 52 Mrs. Dick Francisco bowl.
7" deep by 14½" diameter.
Alan and Bronnie Blaugrund Collection.
Jeff Scovil photographer.

Fig. 51 Mrs. Dick Francisco bottleneck olla.
6" high by 10" diameter.
Alan and Bronnie Blaugrund Collection.
Jeff Scovil photographer.

Fig. 53 Mrs. Dick Francisco gambling tray.
25½" diameter.
Private collection.
Jeff Scovil photographer.

Fig. 54 Mrs. Dick Francisco bowl.
5¼" high by 14" diameter.
Wayne and Stevia Thompson Collection.
Jeff Scovil photographer.

Fig. 55 Mrs. Dick Francisco bowl.
10" diameter.
Bob and Carol Adams Collection.
Jeff Scovil photographer.

Fig. 56 Mrs. Dick Francisco bottleneck olla.
10" diameter.
Greg and Cathy Sarena Collection.
Jeff Scovil photographer.

Fig. 58 Mrs. Dick Francisco jar.
5½" diameter.
Bob and Carol Adams Collection.
Jeff Scovil photographer.

Fig. 57 Mrs. Dick Francisco bottleneck olla.
9" diameter.
Todd Adams Collection.
Jeff Scovil photographer.

Fig. 59* Photograph ca. 1920s showing part of the Helen Harvey Collection of Mrs. Dick Francisco gambling trays in Figs. 39, 60, 61, 64, and 66. Photograph courtesy Bob and Carol Adams.

*See Appendix 3, Figure Notes | Pg. 307

Fig. 60 Mrs. Dick Francisco gambling tray.
30¼" diameter.
Robert and Claire Hardiman Collection.
F. Farah photographer.

Fig. 61 Mrs. Dick Francisco gambling tray.
28" diameter.
Private collection.
Photograph courtesy Gene Quintana.
John Law photographer.

Fig. 62 Mrs. Dick Francisco holding bottleneck jars shown in Figs. 63 and 65, and tray shown in Fig. 64, ca. 1930s. Photograph courtesy Bob and Carol Adams.

Fig. 64 Mrs. Dick Francisco tray.
27" diameter, ca. 1930.
Table Mountain Rancheria Collection.
Photograph courtesy Todd Adams.

Fig. 63 Mrs. Dick Francisco bottleneck olla.
12" diameter.
Todd Adams Collection.
Jeff Scovil photographer.

Fig. 65 Mrs. Dick Francisco bottleneck olla.
11" diameter.
Private collection.
Photograph courtesy Todd Adams.

Fig. 66 Mrs. Dick Francisco gambling tray.
30¼" diameter.
Robert and Claire Hardiman Collection.
F. Farah photographer.

Fig. 67* Mrs. Dick Francisco gambling tray.
26¼" diameter.
Private collection.
Jeff Scovil photographer.

*See Appendix 3, Figure Notes | Pg. 307

Fig. 68 Mrs. Dick Francisco in the 1930s with gambling trays shown in Figs. 64, 69, and 80; bowl shown in Fig. 55; and bottleneck olla shown in Fig. 64. Photograph courtesy Bob and Carol Adams.

Fig. 69 Mrs. Dick Francisco gambling tray.
26½" diameter.
Private collection.
Photograph courtesy Bob and Carol Adams.

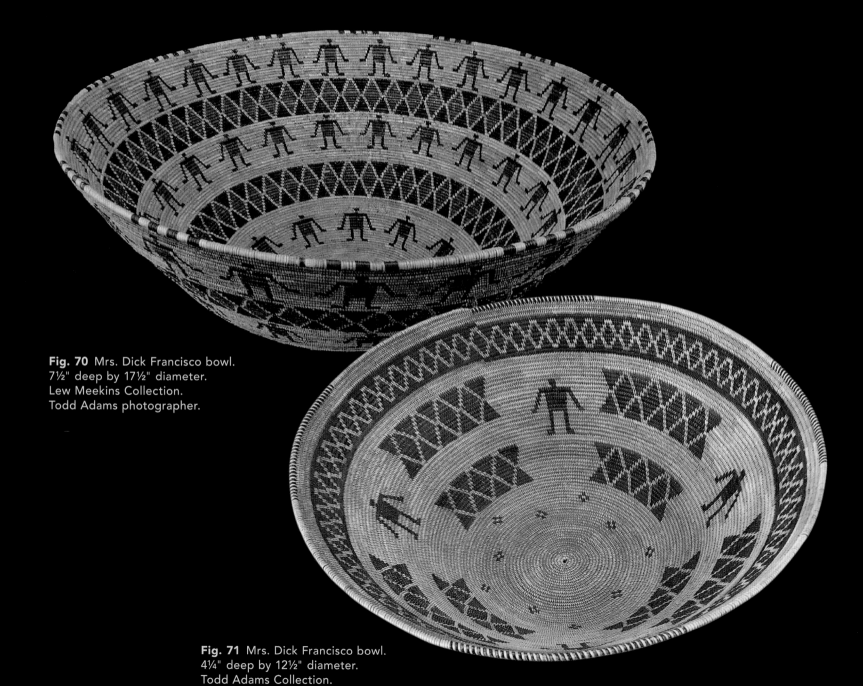

Fig. 70 Mrs. Dick Francisco bowl.
7½" deep by 17½" diameter.
Lew Meekins Collection.
Todd Adams photographer.

Fig. 71 Mrs. Dick Francisco bowl.
4¼" deep by 12½" diameter.
Todd Adams Collection.
Todd Adams photographer.

Fig. 72 Mrs. Dick Francisco bowl.
12¼" diameter.
Private collection.
Ben Watkins photographer.

Fig. 73 Mrs. Dick Francisco bowl.
14" diameter.
Private collection.
Jeff Scovil photographer.

Fig. 74 Mrs. Dick Francisco gambling tray.
26" diameter.
Private collection.
Photograph courtesy Todd Adams.

Fig. 75 Mrs. Dick Francisco gambling tray.
30" diameter.
Todd Adams Collection.
Todd Adams photographer.

Fig. 76 Photograph of a portion of the Helen Harvey Collection, ca. 1920. Included in the photograph is the basket shown in Fig. 78. Photograph courtesy Bob and Carol Adams.

Fig. 79 Mrs. Dick Francisco gambling tray.
26" diameter.
Chicago Institute of Art, Catalogue #1994312.
Jerry Jacka photographer.

Fig. 80 Mrs. Dick Francisco gambling tray.
24¾" diameter.
The Collection of Ken and Judy Siebel.
Gene Meieran photographer.

Fig. 81 Mrs. Dick Francisco with baskets shown in Figs. 63, 64, 69, and 80; basket seen in Fig. 55; and bottleneck basket seen in Fig. 65, ca. 1930s. Photograph courtesy Bob and Carol Adams.

Fig. 82 Mrs. Dick Francisco bowl.
21" diameter.
The Collection of Ken and Judy Siebel.
Gene Meieran photographer.

Fig. 83 Mrs. Dick Francisco gambling tray.
31¼" diameter.
Gift of William K. Jewett.
Photograph courtesy of the Penn Museum.
Image number NA8307A.

Sarah Jim Mayo
Washoe | 1860–1918

Sarah Jim Mayo was born around 1860. Her mother was known as "Doctor" and her father, Captain Jim, was probably the most important nineteenth century Captain or spokesman for the Washoe in their relations with Anglo society. Sarah had one sister, Agnes (Cohodas 1986). Sarah married Big George and they had two children, but by 1888 George had left and Sarah then remarried to Tom Sanco, having one child with him. In 1896, they separated and by about 1900 Sarah married again, this time to Captain Pete Mayo. Captain Pete was the father of Maggie Mayo James, who would later be among the next generation of basketweavers to be influenced by Sarah Jim Mayo's art (Cohodas 1979a, 1981, 1986).

When Captain Pete Mayo traveled to Washington, DC to meet President Woodrow Wilson, Sarah wove a presentation basket with an inscribed message for the President. Sarah's importance in the community is documented through several photographs of her with distinguished politicians and judges. Unfortunately, this "presentation basket," shown in Figs. 96, 97, and 98, has since disappeared. An excellent article about the missing presentation basket is provided by *The Reno Gazette-Journal*, written by Jenny Kane, and appearing in the January 6, 2016 edition of the journal.

Captain Pete Mayo was a victim of the 1918 influenza epidemic and after his death Sarah moved to Mottsville in the Carson Valley in Nevada (Cohodas 1979a; pages 47-49; Cohodas 1981). She died soon after in 1918, also of influenza (*The Reno Gazette-Journal*, December 20, 1918).

Regardless that the technical abilities of other Washoe weavers were considered superior to Sarah's, her innovative approach to imagery was to have a greater influence on later Washoe weavers than even Dat So La Lee. Her use of butterflies, human figures, eagles, trees, horses, deer, and even houses began between 1905/1910 and started a trend in Washoe weaving that lasted nearly two decades (Cohodas 1986).

And although Sarah never enjoyed a full-time artist/patron relationship that a few basketweavers enjoyed, she did sell many of her baskets to Margaretta Dressler, the wife of an important Carson Valley rancher. Margaretta assembled a fine collection of Washoe basketry (Cohodas 1986).

Photographs of Sarah in 1913 and 1916 document five of her baskets; and another basket has an Emporium label. By 1979, Cohodas had attributed 18 more pieces to her basketry inventory (Cohodas 1979a). Subsequently many of her other baskets have since come to light (a few of which showed up on the television program *Antiques Roadshow*, Figs. 86 and 88). Sarah's artistic style had a tremendous influence on many of the great Washoe weavers and set a creative trend on the development of the Florescence.

Fig. 84 Sarah Jim Mayo degikup.
6¾" high by 10¼" diameter.
Robert and Bunny Jochim Collection.
Jeff Scovil photographer.

Fig. 85 Sarah Jim Mayo degikup.
4½" high by 6½" diameter.
Robert and Bunny Jochim Collection.
Jeff Scovil photographer.

Fig. 86 Sarah Jim Mayo and Captain Pete Mayo with grandchildren Loman and Daisy, ca. 1916. Degikup shown in Fig. 87 is in her lap. Photograph courtesy Nevada State Museum, Carson City, Nevada.

Fig. 87* Sarah Jim Mayo degikup.
20" diameter.
Private collection.
Photograph courtesy of *Antiques Roadshow* C1997–2010 © WGBH Educational Foundation.

*See Appendix 3, Figure Notes |
Pg. 307*

Fig. 88 Sarah Jim Mayo with degikup shown in Fig. 87 in her lap. Photograph courtesy Alex Schwed,

Fig. 89 Sarah Jim Mayo degikup.
6" high by 10" diameter.
Photograph courtesy Bob and Darlene Seng
and Greg and Cathy Sarena.
Bob Seng photographer.

Fig. 90 Sarah Jim Mayo degikup.
3½" high by 5½" diameter, ca. 1910.
Elizabeth Cole Butler Collection.
Photograph courtesy Portland Art Museum.
Catalogue number 91 95 36.

Fig. 91 Sarah Jim Mayo on the Dressler Ranch in Carson Valley, Nevada, ca. 1913.

Fig. 92 Sarah Jim Mayo degikup.
7½" high by 11½" diameter.
Eddie and Nadine Basha Collection.
Jeff Scovil photographer.

Fig. 93 Sarah Jim Mayo degikup.
4¾" high by 6½" diameter.
Photograph courtesy Nevada State Museum,
Carson City, Nevada.
Jeff Scovil photographer.

Fig. 94 Sarah Jim Mayo and Captain Pete Mayo. Governor Emmet
D. Boyle is to her left. Photograph is inscribed *To Captain Pete,
Chief of the Washoe Indians, from Emmet D. Boyle, Governor of
Nevada, May 1917.* Photograph courtesy University of Nevada
Research Services. Catalogue number UNRS-P1984-22-0.

Fig. 95 Sarah Jim Mayo and Captain Pete Mayo at the Al Tahoe Inn
with four of her baskets at her feet. Photograph courtesy University
of Nevada Research Services. Catalogue number UNRS-P1986-02-1(1).

Fig. 96* Sarah Jim Mayo and her father Captain Jim, her mother, and her husband Captain Pete Mayo, with the President Woodrow Wilson Presentation Basket, 1913. Dressler Ranch, Carson City, Nevada. Photograph courtesy Alan Dressler.

See Appendix 3, Figure Notes | Pg. 307

Fig. 97* Sarah Jim Mayo with Captain Pete Mayo and the President Woodrow Wilson Presentation Basket. Photograph courtesy Alan Dressler.

*See Appendix 3, Figure Notes | Pg. 307

Fig. 98* Sarah Jim Mayo with Captain Pete Mayo and the President Woodrow Wilson Presentation Basket, 1913. Photograph courtesy Phoebe A. Hearst Museum of Anthropology and the Regents of the University of California.

*See Appendix 3, Figure Notes | Pg. 307

Mary Smith Hill
Chemehuevi | 1873–1975

Little is known of Mary Smith Hill, a Native Chemehuevi. In Blythe, California, at the age of 82, she brought up her grandson John Hill, Jr. as her own. In John's own words to the right, he stated that she raised him to be tolerant and truthful. When she passed away in 1975 at the age of 102, John was "lost" but lived on to become an important personage in his own right in Parker, Arizona, where he now resides.

Mary had at least one son, John S. Hill, John's father.

Based on two documented baskets, she is obviously a fine Chemehuevi artist, but the whereabouts of other examples of her creations are at this writing unknown.

My name is Jonny Hill, Jr. I was born in Blythe, California on March 10, 1954. My mother was the late Leda Lee Paddock and my father was the late John S. Hill, Sr. A month or so after I was born my late grandmother, Mary Smith Hill, took me and raised me on her own. She was approximately 82 years old and she lived on to be 102. I was 21 when she passed away. She raised me in church and she taught me to be strong and to respect others no matter what the color of their skin. She taught me to be honest and to never lie.

When she passed I was lost.

—Jonny Hill, Jr., Mary Smith Hill's grandson

Fig. 99 Mary Smith Hill olla. 5¾" high by 7" diameter. Terry DeWald Collection. Terry DeWald photograph.

Fig. 100 Mary Smith Hill olla. 10" high by 13½" diameter. Eddie and Nadine Basha Collection. Jeff Scovil photographer.

Isabel Hanson was born at Warm Springs (now Indian Ranch), California, which lies in the Panamint Valley, a low and arid region with few human inhabitants. The Panamint Shoshone Indians (also known as the Timbisha) tradition-ally lived in small family units, and moved with seasonal changes (Slater 2000).

By the beginning of the twentieth century, Warm Springs had become known for the fine baskets that were being made there. As the new basket styles spread through California, Isabel Hanson emerged as a master weaver. She would become one of the finest Panamint artists in history (Slater 2000).

Early Panamint basketry displayed influences from the Kawaiisu, Tübatulabal, and Yokuts tribes, but the new styles brought many changes. Vertical elements replaced the older horizontal bands, grass bundle foundations faded, while triple-rod willow construction came to be dominant. Polychrome designs replaced monochrome designs. Isabel's baskets display beautiful color combinations following the new traditions and styles of California Native basketry.

When she was younger, Isabel made large, highly attractive, and very desirable baskets, but as she grew older her baskets became smaller; and the smaller more geometric works were sold to tourists. Basket sales and her herd of angora goats provided a good living (Slater 2000).

After her daughter died in 1938, and with the death of her brother in 1947, Isabel moved to Darwin, California, where she continued to weave nearly every day, creating fine baskets until her death in 1964 (Slater 2000).

Fig. 101 Isabel Hanson with her father Indian George, ca. 1915. Photograph courtesy Eastern California Museum, Independence, California.

Fig. 102 Isabel Hanson bowl.
10" deep by 22" diameter.
E. J. and Mimi Nusrala Collection.
Jeff Scovil photographer.

Fig. 103 Isabel Hanson bowl.
7" deep by 15" diameter.
Greg and Cathy Sarena Collection.
Jeff Scovil photographer.

Fig. 104 Isabel Hanson, ca. 1963.
Photograph courtesy County of
Inyo Eastern California Museum.

Fig. 105 Isabel Hanson bowl.
7" deep by 15" diameter.
Robert and Bunny Jochim Collection.
Jeff Scovil photographer.

Fig. 106 Isabel Hanson bowl.
11" deep by 22" diameter.
Photography © The Art Institute of Chicago.
Mrs. Leonard S. Florsheim, Jr. Endowment.
Curator's Discretionary Fund, 2006.189.

Fig. 107* Isabel Hanson with her daughter.
The two large baskets are Panamint and
characteristic of Isabel's weaving style.
Arizona Historical Society photograph.
Catalogue number OOO no. 110.

See Appendix 3, Figure Notes | Pg. 307

Casilda Saubel Chia

Cahuilla | ca. 1866–ca. 1920

Casilda Saubel Chia lived on the Morongo Reservation near Banning, California. Few details about her life are known, except for a vintage photograph (Fig. 108) of Casilda and her husband. Seven of her shallow bowls and trays are on exhibit in the Malki Museum in southern California.

Two of these bowls have a rattlesnake design, a motif popular with southern California artists after the taboo against rattlesnake designs faded in the early 1900s. Unfortunately, authenticated baskets by Casilda Saubel Chia are rarely available on the collector market. Even so, she is among the finest of the great Cahuilla tribal artists (see Moser 1993:96 for a brief narrative note on Casilda Saubel Chia, along with four accompanying photographs).

Fig. 108 Casilda Saubel Chia and her husband. Photograph courtesy Malki Museum, Banning, California.

Mary Knight Benson is arguably the best known of the Pomo basketweavers from the period 1895–1905 (Williams et al. 2005). She was born Mary E. Knight in Sanel, Mendocino County, California in the late 1870s, the daughter of Irish immigrant John Knight and a Pomo Indian woman named Fion[4] (Sarah).

She lived at the Yokayo Rancheria in Mendocino County, and in 1894 married William Benson (ca. 1862—1937); he was also an Indian artist, the son of an eastern Pomo woman and a white man from Missouri[5]. One of William Benson's famous miniature baskets is on exhibit at the Grace Hudson Museum, Ukiah, California, shown in Fig. 553. Mary and William settled at the Yokayo Rancheria, as did her mother, Sarah, and Mary's siblings. Sarah (Fion) was also a well-known, admired weaver.

Collector Grace Nicholson purchased their baskets and artworks in exchange for an annual stipend (Fane et al. 1991). One of Mary Knight Benson's greatest creations is a degikup made around 1925 that was later part of the Green Collection and sale. This piece is very much in the style of Dat So La Lee's great masterpieces, and of a quality to rival that great artist's finest works, Fig. 112.

Mary Knight Benson was working for the Fred Harvey Company in 1904, demonstrating the weaving of baskets and Pomo items in Albuquerque, New Mexico. Several baskets in the Harvey Collection appear to be her creations (Howard and Pardue 2000:62). Also, Mary was brought by patron Dr. John W. Hudson (a basket collector and husband of artist Grace Hudson) to the 1904 Louisiana Purchase Centennial Exposition in St. Louis, where she demonstrated basketweaving (Shukla 2000). Towards the end of her life, Mary Knight Benson increasingly suffered from ill health and died at the age of 52 in 1930.

Mary Knight Benson was a master weaver—one of the greatest of the Pomo weavers—who are famous throughout the world for their baskets, which include very large baskets (see Figs. 551 and 552) as well as amazingly small woven baskets (Fig. 553), feathered baskets, and beaded baskets.

Fig. 112* Mary Knight Benson degikup-like basket.
7½" high by 12" diameter.
Natalie Linn Collection.
Jeff Scovil photographer.

Fig. 111 Mary Knight Benson, William Benson, and Grace Nicholson. The Huntington Library, San Marino, California.

Fig. 113* William Benson and Mary Knight Benson, standing next to a Diegueño/Kumeyaay storage vessel. Grace Nicholson photo, ca. 1910. The Huntington Library, San Marino, California.

See Appendix 3, Figure Notes | Pg. 307

Fig. 114 Mary Knight Benson, ca. 1900. Photograph courtesy University of Southern California on behalf of the USC Special Collections. Catalogue number CL56.

Fig. 115 Mary Knight Benson, ca. 1900. This item is reproduced by permission of the Huntington Library, San Marino, California.

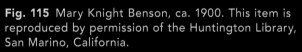

Fig. 116 Mary Knight Benson at Louisiana Purchase Centennial Celebration, St. Louis, Missouri, 1904. Photograph courtesy National Anthropological Archives, Smithsonian Institution. Image number P17579.

Fig. 117 Mary Knight Benson. Photograph courtesy The Huntington Library, San Marino, California. Grace Nicholson collection. Image number CL 56 (347). Grace Nicholson photograph.

Fig. 118 Mary Knight Benson bowl. 5" deep by 9¼" diameter. Photograph courtesy National Museum of the American Indian, Smithsonian Institution. Catalogue number 242120.

Fig. 119 Mary Knight Benson canoe basket. 5" wide by 11¼" long. Photograph courtesy Penn Museum.

Fig. 120 Mary Knight Benson holding "shuwitgie" basket, ca. 1910. Photograph courtesy National Museum of the American Indian, Smithsonian Institution. Catalogue number P34107.

Fig. 121 This is the last known photograph of Mary Knight Benson Photograph courtesy National Museum of the American Indian, Smithsonian Institution. Catalogue number P08349.

Fig. 122 Mary Knight and William Benson, ca. 1910. Photograph courtesy National Museum of the American Indian, Smithsonian Institution. Catalogue number N38238.

Fig. 123 Mary Knight Benson bowl. 9¾" diameter. Photograph courtesy National Museum of the American Indian, Smithsonian Institution. Catalogue number 048767.

Scees (Ceese) Bryant Possack

Washoe | 1858–1918

Scees Bryant Possack was born around 1858; unfortunately, little is known about her ancestry. Her first husband, Jim Bryant, was Dat So La Lee's brother. Scees and Jim had a son, Hugh, who was born in 1898. In 1908, Jim Bryant died and Scees married Indian Charley; she later married George Possack. Neither of her later marriages produced children.

Scees was left-handed but most of her baskets were woven in a right-handed, counter-clockwise style as seen looking down into the basket (Cohodas 1979a, 1986).

A photo from Cohn's Emporium, taken in about 1920, documents six Scees' baskets. The caption reads "The only baskets known to have been made by Scees." At least two of these baskets date to 1904. The last three were made in 1915 and 1918, including LK 64, which was started by Scees,

and finished by Dat So La Lee after Scees' death. A seventh documented basket was completed in 1906 and is in the Smithsonian National Museum of the American Indian. In her later phase, Scees' baskets are so similar to Dat So La Lee's as to be easily and often confused with Dat So La Lee's work (Cohodas 1979a, 1986).

Although she made relatively few baskets, and many were similar in design and style to her more famous sister-in-law's baskets, Scees Bryant Possack is also considered to be one of the finest Washoe basketmakers.

Scees died in the great influenza epidemic of 1918, which was probably spread by soldiers returning from the battlefields of World War I. During this horrendous pandemic, a large number of California Indian people also succumbed (Cohodas 1979a, 1986).

Fig. 124* Scees Bryant Possack degikup.
12¼" diameter, ca. 1918.
Photograph courtesy Gene Quintana.
John Law photographer.
*See Appendix 3, Figure Notes | Pg. 307

Fig. 125* Scees Bryant Possack degikup.
7" deep by 10¾" diameter.

Fig. 126 Scees Bryant Possack. Photograph courtesy Nevada State Museum, Department of Cultural Affairs, Carson City, Nevada.

Fig. 127 Scees Bryant Possack bowl. 6½" deep by 12¾" diameter. Photograph courtesy Nevada State Museum, Carson City, Nevada.

Fig. 128 Scees Bryant Possack. Photograph courtesy Nevada State Museum, Department of Cultural Affairs, Carson City, Nevada.

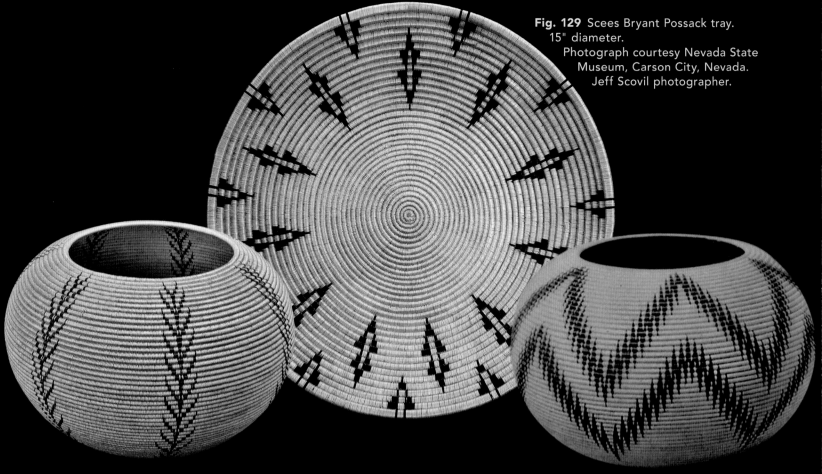

Fig. 129 Scees Bryant Possack tray.
15" diameter.
Photograph courtesy Nevada State
Museum, Carson City, Nevada.
Jeff Scovil photographer.

Fig. 130 Scees Bryant Possack degikup "The Ferns."
7½" high by 10½" diameter.
Thaw Collection, Fenimore Art Museum, Cooperstown, New York.
Gift of Eugene Victor Thaw Art Foundation.
Catalog number T0752.
Richard Walker photographer.

Fig. 131 Scees Bryant Possack degikup.
13" diameter.
Photograph courtesy Nevada Historical
Society, Reno, Nevada.

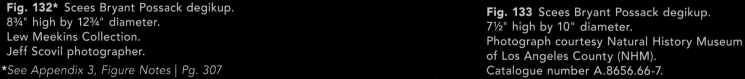

Fig. 132* Scees Bryant Possack degikup.
8¾" high by 12¾" diameter.
Lew Meekins Collection.
Jeff Scovil photographer.

*See Appendix 3, Figure Notes | Pg. 307

Fig. 133 Scees Bryant Possack degikup.
7½" high by 10" diameter.
Photograph courtesy Natural History Museum
of Los Angeles County (NHM).
Catalogue number A.8656.66-7.

Fig. 134 A group of baskets made by Scees Bryant Possack, including baskets shown in Figs. 129 through 133.

Daisy Meadows Baker was born in 1879 in northeastern California near Lassen National Monument, where the eastern shore of Lake Almanor is now located. In spite of experiencing several tragedies throughout her life, she remained an exceptional weaver. Her home in the upper Genesee Valley, where she lived with her husband Billy Baker and her three children, was mysteriously burned to the ground. Billy's allotment of land there was stolen from him and he was murdered in 1924 by unknown assailants, when their family was living in the Honey Lake Valley (Kurtz 2010, 2011).

Daisy created traditional Maidu geometric patterns, but also used elegant butterfly designs in her basketry, which had become popular in the early twentieth century. When her son Bill went overseas in World War II, she made a beautiful commemorative bowl of maple, black fern, and redbud (Kurtz 2010, 2011).

A photograph of Daisy working on one of her last baskets was taken at the Salem Ranch on Lake Almanor in the late 1950s. She never finished the basket in the photograph, but years later it was completed by her daughter Lilly Baker, who also was an exceptional weaver. Like relatives of other fine weavers such as Julia Parker and Margie George, Lilly's weaving career began after the Florescence had already ended in 1940 or so (Kurtz 2010, 2011).

Fig. 135 Daisy Meadows Baker bowl. 8¼" diameter.
Photograph courtesy Pat Kurtz.
David Bozsik photographer.

Fig. 137 Daisy Meadows Baker, late 1950s.
Photograph courtesy Pat Kurtz.

Fig. 136 Daisy Meadows Baker tray. 16½" diameter.
Photograph courtesy Pat Kurtz.
David Bozsik photographer.

Carrie Bethel

Mono Lake Paiute (Kuzedika) | 1898–1974

Carrie Bethel was born in Lee Vining, California, on July 4, 1898. She spent most of her childhood near Bodie in the Mono Basin, California (Bates and Lee 1990).

Her mother was Suzie Bill McGowan and her father was Poker Bill, son of Captain Jim. Suzie McGowan died during childbirth. Carrie, her sisters Minnie Bill (aka Minnie Turner—or more popularly—Minnie Mike), and Sadie were raised by their stepmother Suzie Thompson (Bates and Lee 1990).

She learned to weave as a child, often discarding inferior baskets. Her sister, Minnie Mike, also became an important weaver (see pages 178–180). By the 1920s, Carrie was a master weaver, often competing in the June Lake and Yosemite Indian Field Days. A number of photographs of Carrie at these events have been widely circulated (Bates and Lee 1990). Carrie was married twice; her second husband was Harry Bethel, a Western Mono man (Bates and Lee 1990).

Carrie developed an artist-patron relationship with James Schwabacher, the most important collector of Yosemite baskets. He purchased many of her finest large basket creations (Bates and Lee 1990).

In 1929, she finished a fine 21-inch degikup (Fig. 141) and in the early 1930s she spent four years weaving her largest masterpiece, shown in Fig. 151. As demand for large baskets lessened, she began weaving smaller triple-rod and beaded baskets. In 1958, Carrie delivered one of her most beautiful large masterpieces to Schwabacher, a few months before his death (Fig. 140). She completed her last 14-inch masterpiece in the early 1960s (Fig. 144). Carrie continued to weave smaller pieces until her death in 1974 (Bates and Lee 1990).

Unlike Washoe basketweaver Dat So La Lee (see pages 114–142), Carrie earned much of her living doing domestic work. This limited her ability to create fine baskets, but her relationship with Schwabacher certainly allowed her the luxury of artistic creativity, and at this she excelled, becoming arguably the finest single artist of the Florescence. Indeed, at least three of her five larger baskets have brought prices near or over seven figures, a feat matched only by Dat So La Lee.

Three of her five largest baskets are in museums: specifically, the Yosemite Museum and Autry Museum of the Southwest. The others reside in the finest private collections in the country. Fortunately, her smaller baskets occasionally find their way to the collector's market.

Fig. 138* Carrie Bethel degikup "The Dream Basket." 5¾" high by 8¼" diameter.
Alan and Bronnie Blaugrund Collection.
Jeff Scovil photographer.
*See Appendix 3, Figure Notes | Pg. 307

Minnie and Carrie had favorite secret spots to collect willows for their basket. Since they lived traditional lives, they made working baskets they used for daily life. They made burden baskets for gathering pine nuts and piagi (Pandora moth larvae) off Jeffrey Pines, cooking baskets, winnowing baskets, water jugs, and baby baskets. Minnie made baby baskets for her children, grandchildren, and great-grandchildren.

—William Jerry Andrews, Minnie Mike's grandson and Carrie Bethel's nephew

Fig. 139 Carrie Bethel, Mono Lake Paiute. Braun Research Library Collection. Autry Museum, Los Angeles. Item number N.30966.

Fig. 140* Carrie Bethel degikup.
13" high by 25" diameter, 1956/1958.
Wayne and Stevia Thompson Collection.
Jeff Scovil photographer.

*See Appendix 3, Figure Notes | Pg. 307

Fig. 141 Carrie Bethel degikup.
10" high by 21" diameter, ca. 1928.
Private collection.
Photograph courtesy Gene Quintana.
John Law photographer.

Fig. 142 Carrie Bethel holding
basket shown in Fig. 141, in 1929.
Photograph courtesy Yosemite
Museum and Research Library.
National Park Service.

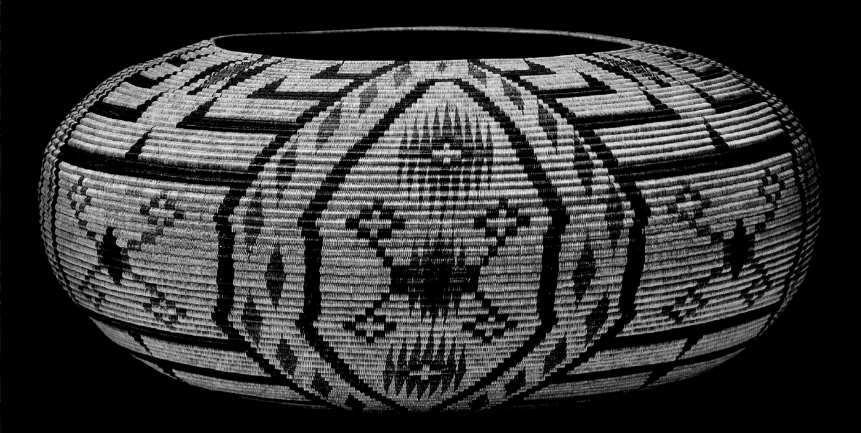

Fig. 143* Carrie Bethel degikup.
10" high by 26" diameter, ca. 1930.
Photograph courtesy Mrs. Gene Autry.
Autry Museum, Los Angeles. Item number LT2013-6-1.
See Appendix 3, Figure Notes | Pg. 307

Fig. 144* Carrie Bethel degikup.
8" high by 13½" diameter, 1961/1962.
The Collection of Ken and Judy Siebel.
Photograph courtesy Gene Quintana.
John Law photographer.

*See Appendix 3, Figure Notes | Pg. 307

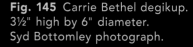

Fig. 145 Carrie Bethel degikup.
3½" high by 6" diameter.
Syd Bottomley photograph.

Fig. 146 The Bill Family—Carrie Bethel's parents with Carrie Bethel (right)
and Minnie Mike (left), ca. 1900 [in the center, unidentified third child or
infant]. Photograph courtesy Yosemite Museum and Research Library.
National Park Service Catalogue number YOSE 27028.

Fig. 147 Carrie Bethel, ca. 1940.
Photograph courtesy Jerry Andrews.

Fig. 148* Carrie Bethel degikup.
14" high by 27" diameter.
The Collection of Ken and Judy Siebel.
Photograph courtesy Gene Quintana.
John Law photographer.

See Appendix 3, Figure Notes | Pg. 307

Fig. 149 Carrie Bethel with basket shown in Fig. 150 at the June Lake Field Days, 1929. Also seen is Nellie Jameson Washington (right) and her basket shown in Fig. 180. Photograph courtesy Alex Schwed.

Fig. 150* Carrie Bethel degikup. 8" high by 17½" diameter, ca. 1929. E. J. and Mimi Nusrala Collection. Jeff Scovil photographer.

Fig. 151* Carrie Bethel degikup.
21" high by 32¼" diameter, 1930s.
Photograph courtesy Yosemite Museum and Research Library.
National Park Service Catalogue number YOSE 66820.
Gene Meieran photographer.

*See Appendix 3, Figure Notes | Pg. 308

Bottom view.

Side view.

Fig. 152* Carrie Bethel degikup.
7½" deep by 14½" diameter, ca. 1925.
Private collection.
© 2012 Bonhams & Butterfields Auctioneers
Corporation. All rights reserved.
German Herrera photographer.

*See Appendix 3, Figure Notes | Pg. 308

Fig. 153 Carrie Bethel with California Governor Friend Richardson,
Yosemite Indian Field Days, 1925. Carrie is holding basket Fig. 152.
Tina Charlie is to the left of Governor Richardson. Photograph courtesy
Yosemite Museum and Research Library, National Park Service.

Fig. 154 Carrie Bethel degikup.
13½" high by 22" diameter, 1930s.
Yosemite Museum and Research Library.
National Park Service Catalogue number YOSE 66821

Carrie Bethel was my great aunt. She was my grandmother Minnie Mike's sister. She lived alone in a two-bedroom house. She had no electricity, so everything she did was during the day. So she did her basket and beading during the day.

In her early years, she worked for Caltrans as a cook for many years. In her spare time, she worked on her baskets and beading. And every time she was making a basket, she had a lot of visitors. That was because they wanted to see who was going to be the first to buy it.

—Violet Dondero, Carrie Bethel's great niece

Fig. 155 Carrie Bethel (right) with her sister Minnie Mike, near Lee Vining, California. Carrie is holding the baskets shown in Figs. 156 and 157, ca. 1962. Photograph courtesy Jim Yoakum

Ramona Lubo (Diego)
Cahuilla | 1853–1922

Ramona Lubo was born right after the Mexican-American War, just as California was on the way to becoming the 31st state in the United States. Her village, Sahatapa, was located in San Timoteo Canyon, near Riverside, California. Ramona's mother died when she was young and she and her brothers were raised by their father, José Maria Lubo (Moser 1993).

When she was about 10 years old, her family fled from the growing smallpox epidemic; unfortunately, her father caught the disease and died. Her grandmother moved again with the children to avoid being exposed. At about age 15, Ramona moved back to her native homeland living in Cahuilla, California, near Riverside. In 1873, she married Juan Diego and through their union gave birth to two children. Both children died at a young age (Moser 1993).

In 1883, Juan Diego was killed by Sam Temple, a Euro-American who accused Juan of stealing a horse. Temple was not charged with the murder, prompting Helen Hunt Jackson to file an official report with the United States government. Helen strongly protested what she recognized as the unjust treatment of the Indians by the Euro-Americans. She later based her 1884 highly popular novel *Ramona* on these events (Jackson 1884). Her book was resoundingly acclaimed and became a runaway international bestseller. The story was also transformed into an annual play (Moser 1993) and into several film versions.

After Juan's death, Ramona lived with her brother, Capitán Dico Cinciono Lubo. She later returned to Cahuilla doing domestic work for white families and weaving baskets. During her time with her brother she again gave birth to another child, who sadly died while young (Moser 1993).

In 1899/1900, George Wharton James photographed Ramona with her famous "star basket" that was made as a memorial to Juan (Fig. 159). This particular basket—as well as many other similar star baskets—has become a symbol of Ramona's basketmaking artistry. By this time, Ramona had become somewhat famous and made appearances at local fairs and other shows as the "Real Ramona." In 1921, she suffered several bouts with influenza and passed away in 1922 (Moser 1993).

A number of documented Ramona baskets, as well as pieces attributed to her, are in the collections of the Malki Museum, Riverside County, and Pomona College, Los Angeles County. Her baskets are primarily juncus and sumac on a grass foundation. The star pattern incorporated in many of her baskets—the symbol for Ramona Lubo—has become widely recognized and helped her to become one of the best known of the Cahuilla weavers.

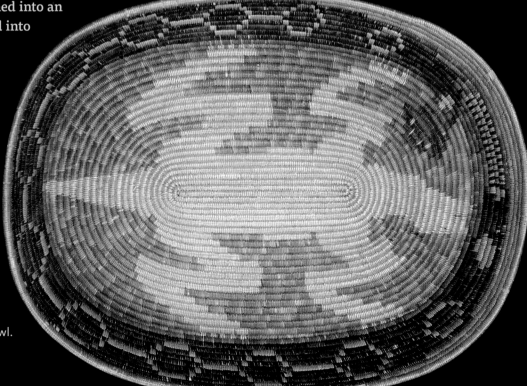

Fig. 158 Ramona Lubo oval bowl.
2½" deep by 12" wide by
16" long, ca. 1916.
Private collection.
Jerry Jacka photographer.

*See Appendix 3, Figure Notes | Pg. 308

Fig. 161 Ramona Lubo bowl.
15½" diameter.
Collection of Agua Caliente Band of Cahuilla Indians.
Catalogue number L2002003076.
Photograph courtesy Gene Quintana.

Fig. 162 Ramona Lubo bowl.
3" deep by 11½" diameter.
Natalie Linn Collection.
Justin Tunis photograph.

Fig. 163 Ramona Lubo. Courtesy of the Agua Caliente Cultural Museum.
Catalogue number 2003032007. All rights reserved.

Fig. 165 Ramona Lubo (right) with Rose Costo.
Photograph courtesy San Jacinto Museum,
San Jacinto, California.

Fig. 167 Ramona Lubo "Star" tray. 8" diameter.
Photograph courtesy Heard Museum, Phoenix, Arizona.

Fig. 168 Ramona Lubo at the grave of her husband, Juan Diego. The Huntington Library, San Marino, California. Image #CL 294 (220). George Wharton James photographer.

Fig. 169 Ramona Lubo, ca. 1895. Photograph courtesy San Jacinto Museum, San Jacinto, California.

Fig. 170 Ramona Lubo. Photograph courtesy National Museum of the American Indian. Smithsonian Institution Item 325137, photo P00499. Edward H. Davis photographer.

Kitty (Kittie) Johnson
Chemehuevi/Paiute | 1873/1878–year of death unknown

Kitty Johnson was born in California, and the U.S. Census lists her as a resident of Victorville, having lived there from 1900 to 1933. Earlier records on Kitty do not exist as that documentation was destroyed in a fire. Her tribal affiliation is surrounded by considerable confusion; nevertheless, most of the official records list her simply as a "Paiute." In the ledger of Grace Nicholson—who knew Kitty Johnson particularly well and regularly purchased baskets from her—Kitty is listed as a Victorville Chemehuevi. However, Mrs. Chlorene Hayward also purchased baskets from Kitty, and in her collection ledger she listed Kitty as Paiute. Kitty's name has also appeared as Katie on some baskets, perhaps an error in some catalogue listings (Kania 2014).

Christopher L. Moser, in his book *Native American Basketry of Southern California* lists Kitty Johnson as a Serrano, since Kitty's husband Juan Johnson also appears in the census records as a Serrano (Moser 1993:117–118). A vintage photograph of Kitty with her famous butterfly olla has a handwritten note on the back: "Chemehuevi Indian." This confusion may be attributable in part to the fact that some tribes were called by more than one name; both "Paiute" and "Chemehuevi" are correct names for the Chemehuevi since the Chemehuevi are a group of Native Americans who spoke the Southern Paiute language.

Grace Nicholson's ledger lists basket #2792 as having been purchased from Kitty Johnson in 1907. This basket was later sold to Homer Sargent and now resides in the Chicago Field Museum Collection as #103040. A very similar basket, now #A5697-17 in the Natural History Museum of Los Angeles County, was in the Cole/Waters' Collection, which was fashioned at the Victorville Native community before the turn of the last century. This basket is clearly the work of Kitty Johnson, as are two shallow trays from the same collection. These early baskets of Kitty's vary significantly from documented pieces she made later in life.

The Ruby Richardson Collection ledger begins in 1907 and ends in 1922. It lists eleven baskets that were purchased from Kitty Johnson (John Kania personal communication 2016).

Mrs. Chlorene Hayward, who began collecting baskets in 1921, lists three baskets that she purchased from Kitty Johnson. Chlorene, who kept detailed records of her collection, relates that Kitty would drive her horse and buggy from Victorville every year to sell baskets to her; she also notes that Kitty Johnson was an excellent weaver (John Kania personal communication 2016).

Most of this early documentation relating to Kitty Johnson was nearly forgotten, with the result being that Kitty Johnson's name had almost faded into the shadows that have enveloped many of the great, now unknown, Native Californian basketweavers. However, when the Ruby Richardson Collection—which had been on loan to the Natural History Museum of Los Angeles County (NHM) since 1950—was returned to its heirs, the collection was placed with Bonhams and Butterfields, which auctioned it in April 2001.

At this auction, many unique and beautiful baskets were unveiled, but the star of the show was Kitty Johnson's butterfly olla, which sold for $146,625. This was then an all-time world-record auction price for any American Indian basket. The Richardson Collection and its sale introduced the Victorville Phenomenon to most of the basket world, and Kitty Johnson's baskets were the focal point. The Victorville Phenomenon is the name given to the confusing events that led to the creation of this new style of basketry—unlike any other in Native Californian basket history, and characteristic of the design and shape of just about all of Kitty Johnson's baskets.

Kitty Johnson appears to have been the most significant artist of the Phenomenon, and quite probably its instigator, although other weavers—among them Annie Brown, Maria Chapula, Suzie Higgins, and Nancy Johnson—also contributed. All of these other weavers were Chemehuevi (aka Southern Paiute) or Kawaiisu, and therefore the Victorville Phenomenon may have been largely a Southern Paiute/Kawaiisu innovation and not the necessary result of the mingling of cultures, as was once believed. However, recent documentation attests to the fact that there were Natives of Serrano, Kawaiisu, and Chemehuevi affiliation all living together at the Native Californian Victorville Indian village (Blomberg 1987; Garfinkel and Williams 2011:66)

Fig. 171 Kitty Johnson holding the butterfly olla shown in Fig. 172, ca. 1907.

Fig. 172* Kitty Johnson butterfly olla.
19½" high by 20½" diameter.
Wayne and Malee Thompson Collection.
Jeff Scovil photographer.

*See Appendix 3, Figure Notes | Pg. 308

A closer look at Kitty Johnson's career shows two distinct phases. Her early, more traditional phase from 1890 to 1910 is defined by the use of grass bundle foundations to produce small, blocky jars and shallow trays. Juncus, dyed juncus, dyed willow, and white sumac were used to brightly color the horizontal banding and for meandering line designs with negative backgrounds (John Kania personal communication 2016).

In her second made-for-sale phase from 1910 to 1935, Kitty Johnson created unusually large ollas, some similar in shape to Apache baskets. She also made large globular jars with short necks. The dominant color was furnished by dark orange juncus, with dynamic new patterns characterized by diagonal or vertical geometric patterns, even containing exceptional figural elements. During this phase, Kitty used both grass bundle and triple-rod foundations, often on the same basket; this technique appears to be her signature and renders her unique among the weavers of Victorville. This beautiful new style of basket was the basis of the Victorville Phenomenon. Kitty Johnson's newly recognized leadership as its most important creator has ensured her a place on the list of California's most influential artists and master weavers (John Kania personal communication 2016).

Fig. 173 Kitty Johnson, ca. 1907, with the butterfly olla shown in Fig. 172. Photograph courtesy Wayne A. Thompson.

Fig. 174 Kitty Johnson with girl. C. Hart Merriam photograph. Photograph courtesy Bancroft Library, University of California, Berkeley. Catalogue number BANC I0011159A.

Fig. 175* Kitty Johnson bowl.
3¾" deep by 12" diameter.
Collection Palm Springs Art Museum.
Gift of Mary Beal.
Catalogue number A554-1974.
Jeff Scovil photographer.
*See Appendix 3, Figure Notes | Pg. 308

Fig. 176 Olla attributed to Kitty Johnson.
12" high by 14½" diameter.
Ned Smith Collection.
Photograph courtesy Ned Smith.

Fig. 177 Kitty Johnson olla.
10¼" high by 14" diameter, ca. 1907.
Photograph courtesy Gene Quintana.
John Law photographer.

Nellie Jameson Washington

Mono Lake Paiute (Kuzedika) | 1903–year of death unknown

In 1928, Nellie Jameson Washington displayed an exceptional degikup (Fig. 180) at the June Lake Field Days competition. The venue for this gathering was June Lake, just south of Mono Lake in eastern California. Competing with entries from Tina Charlie (see pages 15–23), Carrie Bethel (see pages 89–100), and Leanna Tom (see pages 144–147), Nellie's degikup won second place, a distinguished prize considering the eminence of her competitors!

Ella Cain, a prominent collector of Yosemite baskets, purchased this basket for her collection, which is now among the finest of the great Yosemite, new-style baskets ever made. The basket remained in her collection until it was auctioned by Bonhams and Butterfields in 2005.

In the 1930s, Nellie started a much larger degikup, but due to her failing health, she never completed the piece. It was obtained by James Schwabacher who arranged for Carrie Bethel to put a finishing rim stitch on the piece (Bates and Lee 1990:115–116).

Fig. 178 Nellie Jameson Washington degikup. 7¾" high by 13½" diameter.
© 2012 Bonhams & Butterfields Auctioneers Corporation. All rights reserved.
German Herrera photographer.

Fig. 179 Nellie Jameson Washington (second from left) holding the basket shown in Fig. 180 at June Lake Field Days, 1928. Tina Charlie is to Nellie's left and Carrie Bethel to her right. Photograph courtesy Alex Schwed.

Fig. 180* Nellie Jameson Washington degikup.
6½" deep by 11½" diameter, ca. 1928.
Todd Adams Collection.
Todd Adams photograph.
*See Appendix 3, Figure Notes | Pg. 308

Louisa Keyser (Dat So La Lee)
Southern Washoe | ca. 1829–1925

Dat So La Lee, the great Washoe weaver, was born sometime between 1829 and 1850 (most researchers put her year of birth around 1835), the daughter of a union between a Washoe man named Da Da Uongala and an unnamed Washoe woman. Her exact place of birth is unknown. The baby was given the name Dabuda. Dabuda would become an internationally recognized artist named Dat So La Lee (aka Louisa Keyser), the most famous and most documented of all of the California Native basketweavers.

Dabuda was born a member of the Southern Washoe tribe that lived in the Carson Valley of Alpine County near the Nevada-California border, not far from the mining town of Sheridan. She grew up in both Carson Valley and on the southeastern shore of Lake Tahoe, as the Washoe people of that time migrated with the seasons (Cohodas 1976, 1979a; Hickson 1967; Quintana 2010).

When she was young, she worked for a white family doing laundry and other household chores. In 1871, she is reported in many biographies to have gone to the town of Monitor in Alpine County, California, where she was employed by the Harris Cohn family (Cohodas 1976, 1979a; Hickson 1967; Quintana 2010). However, as is the situation with many of the weavers featured in this book, there is strong doubt as to the factual evidence that this indeed took place! Even for a personality such as Dat So La Lee—regarded as one of the finest and most famous of the Florescence basketweavers, who had strong patrons (the Cohns), who was extensively written about during her life, and who had a ledger detailing her basketry—her story has modern historical biographies full of contradictions, misstatements, and myths (Cohodas 1992).

In 1888, she married Charlie Keyser, a man 24 years younger than she was. Charlie had two children from his previous marriages. At that time, Dabuda took the name Louisa Keyser. In 1895, she sold four of her baskets to Abe Cohn, Harris Cohn's son. That transaction would change the course of not only their lives but would also alter the lives of numerous California basketweavers and the history of the art of California Native basketry.

Abe and his wife Amy owned a clothing store in Carson City called "The Emporium." Amy's interest in Indian crafts, combined with Abe's business instincts led to an arrangement where they would provide a home, food, and all other necessities to Dabuda. In 1895, she changed her name to Dat So La Lee—it is reported that the name derived from her early association with Dr. S. L. Lee, although this is also in question (Cohodas 1992). In return, Dat So La Lee would weave baskets full time, exclusively for the Cohns (Cohodas 1976, 1979a; Hickson 1967; Quintana 2010).

This was the first example of a patron/artist relationship with a Native American basketweaver, and the results had a widespread impact. During their 30-year relationship, Dat So La Lee would make famous the "degikup" (a shape adapted from Maidu/Pomo Indians to the north and west), introduce a polychrome color scheme to Washoe basketry using redbud as a third color, and develop a dimensional appearance for her baskets where the patterns would be smaller at the base and top and larger in the bulbous center. Her stitch count on larger baskets was over 30 per inch and her weaving impeccable.

Meanwhile, the Cohn's ingenious marketing strategies, including stories about Dat So La Lee's "princess status" in the Washoe tribe and about the meaning of the designs; cataloging each piece with an LK number including basket dimensions, number of stitches, and length of time it took to make, elevated her work to an art form and made her an internationally renowned artist—a star of the Native Californian basketry world (Cohodas 1976, 1979a; Hickson 1967).

During her 30-year career, which ended with her death in December 1925, over 100 baskets were catalogued (Cohodas 1976, 1979a; Hickson 1967). The original ledger containing details of Dat So La Lee's baskets can be seen at the Nevada Historical Society in Reno.

Her masterpieces were both an artistic inspiration to later artists and a financial incentive. Dat So La Lee's pieces have always been at the top of the value scale. In 1914, one sold for $1,400 to Gottlieb Adam Steiner and at the Green sale in 1971 (a Sotheby's auction), several of Dat So La Lee's pieces sold for $4,500 to $6,000 each, which at the time was an unheard-of price (Cohodas 1976, 1979a).

Between 2000 and 2011, prices of greater than $1,000,000 have been paid for her baskets, and even higher values have recently been attributed to some of her most significant pieces. The overwhelming majority of her art is already

Fig. 181* Dat So La Lee, ca. 1910. Photograph courtesy Nevada Historical Society.
Catalogue number eth00090. Edward S. Curtis photograph.
*See Appendix 3, Figure Notes | Pg. 309

in museums and other institutions, but a few pieces are still in private hands and occasionally come up for sale by dealers or at auctions. However, there have also been many baskets attributed incorrectly to Dat So La Lee as a result of her fame, so potential buyers must be careful when looking at baskets for possible purchase.

In addition to the 100+ larger LK pieces, she made a number of smaller or miniature pieces, many of which were kept in a collection by Amy Cohn. This collection is now owned by Gene Quintana and much of it has been displayed at the Gatekeeper's Museum in North Lake Tahoe, California (Quintana 2010). See Figs. 242 to 246.

Numerous photographs were taken of Dat So La Lee; original negatives as well as a video about Dat So La Lee are available at the Nevada State Museum in Carson City and at the Nevada Historical Society in Reno.

The photographs in this volume show a significant portion of Dat So La Lee's LK basket series, as well as a number of baskets that can be seen in original vintage photographs. Dat So La Lee made a uniquely important contribution to the transition of Central California/Western Nevada Indian basketry—from being a craft to being recognized as a valuable and collectible art form. Although several other artists created baskets which were the equal of her finest works, Dat So La Lee will always be recognized as an "ikon of the ikons."

Fig. 182 Dat So La Lee with baskets shown in Figs. 183 and 185. Photograph courtesy Nevada State Museum, Carson City, Nevada. Catalogue number NSM-266-23.

Fig. 183 Dat So La Lee degikup (LK 44). 13" high by 17" diameter, 1907. Private collection.

Fig. 184 Dat So La Lee with baskets shown in Figs. 183 and 185. Photograph courtesy Nevada State Museum, Carson City, Nevada. Photo number 26615-2.

DATSOLALEE
WASHOE INDIAN BASKET ARTIST
A. COHN   CARSON NEVADA

105

Fig. 185* Dat So La Lee degikup (LK 59). 8" high by 12" diameter, 1916. Photograph courtesy Nevada Historical Society.

*See Appendix 3, Figure Notes | Pg. 308

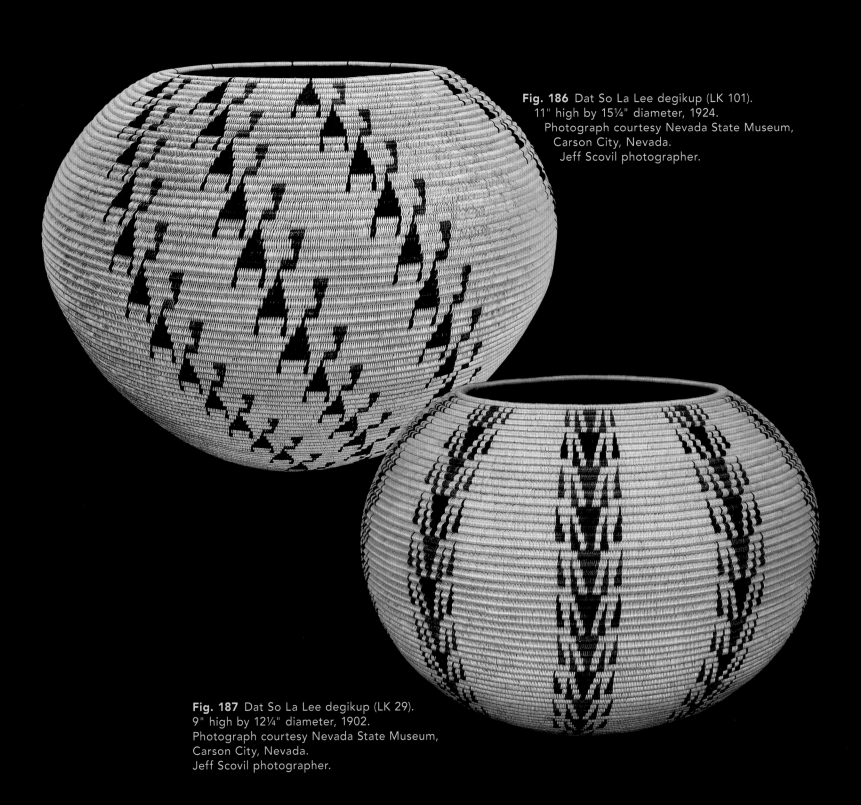

Fig. 186 Dat So La Lee degikup (LK 101).
11" high by 15¼" diameter, 1924.
Photograph courtesy Nevada State Museum,
Carson City, Nevada.
Jeff Scovil photographer.

Fig. 187 Dat So La Lee degikup (LK 29).
9" high by 12¼" diameter, 1902.
Photograph courtesy Nevada State Museum,
Carson City, Nevada.
Jeff Scovil photographer.

Fig. 188 Dat So La Lee, ca. 1921, weaving basket shown in Fig. 189. Nevada State Museum photograph. Catalog number 266030.

Fig. 189 Dat So La Lee degikup (LK 81). 10¾" high by 14½" diameter, 1922. Robert and Bunny Jochim Collection. Jeff Scovil photographer.

Fig. 190 Dat So La Lee, holding basket shown in Fig. 191. Photograph courtesy *St. Louis Globe-Democrat*, St. Louis, Missouri, 1919.

Fig. 191 Dat So La Lee degikup (LK 32).
12" high by 14" diameter, 1903.
Photograph courtesy Nevada State Museum,
Carson City, Nevada.
Jeff Scovil photographer.

Fig. 192 Dat So La Lee degikup (LK 63).
13½" high by 15¼" diameter, 1919.
Photograph courtesy Nevada State Museum,
Carson City, Nevada.
Jeff Scovil photographer.

Fig. 193 Dat So La Lee degikup (LK 58).
10¼" high by 12¾" diameter, 1916.
Photograph courtesy Nevada State Museum,
Carson City, Nevada.
Jeff Scovil photographer.

Fig. 194 Dat So La Lee lidded degikup (LK 95).
8" high by 10" diameter, 1924.
Marc and Pam Rudick Collection.
Gene Quintana photograph.
John Law photographer.

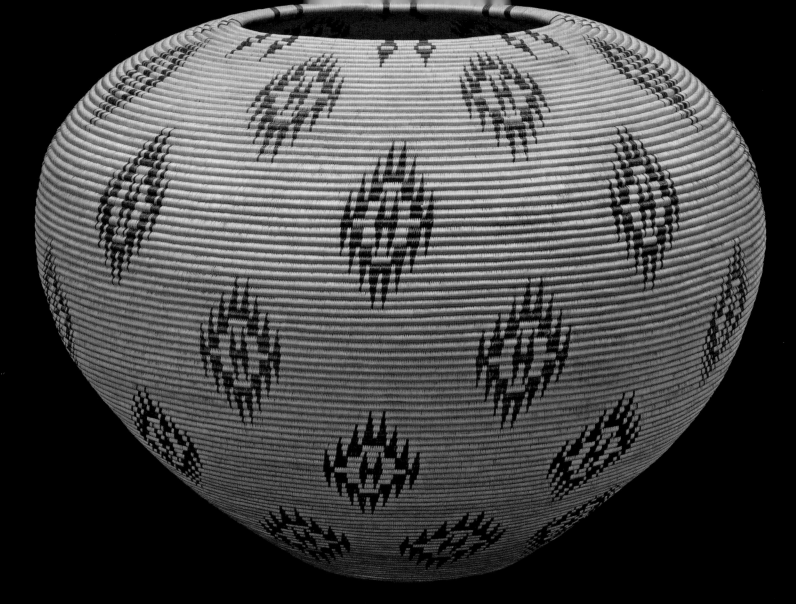

Fig. 195* Dat So La Lee degikup (LK 52).
12¾" high by 17¾" diameter, 1912.
Private collection.
Photograph courtesy Donald Ellis Gallery, Ltd.,
Dundas, Ontario, Canada and New York.

*See Appendix 3, Figure Notes | Pg. 308

Fig. 196 Dat So La Lee degikup (LK 107).
11¼" high by 15 1/8" diameter, 1925.
Photograph courtesy Nevada State Museum,
Carson City, Nevada.
Jeff Scovil photographer.

Fig. 197 Dat So La Lee degikup (LK 38).
7½" high by 11" diameter, 1900.
Photograph courtesy Nevada State Museum,
Carson City, Nevada.
Jeff Scovil photographer.

Fig. 198* Dat So La Lee degikup (LK 50).
11" high by 15¼" diameter, 1911.
Lew Meekins Collection.
Jeff Scovil photographer.

*See Appendix 3, Figure Notes | Pg. 308

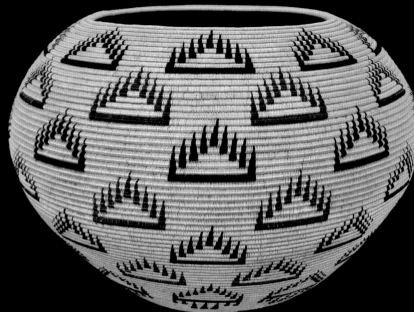

Fig. 199* Dat So La Lee degikup (LK 22).
7" high by 10½" diameter, 1899.
Photograph courtesy University of Nevada, Reno.
Catalogue number UNRS 2-P1985-08-1611.

*See Appendix 3, Figure Notes | Pg. 308

Fig. 200 Dat So La Lee degikup (LK 37).
8½" high by 12¼" diameter, 1904.
Photograph courtesy Nevada State Museum,
Carson City, Nevada.
Jeff Scovil photographer.

Fig. 201 Dat So La Lee and Charlie Keyser with her baskets (LK 44, Fig. 183; LK 22, Fig. 199;
and LK 37, Fig. 200), 1904. Photograph courtesy Nevada State Museum, Carson City, Nevada.
Catalogue number NSM 266-28.

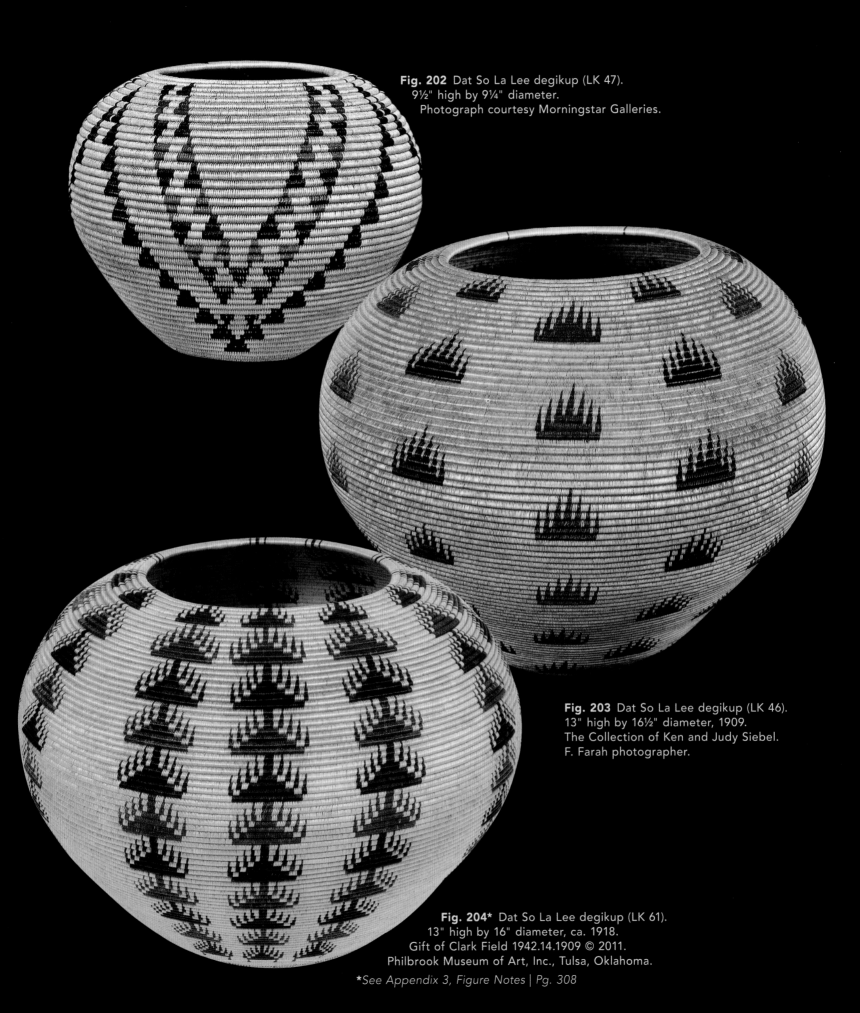

Fig. 202 Dat So La Lee degikup (LK 47).
9½" high by 9¼" diameter.
Photograph courtesy Morningstar Galleries.

Fig. 203 Dat So La Lee degikup (LK 46).
13" high by 16½" diameter, 1909.
The Collection of Ken and Judy Siebel.
F. Farah photographer.

Fig. 204* Dat So La Lee degikup (LK 61).
13" high by 16" diameter, ca. 1918.
Gift of Clark Field 1942.14.1909 © 2011.
Philbrook Museum of Art, Inc., Tulsa, Oklahoma.
*See Appendix 3, Figure Notes | Pg. 308

Fig. 205 Dat So La Lee degikup (LK 28).
10" high by 12¼" diameter, 1901.
Photograph courtesy Nevada State Museum,
Carson City, Nevada.
Jeff Scovil photographer.

Fig. 206 Dat So La Lee degikup (LK 88).
13½" high by 17¼" diameter, 1922.
Photograph courtesy Nevada Historical Society.

Fig. 207* Dat So La Lee degikup (LK 41-42) "Beacon Lights."
11¼" high by 16" diameter, 1905.
Thaw Collection, Fenimore Art Museum, Cooperstown, New York.
Gift of Eugene Victor Thaw Art Foundation.
Catalogue number T0751.

*See Appendix 3, Figure Notes | Pg. 308

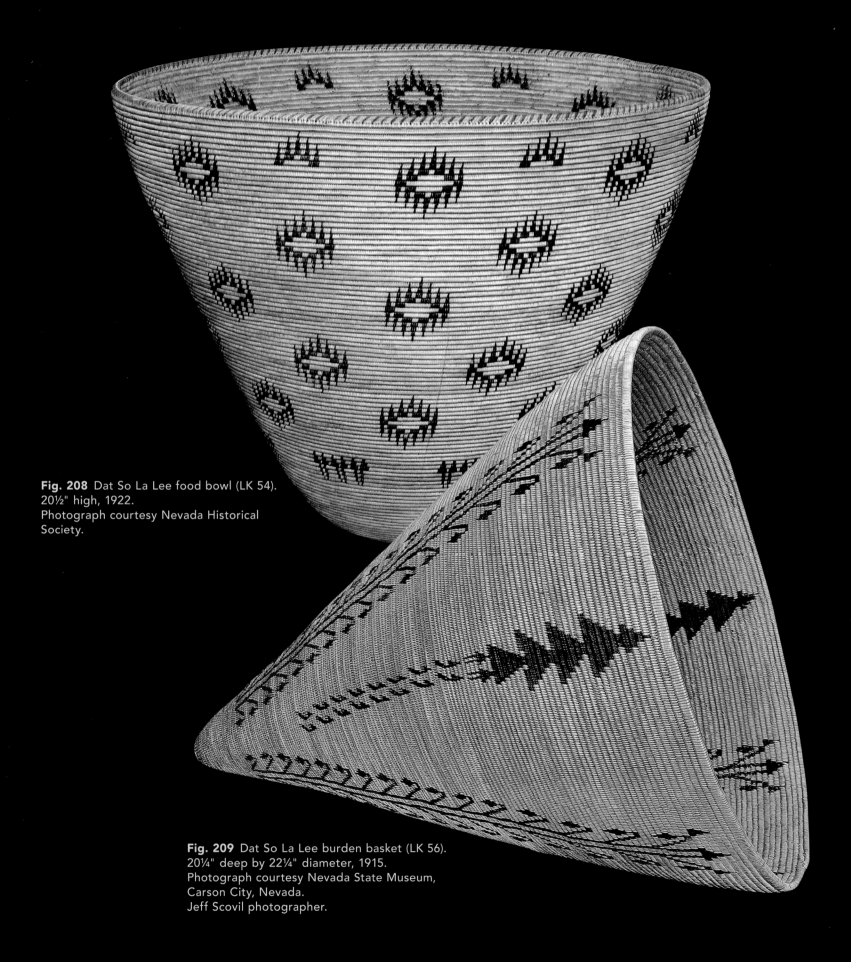

Fig. 208 Dat So La Lee food bowl (LK 54).
20½" high, 1922.
Photograph courtesy Nevada Historical
Society.

Fig. 209 Dat So La Lee burden basket (LK 56).
20¼" deep by 22¼" diameter, 1915.
Photograph courtesy Nevada State Museum,
Carson City, Nevada.
Jeff Scovil photographer.

Fig. 210 Dat So La Lee, ca. 1898, weaving basket shown in Fig. 211 and with baskets seen in Fig. 199 (LK 22) and LK 23. Braun Research Library Collection. Autry Museum, Los Angeles. Item number P2200A.

Fig. 211* Basket made by Dat So La Lee. 8½" high by 11" diameter (LK 24). Carson City, Nevada, ca. 1899. Southwest Museum of the American Indian Collection. Autry Museum, Los Angeles. Item number 2011.21.4.

*See Appendix 3, Figure Notes | Pg. 308

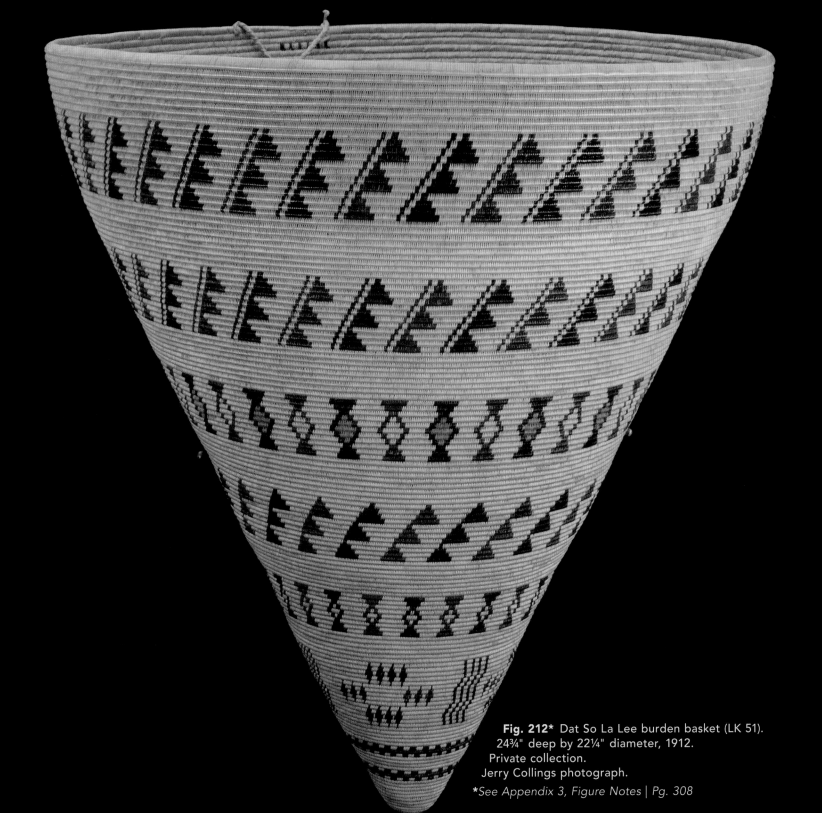

Fig. 212* Dat So La Lee burden basket (LK 51).
24¾" deep by 22¼" diameter, 1912.
Private collection.
Jerry Collings photograph.

*See Appendix 3, Figure Notes | Pg. 308

Fig. 213 Dat So La Lee lidded jar (LK 62).
15½" high by 9¼" diameter, 1918.
Photography courtesy of Heritage Auctions (HA.com),
Dallas, Texas.

Fig. 214 Dat So La Lee degikup (LK 48).
11½" high by 15¼" diameter, 190.
Photograph courtesy Nevada Historical Society.
Gene Meieran photographer.

Fig. 215 Dat So La Lee degikup (LK 116).
9¼" high by 12¾" diameter, 1925.
Photograph courtesy Nevada Historical Society.

Fig. 216 Dat So La Lee degikup (LK 31).
10" high by 13" diameter, 1902.
Private collection.

Fig. 217 Dat So La Lee degikup (LK 69).
8¾" high by 12" diameter, 1920.
Photograph courtesy Nevada Historical Society.

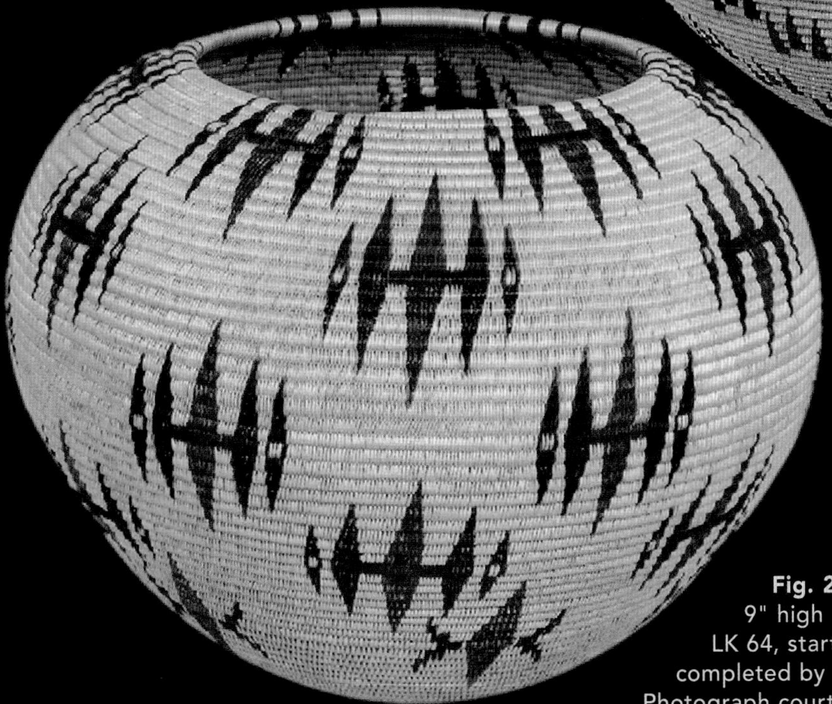

Fig. 218 Dat So La Lee degikup (LK 64).
9" high by 10¼" diameter, 1919.
LK 64, started by Scees Bryant Possack, was
completed by Dat So La Lee after Scees' death in 1918.
Photograph courtesy Nevada Historical Society.

Fig. 219 Dat So La Lee degikup (LK 43).
12" high by 16" diameter, 1923.
Nevada Historical Society Collection.
Gene Meieran photographer.

Fig. 220* Dat So La Lee degikup (LK 96).
13¼" high by 12" diameter, 1905.
Private collection.
Jerry Jacka photographer.

*See Appendix 3, Figure Notes | Pg. 308

Fig. 221 Abe Cohn in 1923 with Dat So La Lee
basket (LK 96) Fig. 220 and (LK 43 [1923] Fig. 219.
Photograph courtesy Nevada State Museum,
Carson City, Nevada Department of Cultural Affairs.
Catalogue number NSM-259-1.

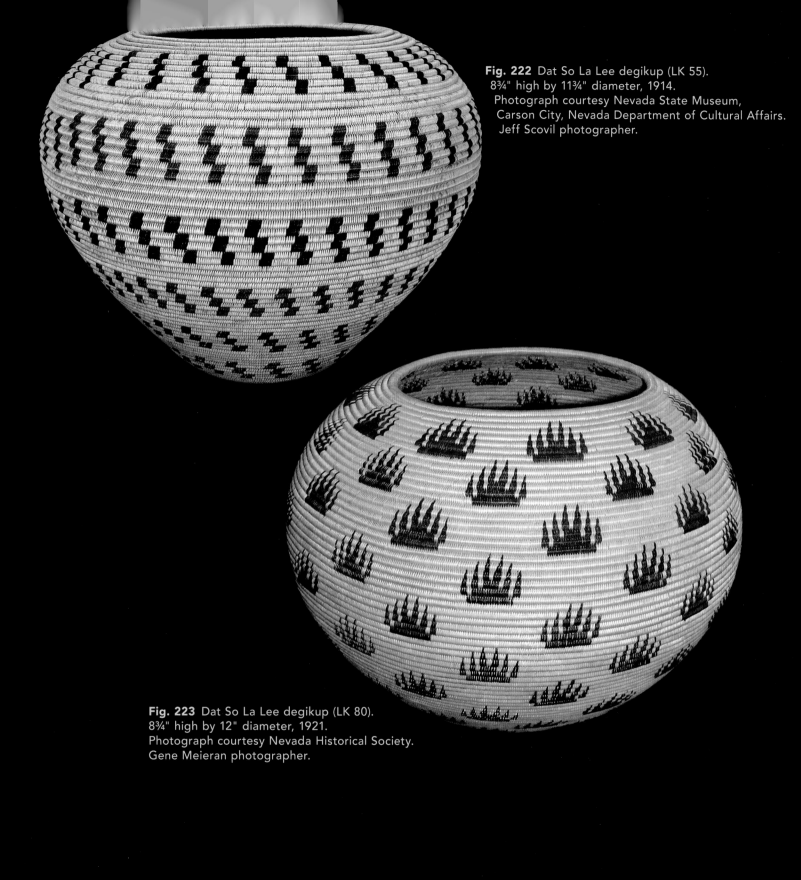

Fig. 222 Dat So La Lee degikup (LK 55).
8¾" high by 11¾" diameter, 1914.
Photograph courtesy Nevada State Museum,
Carson City, Nevada Department of Cultural Affairs.
Jeff Scovil photographer.

Fig. 223 Dat So La Lee degikup (LK 80).
8¾" high by 12" diameter, 1921.
Photograph courtesy Nevada Historical Society.
Gene Meieran photographer.

Fig. 224 Edward S. Curtis, photographer, photographic postcard. Dat So La Lee baskets, made between 1895–1923. The baskets in this photograph postcard include LK 29 [1920], LK 37 [1904], LK 50 [1911], LK 51 [1912], LK 61 [1918], LK 96 [1923], and LK 101 [1924]. Braun Research Library Collection. Autry Museum, Los Angeles. Item number P.2185.

Fig. 225 Photographic postcard, Dat So La Lee, 1895–1923. Braun Research Library

Fig. 226 Dat So La Lee degikup (LK 33).
13½" diameter, 1903.
Photograph courtesy Penn Museum.
Image number 195213, Object NA8800.

Fig. 227 Dat So La Lee degikup (LK 27).
7" high by 10" diameter, 1901.
Photograph courtesy Penn Museum.
Image number 195214, Object 38-26-1.

Fig. 228 Dat So La Lee degikup (LK 36).
5" high by 7" diameter, 1904.
Photograph courtesy Penn Museum.
Image #195212, Object 31-45-15.

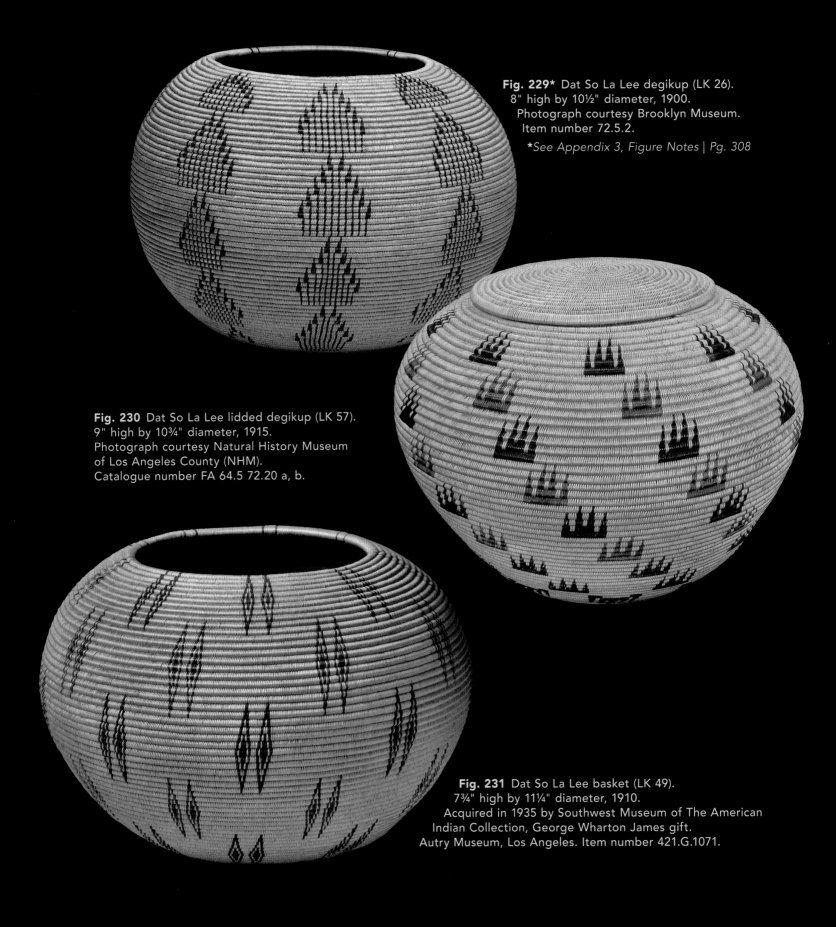

Fig. 229* Dat So La Lee degikup (LK 26).
8" high by 10½" diameter, 1900.
Photograph courtesy Brooklyn Museum.
Item number 72.5.2.

**See Appendix 3, Figure Notes | Pg. 308*

Fig. 230 Dat So La Lee lidded degikup (LK 57).
9" high by 10¾" diameter, 1915.
Photograph courtesy Natural History Museum
of Los Angeles County (NHM).
Catalogue number FA 64.5 72.20 a, b.

Fig. 231 Dat So La Lee basket (LK 49).
7¾" high by 11¼" diameter, 1910.
Acquired in 1935 by Southwest Museum of The American
Indian Collection, George Wharton James gift.
Autry Museum, Los Angeles. Item number 421.G.1071.

Fig. 232* Dat So La Lee with nine baskets at her feet, ca. 1899. Braun Research Library Collection. Autry Museum, Los Angeles. Item number P.2197.

See Appendix 3, Figure Notes | Pg. 308

Fig. 233 Dat So La Lee basket (LK 14?). 5¼" high by 7¼" diameter, 1897. Photograph courtesy Yale Peabody Museum of Natural History. Catalogue number 17026.

Fig. 234 Dat So La Lee basket (LK 15?). 4½" high by 7¼" diameter. Photograph courtesy Phoebe A. Hearst Museum of Anthropology and the Regents of the University of California. Catalogue number I-20897.

Fig. 235 Dat So La Lee basket. 6½" diameter. Photograph courtesy National Museum of the American Indian, Smithsonian Institution. Photograph number 090168.

Fig. 236 Dat So La Lee pedestaled basket (LK 21). 8½" high, 1898. Carnegie Museum of Natural History. Catalogue number 36452-1.

Fig. 237 Dat So La Lee basket (LK 30). 4¾" high by 6¾" diameter, 1902. Photograph courtesy National Museum of the American Indian, Smithsonian Institution. Item number 9/167.

Fig. 238 Dat So La Lee basket 5" high by 7¼" diameter, 1895. Photograph courtesy Nevada Art Museum. Alan and Bronnie Blaugrund Collection. Scott Werschky photographer.

Fig. 239 Dat So La Lee basket 4¾" high by 7¼" diameter. Photograph courtesy Yale Peabody Museum of Natural History. Catalogue number 17025.

Fig. 240 Dat So La Lee basket, pre-1922. 4¼" high by 7" diameter. Southwest Museum of the American Indian Collection Autry Museum, Los Angeles. Item number 116.L.182.

Fig. 241* LK 52-3 3¼" by 4¾".
Photograph courtesy of North
Lake Tahoe Historical Society.
Gene and Julie Quintana Collection.
Marion Steinbach Indian Basket Museum
and Gatekeeper's Museum,
Tahoe City, California.
Gene Meieran photographer.

*See Appendix 3, Figure Notes | Pg. 308

Fig. 242* LK 63-6 3¼" by 5".
Photograph courtesy of North
Lake Tahoe Historical Society.
Gene and Julie Quintana Collection.
Marion Steinbach Indian Basket Museum
and Gatekeeper's Museum,
Tahoe City, California.
Gene Meieran photographer.

*See Appendix 3, Figure Notes | Pg. 308

Fig. 243* LK 44-1 2¾" by 4¼".
Photograph courtesy of North
Lake Tahoe Historical Society.
Gene and Julie Quintana Collection.
Marion Steinbach Indian Basket Museum
and Gatekeeper's Museum,
Tahoe City, California.
Gene Meieran photographer.

*See Appendix 3, Figure Notes | Pg. 308

Fig. 244* LK 59-3 3¼" by 4".
Photograph courtesy of North
Lake Tahoe Historical Society.
Gene and Julie Quintana Collection.
Marion Steinbach Indian Basket Museum
and Gatekeeper's Museum,
Tahoe City, California.
Gene Meieran photographer.

*See Appendix 3, Figure Notes | Pg. 308

Fig. 245 Dat So La Lee degikup (LK 60).
14" high by 15" diameter, 1917.
Private collection.
Jerry Collings photograph.

Fig. 246 Dat So La Lee. Photograph courtesy Nevada Historical Society.

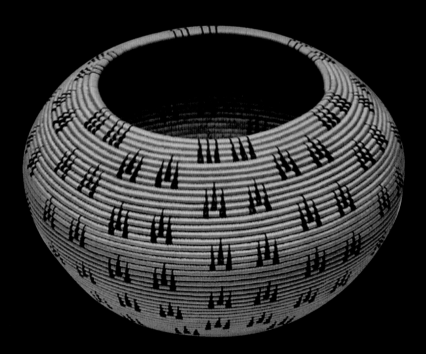

Fig. 247 Dat So La Lee degikup (LK 20).
6½" high by 10" diameter, 1898.
Photograph courtesy Douglas Museum, Douglas County, Nevada.

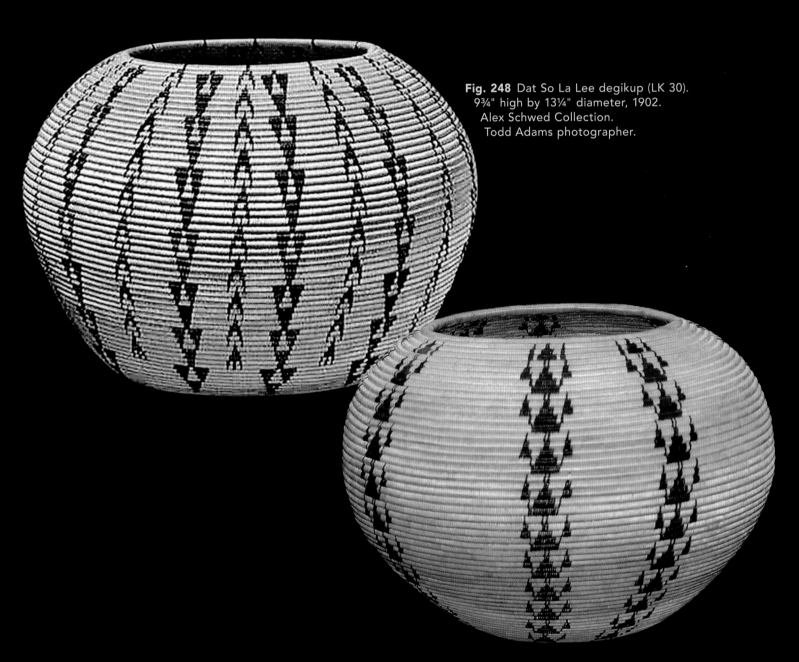

Fig. 248 Dat So La Lee degikup (LK 30).
9¾" high by 13¼" diameter, 1902.
Alex Schwed Collection.
Todd Adams photographer.

Fig. 248 Dat So La Lee degikup (LK 102).
10" high by 12" diameter, 1924.
Photograph courtesy Nevada Historical Society.

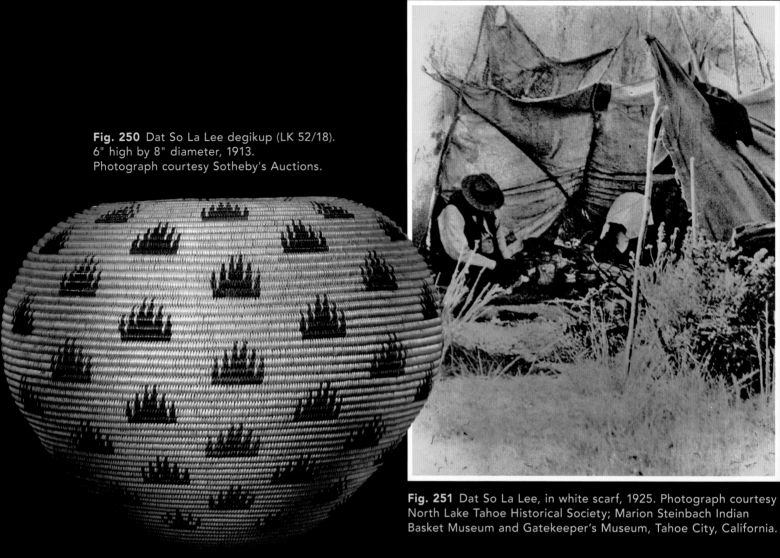

Fig. 250 Dat So La Lee degikup (LK 52/18).
6" high by 8" diameter, 1913.
Photograph courtesy Sotheby's Auctions.

Fig. 251 Dat So La Lee, in white scarf, 1925. Photograph courtesy
North Lake Tahoe Historical Society; Marion Steinbach Indian
Basket Museum and Gatekeeper's Museum, Tahoe City, California.

Fig. 252 Abe Cohn with (LK 59) Fig. 185. Photograph courtesy North Lake Tahoe
Historical Society; Marion Steinbach Indian Basket Museum and Gatekeeper's Museum,
Tahoe City, California.

Magdalena Augustine
Chemehuevi | 1867–1945

Magdalena Augustine was a Chemehuevi Indian who spent much of her life on the Augustine Reservation, in Coachella, California. She was born Magdalena Helena Alvaldo (or Avalado) in Needles, California in 1867[6]. Around 1900, she married Albert Augustine, a farm laborer[7], and they had three children: Amelia (b. 1891/1892), Rodriguez (b. 1900, died in infancy) and Roy Rodriguez Augustine (b. 1909)[8].

The family lived on the Martinez Reservation following their marriage, moved to the Cabazon Reservation in 1910, then to Soboba Reservation in 1920, and finally the Mission Reservation for Augustine Indians from 1922 through at least the 1930s (Indian Census 1902, 1920, 1922–1937; Federal Census 1910, 1920). Magdalena passed away in Riverside County on March 15, 1945[9].

Fig. 253 Magdalena Augustine bowl.
12¼" diameter.
Courtesy Sherwoods Spirit of America, Santa Fe, New Mexico.

Her work differed from that of other Chemehuevi weavers living on the Colorado River, as it tended to show influences from the California tribes[10], including their use of materials such as yellow and orange juncus (Bibby 1996:93). Magdalena's designs are unusually bold and bright, and most are easily recognizable.

In 1914, Emil P. Steffa purchased three of Magdalena's globular baskets; and in 1938, her grandson sold one of her baskets to Chlorene Hayward. Two of the baskets purchased by Steffa include rattlesnakes in their designs. Two other baskets by Magdalena appear in Plate 161 of Gregory Schaff's book *American Indian Baskets I* (Schaff 2006). One of these is a beautiful tray, the other a globular bowl. Two of the Steffa baskets—now in the Pomona College Collection—are also photographed in Schaff's book (Schaff 2006:161) and are seen in Figs. 254 and 255.

Baskets made by this innovative artist and master weaver are rarely available and are highly desirable and collectible.

Fig. 254 Magdalena Augustine bowl.
11" high by 12½" diameter.
Photograph courtesy Pomona College.

Fig. 255 Magdalena Augustine bowl.
10¼" deep by 11½" diameter.
Photograph courtesy Pomona College.

Leanna Tom was born in the Yosemite Valley just after the great California Gold Rush. Her parents, Captain Sam and Suzie Sam, were probably of mixed Miwok and Mono Lake Paiute ancestry. Both parents were bilingual, speaking their native language and the language of their spouse. Leanna had a sister, Louisa, and both grew up in Yosemite Valley (Bates and Lee 1990).

Leanna's first husband is unknown, but after his death she married Bridgeport Tom. Her sister Louisa also married Bridgeport Tom and the three of them lived together in Yosemite in the summer. In the winter they lived in Bridgeport Tom's ranch at Bloody Canyon in the Mono Basin, on the eastern side of the Sierra Nevada, raising horses and cattle. They later moved to Coleville, California. After Bridgeport Tom passed away in 1937, Louisa moved back to Yosemite. Leanna however stayed in Coleville (Bates and Lee 1990).

Leanna became a talented weaver when she was young, and by 1916 was weaving in the new style, which her niece—Lucy Parker Telles—had pioneered around 1912. Leanna was a regular at the Yosemite Indian Field Days, often winning prizes for her baskets. She continued to weave until her death in 1965 (Bates and Lee 1990).

Leanna was a master weaver and her works are well documented, as she is included in the world-famous photographic volumes (1907–1930) fashioned by the eminent Edward S. Curtis. However, unlike her contemporaries, she made very few large baskets, and as a result, only a few collections contain important large

Fig. 256 Leanna Tom with weavers at Yosemite Indian Field Days, 1929, with baskets shown in Figs. 257, 258, and 262. Forest Townsley and James Schwabacher in the rear. Weavers left to right: Tina Charlie, Carrie Bethel, Alice Wilson, Leanna Tom, and Maggie Howard. Photograph courtesy Yosemite Museum and Research Library. National Park Service Catalogue number YOSE RL 2122.

Fig. 257* Leanna Tom degikup.
7" high by 16" diameter, 1928/1929.
Lew Meekins Collection.
Jeff Scovil photographer.

*See Appendix 3, Figure Notes | Pg. 308

Fig. 258* Leanna Tom degikup.
6½" high by 11¼" diameter, ca. 1929.
Natalie Linn Collection.
Jeff Scovil photographer.

*See Appendix 3, Figure Notes | Pg. 308

Fig. 259 Leanna Tom with basket shown in Fig. 260, 1924. Edward S. Curtis Photograph. Photograph courtesy Yosemite Museum and Research Library. National Park Service Catalogue number YOSE 79855.

Fig. 260* Leanna Tom degikup.
8" high by 13" diameter.
Photograph courtesy Yosemite Museum and Research Library. National Park Service Catalogue number YOSE 66828.

*See Appendix 3, Figure Notes | Pg. 308

Fig. 261 Carl Russell and Leanna Tom. Indian Field Days, 1924. She is looking at her basket shown in Fig. 260. Photograph courtesy Honey Lake Maidu,

Fig. 262* Leanna Tom degikup.
8¼" high by 16¼" diameter, 1925.
Photograph courtesy Yosemite
Museum and Research Library.
National Park Service Catalogue
number YOSE 67434.

*See Appendix 3, Figure Notes | Pg. 308

Fig. 263 Leanna Tom and Bureau
of Indian Affairs Superintendent
Colonel L. A. Dorrington with basket
shown in Fig. 262. Photographed at
Yosemite Indian Field Days, 1925.
Photograph courtesy Yosemite
Museum and Research Library.
National Park Service Catalogue
number YOSE RL 17830.

Casilda Welmas

Cupeño | ca. 1870–ca. 1935

Casilda Welmas lived on the Pala Reservation in 1935, located in the middle of San Luis Rey River Valley of northern San Diego County, east of Fallbrook. As a result of several years of legal actions, the Cupeño Indian tribal members were ordered by the California Supreme Court to move from their home at Warner's Ranch (Hot Springs), just west of Lake Henshaw in San Diego County, California, to the Pala Indian Reservation in Luiseño territory in 1903. During her time at Pala, she wove a beautiful floral design basket eventually sold at a Sotheby's auction in 1983 (Moser 1993:74).

Noted author George Wharton James, who visited the area in the early 1900s, took a photo of the collection of Mrs. H. H. Baggy, a school teacher (Moser 1993:74), in which a basket with a radiating star design closely resembles one held by Casilda Welmas in a photo of her taken in the 1930s, Fig. 269. In this photo, Casilda holds two other baskets. Another of her beautiful baskets is in the collection of the Philbrook Museum in Tulsa, Oklahoma.

The three baskets featured in this book—Figs. 265 to 267—display a bold artistic talent with a basic design that is pleasing and very collectible.

Casilda Welmas passed in about the year 1935.

Fig. 264 Casilda Welmas and Cayatano Welmas. Courtesy Agua Caliente Cultural Museum. M. Kashower Co., Los Angeles postcard. Catalogue number 2007148014.

Fig. 265 Casilda Welmas oval bowl.
13" long by 11¼" wide by 2¼" high.
Collection of Agua Caliente Band of Cahuilla Indians.
Courtesy Agua Caliente Cultural Museum.
Catalogue number L1998001032.

Fig. 266 Casilda Welmas bowl, 1920.
9" deep by 18½" diameter.
Courtesy Agua Caliente Cultural Museum.
Catalogue number 1991003001.

Top view.

Side view.

Fig. 267* Casilda Welmas bowl.
11¾" deep by 12½" diameter.
Gift of Clark Field, 1948.27.52 © 2011.
Philbrook Museum of Art, Inc., Tulsa, Oklahoma.

See Appendix 3, Figure Notes | Pg. 308

Fig. 268 Mr. and Mrs. Gabriel, Casilda Welmas, Rose Lima Welmas, Sarah Welmas, Clara St. Marie, and Juan Welmas, January 1, 1925. Courtesy of the Agua Caliente Cultural Museum. Catalogue number 2007020001.

Fig. 269 Casilda Welmas with basket, 1927–1936, similar to basket shown in Fig. 267. Braun Research Library Collection. Autry Museum, Los Angeles. Item number P.944.

Aida Icho (Wahnomkot)

Wukchumni Yokuts | 1878–1964

Aida Icho's family was from the Kaweah River east of Visalia (Latta 1949:438), though she was born near Squaw Valley, Fresno County, California. Her Yokuts name was Wahnomkot, and she was a Wukchumni Yokuts (Latta 1949:298), She was identified as the last "head lady" of the Wukchumni, and her husband Henry was their last chief (Latta 1949:176). She was the daughter of Mary Topino (Mrs. Britches, see pages 238–252), who was one of the finest basketmakers in California history. Aida Icho herself was a master weaver—considered one of the finest of all Yokuts weavers—who balanced design and shape to near perfection while weaving fine, tight, even stitches. She wove only classic Yokuts shapes and designs and is most respected for her bottleneck baskets with rattlesnake bands (Bob Adams personal communication 2009).

Aida Icho was an important source of information for Frank Latta, as she demonstrated for him the Yokuts techniques of gathering and preparing basketry materials (Latta 1949). Several of her baskets appear in his *Handbook of the Yokuts Indians*. An Aida Icho bowl and bottleneck are shown on pages 574 and 579 of Latta's book and are also shown here in the present volume. In Latta's book (1949:460–461) there is a photograph of one of Aida's large gambling trays. She made at least two of these trays; a photograph of one of these trays is also shown here in Fig. 273.

Fig. 271 Aida Icho (Wahnomkot) ca. 1925. Photograph courtesy Chris Brewer, Bear State Books, Exeter, California. Frank Latta photographer.

Fig. 272 Aida Icho bowl. 7¾" deep by 15½" diameter. Bob and Carol Adams Collection. Jeff Scovil photographer.

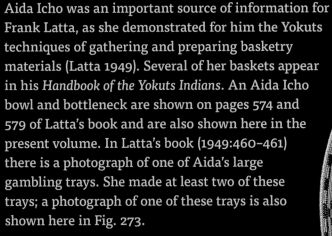

Fig. 270 Aida Icho bottleneck olla with feathers circling the shoulder. 6½" deep by 11¾" diameter. Bob and Carol Adams Collection. Jeff Scovil photographer.

Fig. 273 Aida Icho gambling tray.
29" diameter.
Bob and Carol Adams Collection.
Jeff Scovil photographer.

Fig. 274 Aida Icho with gambling tray shown in Fig. 273. Photograph courtesy Yosemite Museum and Research Library. National Park Service Catalogue number YOSE RL 19411.

Lizzie (Lizzy) Toby Peters
Washoe | 1865/70–1943

Lizzie Toby Peters was born sometime between 1865 and 1870 to Mariah and Toby. Her father Toby had four other children with another woman before Mariah; they were raised with Lizzie. One of them, Suzie Washo was a fine weaver (Cohodas 1979a). Lizzie married three times—her second union was to Ben Peters who died in 1913. Lizzie never had any children of her own. Her best baskets were made early in her career between approximately 1900 and 1915. She died in 1943 (Cohodas 1979a).

Dr. S. L. Lee, a noted early collector of Washoe basketry considered Lizzie to be the third finest Washoe artist after Dat So La Lee (see pages 114–142), and her sister-in-law, Scees Bryant Possack (see pages 84–87), but that was before the emergence of the later weavers, particularly Tootsie Dick and Lena Frank Dick (Cohodas 1979a).

Dr. Lee's collection included five documented Lizzie Toby Peters' baskets, all now in the Nevada State Museum. Four of these were made between 1900 and 1904. Several other baskets have been attributed to her, based on comparison with the five documented baskets from Dr. Lee's collection. Most of Lizzie Toby Peters' production coincides with Dat So La Lee's early phase, although Peters' style was much more traditional. Lizzie had considerable influence on later Washoe artists (Cohodas 1979a).

Fig. 275 Lizzie Toby Peters with degikup shown in Fig. 276. Photograph courtesy Chicago Field Museum. Catalogue number CSA 1872.

Fig. 276 Lizzie Toby Peters degikup.
4¾" high by 9½" diameter, ca. 1910.
Photograph courtesy Phoebe A. Hearst Museum of Anthropology and the Regents of the University of California.
Catalogue number I-72861.

Fig. 277 Lizzie Toby Peters degikup.
5½" high by 8½" diameter.
Photograph courtesy Nevada State Museum,
Department of Cultural Affairs, Carson City, Nevada.
Catalogue number 38 G 466.
Jeff Scovil photographer.

Fig. 278 Lizzie Toby Peters degikup.
6¾" high by 8" diameter.
Photograph courtesy Nevada State Museum,
Department of Cultural Affairs, Carson City, Nevada.
Catalogue number 38 G 1215.
Jeff Scovil photographer.

Fig. 279 Lizzie Toby Peters degikup.
7½" high by 9½" diameter.
Photograph courtesy Nevada State Museum,
Department of Cultural Affairs, Carson City, Nevada.
Catalogue number 38 G 463.
Jeff Scovil photographer.

Fig. 280 Possibly Lizzie Toby Peters degikup.
7" high by 11" diameter.
Photograph courtesy National Museum of
the American Indian, Smithsonian Institution.

Annie Laird

Chemehuevi | 1871–year of death unknown (after 1945)

Mary Anna ("Annie") Laird was a Chemehuevi Indian from the Colorado River Reservation near Parker, Arizona. Her maiden name is unknown, but she was born in Arizona in 1871 and married William Eddy in 1905[11]. After Eddy's death around 1914, she married George Laird sometime between 1917 and 1920[12]. (Laird had lost his first wife, Sally, in 1906 or 1907). Annie Laird died after 1945.

Annie Laird is best known for a magnificent olla, which she made around 1905. The design is said to represent the "tree of life" (Stacey 1975:29). This masterpiece alone qualifies Annie Laird as a master weaver and an exceptional artist.

Fig. 281 Annie Laird (seated, center) with Alice Waco (left), Mary Snyder (right), and collector Birdie Brown (standing), ca. 1945. Photograph courtesy Fred Harvey Company Association Files. Heard Museum photograph, Phoenix, Arizona.

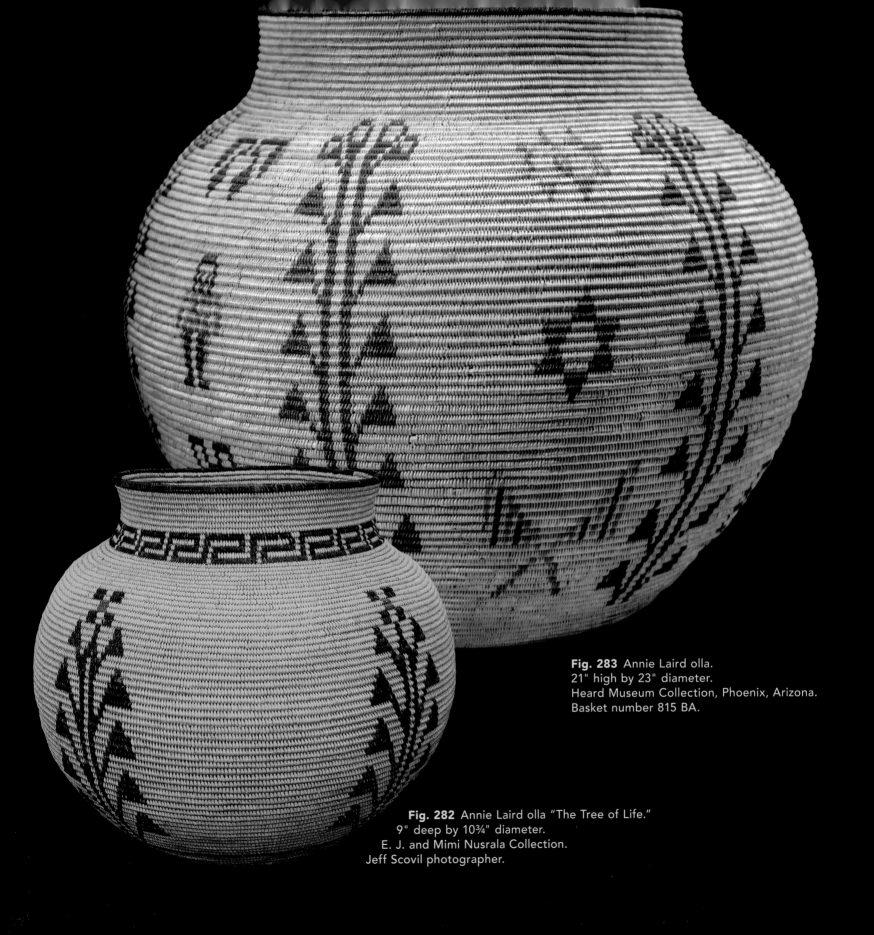

Fig. 283 Annie Laird olla.
21" high by 23" diameter.
Heard Museum Collection, Phoenix, Arizona.
Basket number 815 BA.

Fig. 282 Annie Laird olla "The Tree of Life."
9" deep by 10¾" diameter.
E. J. and Mimi Nusrala Collection.
Jeff Scovil photographer.

Lena Frank Dick

Washoe | 1889–1965

Lena Frank Dick was born in Coleville, which is in Antelope Valley, Mono County, California. Her parents were Charley and Lucy Frank. She had several siblings, many who died while young. Her two sisters, Lillie Frank James and Jessie Frank Wade, would also become recognized weavers. Lena married George Emm, but after the birth of their daughter Juanita, he left in about 1910 (Cohodas 1979a, 1979b, 1986).

Lena was then remarried to Levi Dick and they lived in Coleville for most of their lives. Levi had a construction job that provided a good and steady income, allowing Lena time to weave baskets. The Cohn's labels document three of Lena's baskets made during the period between 1916 and 1921 (Cohodas 1979a, 1979b, 1986).

Facilitated through Fred Settlemeyer, a Carson Valley rancher in the mid to late 1920s, Lena had a patron, Dr. Roscoe A. Day, who purchased all her baskets. In 1934, Dr. Day suffered a serious heart attack, ending the arrangement. At about the same time, Lena's eyesight began to fail, and for the rest of her life she could only weave utilitarian baskets (Cohodas 1979a, 1979b, 1986).

During the years of Dr. Day's patronage, Lena developed her technical and aesthetic skills, creating baskets regarded as equal to those of Dat So La Lee, Carrie Bethel, and Tina Charlie. Her stitch counts were equal to Dat So La Lee's and the shapes and designs excelled to near perfection.

She wove at least two large degikups (Figs. 284 and 288), but most of her baskets were smaller—under 12 inches in diameter. Unfortunately, neither Fred Settlemeyer nor Dr. Day promoted Lena, and for many years her creations were credited to Dat So La Lee! The research of scholars such as Dr. Marvin Cohodas later corrected this oversight and Lena Dick is today recognized as another of the very finest of the gifted artists of the Florescence (Cohodas 1979a; 1979b, 1986).

By 1979, 17 baskets were formally documented and attributed to her; three were identified as having Emporium Company certificates. Twelve were in the Dr. Day collection, which was donated to the California State Indian Museum in 1945 by his widow. Two more were in a private collection that rancher Fred Settlemeyer purchased from Lena. Finally, several other pieces have come to light in recent years (Cohodas 1979a; 1979b, 1986).

Lena's art is highly prized and valued. One larger piece was recently offered for sale in the low- to mid-six figure range.

I think I was 2 years old when my great-grandmother and I went to a Peyote ceremonial event when a girl becomes a woman. And also going to Minden to have meals with my great-grandparents. Her strength of living throughout her life, and her love of family, has always inspired me.

—Juanita Marie Tyler, great-granddaughter of Lena Frank Dick

Fig. 287 Lena Frank Dick with husband Levi, ca. 1960. Lena is holding great-granddaughter Juanita (Tyler) Preciado. Photograph courtesy Juanita Preciado.

Fig. 288 Lena Frank Dick degikup. 9¼" high by 14¾" diameter, ca. 1921. Photograph courtesy Nevada State Museum, Department of Cultural Affairs, Carson City, Nevada. Jeff Scovil photographer.

Fig. 286 Lena Frank Dick, ca. 1942. Photograph courtesy Juanita Preciado.

Fig. 289 Lena Frank Dick degikup.
6½" high by 9½" diameter, ca. 1925.
Photograph courtesy Charles and
Valerie Diker.
Catalogue number 38G457.

Fig. 290 Lena Frank Dick degikup.
4¾" high by 7¼" diameter.
California Department of Parks and
Recreation.
Catalogue number BWH 16B2-156.

Fig. 291 Lena Frank Dick degikup.
4" high by 8" diameter.
New York Metropolitan Museum of Art.
Ralph T. Coe Collection.
Catalogue number 2011.154.130.

Fig. 292 Lena Frank Dick degikup.
7½" high by 11" diameter.
Donner Museum, Donner Pass,
California State Parks.
Gene Meieran photographer.

Fig. 293 Lena Frank Dick (seated), ca. 1960
with (left to right) daughter Juanita Summers,
granddaughter Bernice H. Tyler, and great-
granddaughter Juanita M. Tyler. Photograph
courtesy Juanita (Tyler) Preciado.

Bridgita Castro

Cahuilla | Year of birth unknown–year of death unknown

While little is known about Bridgita Castro, Moser (Moser 1993:95) does have a brief note on her life. She lived on the Morongo Reservation near Banning, California, in the first part of the twentieth century.

Fig. 294 shows Bridgita holding a large oval bowl but unfortunately the photograph is undated. Fig. 295 shows an exceptional large olla with a Palm Springs trading post tag that identifies the weaver to be Mrs. Castro of the Morongo Reservation. Both baskets have similar aesthetic appeal. The basket in Fig. 295 is decorated with eagles, especially revered in Cahuilla ceremony. Based on these two baskets, Bridgita Castro is high on the list of great Cahuilla tribal artists.

Bridgita Castro.

Fig. 294 Bridgita Castro, early to mid-1900s. Braun Research Library Collection. Autry Museum, Los Angeles. Item number P.125.

Rose Meadows Salem
Mountain Maidu | 1883–1969

Rose Meadows Salem was born on the eastern side of Big Meadows near Lake Almanor, in Plumas County, California. Her mother, Kate Meadows McKinney, was an accomplished weaver and Rose continued the family tradition of great weavers. Rose learned to weave in that environment (Kurtz 2010, 2011).

Rose married Ole Salem, whose previous three wives had all died in childbirth; Rose raised his three sons and also her sister's daughter, Jennie. Rose had no children of her own. They lived on the Salem Ranch at Lake Almanor along with Rose's mother Kate and her sister. Living nearby were Daisy Frank and Rilla Cady of Susanville, who were both early collectors of Maidu basketry (Kurtz 2010, 2011).

In the 1890s, Rilla Cady would often tour Plumas County in her horse-drawn buggy, collecting Native Californian Indian baskets. The Cady collection included basketry obtained from Rose Meadows Salem, and when a portion of that great collection was donated to the California State Indian Museum, Rose along with many other fine weavers were well represented. At least two of her baskets were decorated with butterflies (Bob Adams personal communication 2009).

A vintage photograph of Rose with an exceptional degikup showing stylized butterflies (Figs. 297, 299) is now in the Greg and Cathy Sarena collection. That basket displays technical skills comparable to the finest of California Indian weavers.

Unfortunately, Rose Meadows Salem's baskets are seldom available to the collector's market, since most are in museums or in private collections and rarely become available for sale.

Fig. 297 Rose Meadows Salem tray.
7" diameter.
Photograph courtesy Pat Kurtz.
David Bozsik photographer.

Fig. 298 Rose Meadows Salem with degikup shown in Fig. 299. Photograph courtesy California State University, Chico, California.

Fig. 299 Rose Meadows Salem degikup. 7" high by 13" diameter, ca. 1915. Greg and Cathy Sarena Collection. Todd Adams photographer.

Minnie Wilcox Hancock was a member of the Wukchumni Yokuts; her Yokuts name was Waysheemlet (Latta 1949:585). She was born in Drum Valley and lived in Squaw Valley within the larger Tivy Valley area of Central California. Minnie's sister, Mary Sampson, was also a master weaver.

Technically, Minnie Hancock remains one of the finest weavers in California basket history and knowledgeable collectors prize her artistic style very highly. Her creation baskets—named for the designs that tell the story of the Yokuts nation's creation—with eagle and spirit designs, are especially valued for their perfection and elegance. Frank Latta credits her as having been the finest weaver in Yokuts territory (Latta 1949:549), with coil counts of 20 per inch and stitch counts of 50 per inch (Latta 1949:586).

Photographs of two of her ceremonial creation baskets are shown on pages 549, 586, and 587 of Latta's *Handbook* (Latta 1949), and in Fig. 300 of this book. Fig. 301 shows Minnie holding in her left hand one of her bottleneck baskets, now part of the Bob Adams' collection. It has 20 coils per inch and over 40 stitches per inch.

Minnie married Ben Hancock after the death of his first wife, Lucinda Hancock (Bob Adams personal communication 2009) who was another of the famous Yokuts weavers (see pages 222–235).

One basket woven by Minnie and two baskets woven by Lucinda have similar designs, and all three were probably influenced by Ben Hancock (for example, some of their baskets exhibit an Apache-style weaving).

Minnie's greatest masterpieces are only hand-size, but they bring prices equal to those of important larger baskets by other great weavers.

Fig. 301 Minnie Hancock, right, ca. 1930, with basket shown in Fig. 300. Photograph courtesy Bob and Carol Adams.

Fig. 300* Minnie Hancock bottleneck olla.
9" diameter, ca. 1925.
Bob and Carol Adams Collection.
Jeff Scovil photographer.
See Appendix 3, Figure Notes | Pg. 308

Fig. 302 Minnie Hancock bowl.
3" high by 8" diameter.
The Collection of Ken and Judy Siebel.
Gene Meieran photographer.

Fig. 303 Minnie Hancock bowl.
6½" diameter.
Table Mountain Rancheria Yokuts Tribe Collection.
Gene Meieran photographer.

Fig. 304 Minnie Hancock bottleneck olla.
6½" high by 9½" diameter.
Todd Adams Collection.
Photograph courtesy Todd Adams.

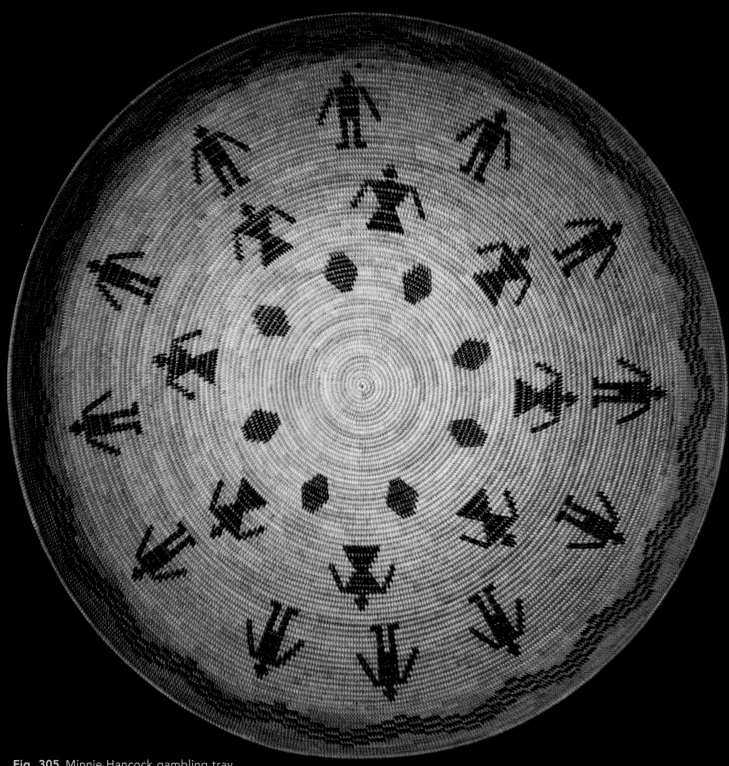

Fig. 305 Minnie Hancock gambling tray.
24½" diameter, ca. 1918.
Private collection.
Ben Watkins photographer.

Fig. 306 Minnie Hancock bottleneck olla.
7" high by 9" diameter.
Sanger Depot Museum, Sanger, California.

Fig. 307 Minnie Hancock, ca. 1930s. Photograph courtesy Bob and Carol Adams.

Fig. 308 Minnie Hancock. Photograph courtesy Sanger Depot Museum, Sanger, California.

Guadalupe Arenas
Cahuilla | 1880–1937

Guadalupe ("Lupe") Arenas was a Cahuilla Native who lived much of her life in the vicinity of Palm Springs, California. She was born Guadalupe Chevedore[13] around 1876[14] and was raised on the Tule River Reservation by her grandparents, Joseph and Maria Rice, whose surname she took.

She married Lee Arenas, a Cahuilla fruit farmer, around 1901[15], and they lived on the Tule River Reservation until 1904[16], when her family moved to Thermal Township on the Torres Reservation near Indio, California[17]. They later moved to San Gorgonio Township[18] in the Palm Springs area, where she did domestic work as well as continuing to weave fine baskets. Guadalupe and Lee lived together in San Gorgonio until her death. There is some controversy regarding the date of her death; in a photograph at the Palm Springs Art Museum, the date is given as 1958, but a hand-written note appended to the 1937 Census Schedule for Palm Springs says she passed away in 1937[19].

Guadalupe was especially renowned for her skill in weaving diamondback rattlesnakes into her dynamic basket designs; two of Guadalupe's rattlesnake baskets, juncus on a grass foundation, are in the collection of the Palm Springs Art Museum. The dark spiral form of the snake creates a sharp contrast against the lighter mottled yellow and orange juncus background. One of these—which shows an eagle above the snake—is included as an illustration in Brian Bibby's book (Bibby 1996). Christopher Moser's book (Moser 1993) shows two snake baskets attributed to Guadalupe in Fig. 100. Moser also attributes two other pieces in a private collection to this artist. A 1920 vintage photograph shows Guadalupe working on a large bowl or olla.

Guadalupe's snake baskets are among the finest made in southern California, and, to judge from the few documented or attributed examples of her work, she was indeed a master weaver.

Fig. 311 Guadalupe Arenas bowl.
4¾" deep by 10¼" diameter, ca. 1910.
Collection Palm Springs Art Museum.
Gift of J. Smeaton Chase.
Catalogue number A91-1974.
Jeff Scovil photographer.

Fig. 312 Guadalupe Arenas with baskets. Braun Research Library Collection. Autry Museum, Los Angeles. Catalog number PO.4278.

Fig. 313 Guadalupe Arenas with Lee Arenas and Della Brown. Courtesy of the Agua Caliente Cultural Museum. Catalogue number 199104006.

Fig. 314 Guadalupe Arenas with Margaret Pablo Saubel, early- to mid-1900s. Braun Research Library Collection. Autry Museum, Los Angeles. Item number P1711.

Fig. 315 Guadalupe Arenas.
Braun Research Library Collection.
Autry Museum, Los Angeles. Item number PO.4279.

Fig. 316 Guadalupe Arenas bowl.
3" deep by 11½" diameter.
Collection Palm Springs Art Museum.
Gift of Jack Wentworth.

Laura Burris Willum
Pomo | 1859–1919

Laura Burris Willum was born in 1859[20], near Shigom, barely nine years after the massacre of the Pomo Indians at the hands of the U.S. Cavalry at Badon Batin—also known as Bloody Island (McLendon 1998). She was the eldest daughter of Jim and Sally Burris (born ca. 1840[21]). Sally herself was an important basketweaver (McLendon 1998) from Shigom (across Clear Lake in Big Valley).

Laura married Willum Dick around 1877[22], at a time when her parents and other relatives were buying back their former lands to establish the self-owned community of Habematolel near the town of Upper Lake. Her sister, Rosa Burris Smith (see pages 218–219), was also a skilled weaver (McLendon 1998). Laura had at least four children, one of whom—Annie Willum Boone (born 1855[23])—became a skilled basketweaver as well.

Fig. 317 Laura Burris Willum, ca. 1905, with large boat-shaped basket shown in Fig. 318. Photograph courtesy Penn Museum. Image number 140386.

Fig. 318* Laura Burris Willum oval basket. 9½" high by 21¼" wide by 34¼" long. Photograph courtesy Penn Museum. Image number 194245.

*See Appendix 3, Figure Notes | Pg. 308

Her mother, Sally Burris, wove mostly twined baskets, while Laura and Rosa wove mostly coiled pieces. This change in weaving technique was probably a result of the influence of non-Indian buyers. In general, weavers born in the 1880s and 1890s shifted to making small coiled baskets, which took less time to make and sold very easily (McLendon 1998).

A vintage photograph of Laura Burris Willum holding a magnificent, large oval basket appears on the cover of Volume 40, No. 1 (1998) of *Expedition Magazine* (McLendon

1998). The basket itself—now in the University of Pennsylvania Museum of Anthropology—is considered to be one of the finest and perhaps the largest of the Pomo boat baskets ever made. It took three years to complete and is shown here in Fig. 318.

There were at least 30 weavers in Habematolel. Many were very talented, but Laura Burris Willum was exceptional, and her large basket qualifies as one of the finest baskets ever made.

Fig. 319 Laura Burris Willum, ca. 1905, with basket shown in Fig. 318. Photograph courtesy Penn Museum. Image number 140585.

Mary Snyder
Chemehuevi | 1852–1951

Mary Snyder was born on the Colorado River that borders California and Arizona during the era of the California Gold Rush. In the 1870s, she moved with a group of Chemehuevi to the Twentynine Palms area of California. She lived there for several years, then moved to the Morongo Reservation near Banning, California. After 1910, Mary divided her time between her early home on the Colorado River and the Morongo Reservation. She also spent time in Victorville in the Mojave Desert adjacent to the Mojave River, where the new weaving styles of Kitty Johnson and others were evolving (Dalrymple 2000b).

Mary was a creative weaver, credited with being the first of the Chemehuevi tribe—around 1896—to incorporate the rattlesnake design in her baskets. Until then, depicting the rattlesnake had been forbidden, as it was believed to bring the offender blindness or death. For years Mary was the only Chemehuevi who was considered powerful enough to use the design, but in time other weavers adopted it as well (Robinson 1954).

Mary also created the "bug" basket (Figs. 323, 325, 330): trays with stink bugs crawling out from the center. This eventually became her signature basket, along with the rattlesnake basket, and for the rest of her life she fashioned numerous variations of both (Robinson 1954).

Her style varied as a function of where she was living: while on the Colorado River she wove traditional Chemehuevi basketry, but on the Morongo Reservation she created "Mission-style" baskets using local materials and designs. When she was younger she was an exceptional weaver, but as she aged, the quality of her work declined.

Mary Snyder is the most famous and most collectible artist of all the great Chemehuevi weavers. Many great collections, public and private, proudly display this master weaver's works.

Fig. 321 Mary Snyder, ca. 1940, from *The Basket Weavers of Arizona.* Bert Robinson, New Mexico Press. © 1954 University of New Mexico Press. Mary is also seen on the right in Fig. 281.

Fig. 320* Mary Snyder tray.
13½" diameter.
Alan and Bronnie Blaugrund Collection.
Jeff Scovil photographer.
*See Appendix 3, Figure Notes | Pg. 308

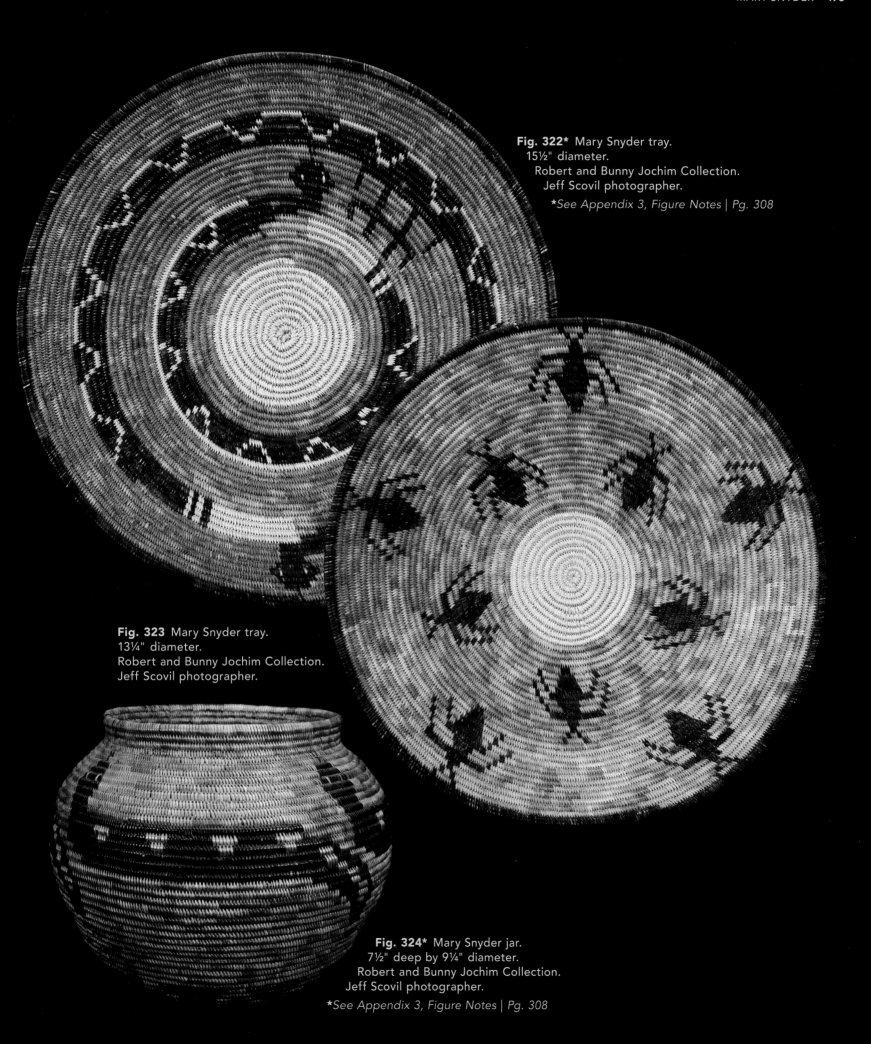

Fig. 322* Mary Snyder tray.
15½" diameter.
Robert and Bunny Jochim Collection.
Jeff Scovil photographer.
*See Appendix 3, Figure Notes | Pg. 308

Fig. 323 Mary Snyder tray.
13¼" diameter.
Robert and Bunny Jochim Collection.
Jeff Scovil photographer.

Fig. 324* Mary Snyder jar.
7½" deep by 9¼" diameter.
Robert and Bunny Jochim Collection.
Jeff Scovil photographer.
*See Appendix 3, Figure Notes | Pg. 308

Fig. 325 Mary Snyder tray.
15¾" diameter.
Natalie Linn Collection.
Justin Tunis photographer.

Fig. 326* Mary Snyder tray.
15" diameter.
Natalie Linn Collection.
Justin Tunis photographer.

See Appendix 3, Figure Notes | Pg. 308

Fig. 327 Mary Snyder jar.
6½" deep by 10" diameter.
Natalie Linn Collection.
Justin Tunis photographer.

Fig. 328 Mary Snyder tray.
15" diameter, ca. 1910.
Collection of Agua Caliente Band of Cahuilla Indians.
Courtesy of the Agua Caliente Cultural Museum.
Catalogue number L2002003078.

Fig. 329 Mary Snyder olla.
13" deep by 13" diameter.
Terry DeWald Collection.
Jeff Scovil photographer.

Fig. 330 Mary Snyder shallow bowl.
3" deep by 14¾" diameter.
Gift of Clark Field, 1942.14.1995 © 2011.
Philbrook Museum of Art, Inc., Tulsa, Oklahoma.

Fig. 331* Mary Snyder shallow bowl.
3½" deep by 16" diameter.
Gift of Clark Field, 1942.14.2014 © 2011.
Philbrook Museum of Art, Inc.,
Tulsa, Oklahoma.
*See Appendix 3, Figure Notes | Pg. 308

Fig. 332* Mary Snyder bowl.
3½" deep by 16¼" diameter.
Terry DeWald Collection.
Terry DeWald photographer.
*See Appendix 3, Figure Notes | Pg. 308

Fig. 333 Mary Snyder "The Diamondback Rattlesnake Olla"
20" high by 21" diameter, ca. 1910.
Wayne and Malee Thompson Collection.
Jeff Scovil photographer.

Fig. 334 Mary Snyder olla.
9" deep by 9½" diameter,
ca. 1910.
Collection of Agua Caliente
Band of Cahuilla Indians.
Courtesy Agua Caliente
Cultural Museum.
Catalogue number L2002003077.
All rights reserved.

Fig. 335 Mary Snyder olla.
7⅞" deep by 10" diameter.
Terry DeWald Collection.
Terry DeWald photographer.

Minnie Mike was born in Lee Vining near Mono Lake on the eastern side of the Sierra Nevada in eastern California in Mono County. After the death of her mother, Suzie McGowan, Minnie was raised by her stepmother, Suzie Thompson. Minnie lived most of her life in the Mono Lake area, and was married twice, the second time to Caroose Mike, a Mono Lake Paiute (Bates and Lee 1990).

Like her famous sister, Carrie Bethel (see pages 89–100), Minnie wove in the new style of fancy baskets. Although a master weaver, she never attained the recognition that her sister Carrie did. She continued to weave throughout her life. Unfortunately, very few documented Minnie Mike baskets are known. Most of her baskets are small, yet finely made pieces. One documented basket from the Ella Cain Collection, Fig. 339, is now in the Stevia Thompson Collection.

Photographer Jim Yoakum of Nevada was fortunate enough to meet with both Minnie Mike and her sister Carrie Bethel He took a few color photographs of the two sisters with some of their baskets—which are now in the Natalie Linn Collection.

My grandma got her willows during the fall season for making her baskets. She did her baskets during the daylight hours since she didn't have any electricity. She never burned her shavings from her willows; that was a bad omen. She made beautiful baskets.

— Erma Andrews, Minnie Mike's granddaughter and
   Carrie Bethel's great grand-niece

Fig. 336 Minnie Mike with her sister Carrie Bethel. Minnie Mike is holding the large basket tray shown in Fig. 337, ca. 1965. Photograph courtesy Jerry Andrews.

Fig. 337 Minnie Mike tray.
About 23" diameter.
Photograph courtesy Jerry Andrews.

Fig. 339 Minnie Mike degikup. 3½" high by 7¼" diameter. Stevia Thompson Collection. Jeff Scovil photographer.

Fig. 338 Minnie Mike in the process of weaving a basket, ca. 1965. Photograph courtesy Jerry Andrews.

Fig. 340 Minnie Mike degikup. 4" high by 6½" diameter. © 2012. Bonhams & Butterfields Auctioneers Corporation. All rights reserved. German Herrera photographer.

Fig. 341 Minnie Mike degikup. 6½" diameter, ca. 1960. Natalie Linn Collection. Jeff Scovil photographer.

Fig. 342 Minnie Mike holding basket shown in Fig. 341, ca. 1962. Carrie Bethel is to her left. Photograph courtesy Jim Yoakum.

Tootsie Dick
Washoe | 1855–1928

Tootsie Dick was born around 1855 and lived in the Antelope Valley, south of Carson Valley. Her father was Euro-American and was never really considered part of her family. The Antelope Valley is somewhat isolated from the Lake Tahoe region, and weavers in the Antelope Valley developed their own new specialized, signature style of fancy basketweaving.

Tootsie began selling her pieces through the Emporium around 1913, and was influenced by Minnie Dick, another Antelope Valley weaver. She expanded on Minnie's innovations and by 1915 had adapted decorative birds, butterflies, and insects—as well as plants, vines, trees, and shrubs based on Sarah Jim Mayo's work. Tootsie did some work for the owners of a general store in Coleville (the Hardys and the Chichesters, who owned a large ranch in the Antelope Valley), but most of her better works were sold to the Cohns. Dat So La Lee even sold a few of Tootsie's baskets to William Breitholle, who also bought a few unnumbered Dat So La Lee baskets, which therefore were independent of the Cohn relationship (Cohodas 1979, 1981, 1986).

The Cohns recognized Tootsie's work as outstanding and had Edward S. Curtis photograph several of her baskets. They never promoted Tootsie as an artist while Dat So La Lee was alive. When Dat So La Lee died in December 1925, the Cohns then decided that Tootsie Dick would be their new star, identifying her as the second finest Washoe weaver after Dat So La Lee. Many of Tootsie Dick's baskets are represented in numerous collections. But unfortunately—and unlike Dat So La Lee—there do not seem to be any photos of Tootsie herself! (Cohodas 1979, 1986)

After Tootsie's six-year-old daughter died of spinal meningitis in 1928, a grief-stricken Tootsie Dick took her own life.

Tootsie was nearly forgotten until Marvin Cohodas and other scholars rediscovered her, and today, she is recognized as one of the great Washoe artists (Cohodas 1986).

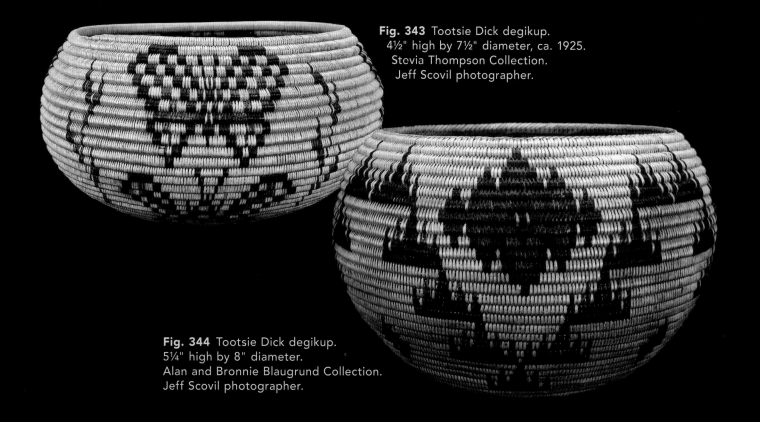

Fig. 343 Tootsie Dick degikup.
4½" high by 7½" diameter, ca. 1925.
Stevia Thompson Collection.
Jeff Scovil photographer.

Fig. 344 Tootsie Dick degikup.
5¼" high by 8" diameter.
Alan and Bronnie Blaugrund Collection.
Jeff Scovil photographer.

Fig. 345 Tootsie Dick degikup.
7¾" high by 12" diameter, ca. 1925.
Photograph courtesy Nevada State Museum,
Carson City, Nevada Collection.
Jeff Scovil photographer.

Fig. 346 Tootsie Dick degikup.
5¾" high by 8¼" diameter, ca. 1925.
Robert and Bunny Jochim Collection.
Jeff Scovil photographer.

Fig. 347 Tootsie Dick degikup.
5½" high by 10½" diameter.
Thaw Collection, Fenimore Art Museum,
Cooperstown, New York.
Gift of Eugene V. and Claire F. Thaw.
Catalogue number T0142.
John Bigelow Taylor photographer.

Fig. 348 Tootsie Dick degikup.
4¾" high by 8¾" diameter, ca. 1925.
Robert and Bunny Jochim Collection.
Jeff Scovil photographer.

Fig. 349 Tootsie Dick degikup.
3" high by 5¾" diameter, 1925.
David Salk Collection.
Jeff Scovil photographer.

Fig. 350 Tootsie Dick degikup.
6½" high by 12" diameter.
Photograph courtesy Fine Arts Museums
of San Francisco, de Young Museum.
Gift of Mrs. T. C. Tilden.

Fig. 351 Tootsie Dick degikup.
9½" diameter.
Photograph courtesy Gene Quintana.
John Law photographer.

Fig. 352 Tootsie Dick degikup.
9" diameter.
Photograph courtesy North Lake Tahoe
Historical Society; Marion Steinbach Indian
Basket Museum and Gatekeeper's Museum,
Tahoe City, California.

Sartonia Emeterio

Yawelmani (Yowlumni) Yokuts | 1798–1905

Sartonia Romana Emeterio (Mrs. Emeterio) is one of the earliest and greatest weavers of the Florescence but is also perhaps one of the least well known. She was born in 1798[24], probably in the Yawelmani[25] Yokuts settlement of Tubampet (Tulamniu) on Buena Vista Lake near Bakersfield, California. Her Indian name is unknown, but it was there at Tubampet that she married Francisco Emeterio, a local tribal leader[26], and together they had three children, including Juan Emeterio.[27] Following the signing of the Tejon Treaty by Francisco Emeterio and others in 1851, Sartonia and her people moved to Alta Vista near Porterville in Tulare County (Nicola Larsen personal communication 2013; Phillips 2004:25, 123–124) Her son Juan (1845–1909) and his family relocated to the Tule River Reservation, where she occasionally visited.[28]

One of the finest gambling trays known, Fig. 357, is documented as woven by Mrs. Emeterio through the records of Helen Harvey, a turn-of-the-century collector in Porterville, California (Bob Adams personal communication 2009). A few other bottlenecks and bowls are also attributed to her, but the true scope of her accomplishments remains a matter of some speculation, since there is only a limited number of pieces that she is known or believed to have created.

Fig. 353 Sartonia Emeterio bottleneck olla.
6¾" deep by 11" diameter.
Alan and Bronnie Blaugrund Collection.
Jeff Scovil photographer.

Fig. 354 Sartonia Emeterio, ca. 1895, with basket shown in Fig. 355. Photograph courtesy Bob and Carol Adams.

Fig. 355 Sartonia Emeterio bowl. 7¾" deep by 17¼" diameter. Lew Meekins Collection. Jeff Scovil photographer.

Fig. 356 Sartonia Emeterio gambling tray.
27" diameter, ca. 1900.
Private collection.
Ben Watkins photographer.

Fig. 357* Sartonia Emeterio
gambling tray.
33" diameter.
Janis and Dennis Lyon Collection.
Jeff Scovil photographer.
*See Appendix 3, Figure Notes | Pg. 308

Mary Wrinkle

Panamint Shoshone (Timbisha) | 1876–1940

Mary Wrinkle was born in the Saline Valley, California which lies on the western edge of Death Valley. Her husband, Charlie Wrinkle, took his name from the owner of the old soda works in Keeler where Charlie was employed. Mary's sister, Mamie Gregory, also was an accomplished weaver (Slater 2000).

In 1910, Mary and Charlie moved to Darwin, where Mary would be exposed to the new style of basketry sweeping through California. She shifted from the old, traditional style of basketweaving and began to develop her own version of the new style. She soon distinguished herself as an exceptional weaver and became one of the more influential artists in California Native basket history.

Her earlier works were two-color pieces with stitch counts of over 50 per inch and coil counts of 12 per inch. She later expanded her use of color to include yellow juncus, red yucca root, white porcupine quill, and the pink quill from woodpecker feathers.

She collected the yucca root and woodpecker feathers found only at higher elevations—Darwin lies 4,700 feet above sea level. Also found at these upper elevations were a variety of colorful birds, many of which are depicted on her baskets.

From the time when she first began weaving baskets with scenes of birds in trees, squirrels, turtles, and high-desert panoramas, collectors prized them. Aurelia McLean, who built one of the finest collections of Panamint basketry, noted that Mary Wrinkle was an extraordinary weaver. Mary was one of the featured basketmakers at the Golden Gate Exposition of 1939 (Slater 2000). Although Mary never made large, overpowering baskets, her creations still rate among the finest baskets ever made in California.

Unfortunately, our research was unable to locate any photographs of Mary Wrinkle.

Fig. 358 Mary Wrinkle olla. 8" deep by 11" diameter. Charles and Valerie Diker Collection.

Fig. 359 Mary Wrinkle bowl. 4" deep by 7¼" diameter. Natalie Linn Collection. Justin Tunis photographer.

Fig. 360 Mary Wrinkle bowl. 6" diameter. Photograph courtesy Timbisha Shoshone Tribe, Ridgecrest, California.

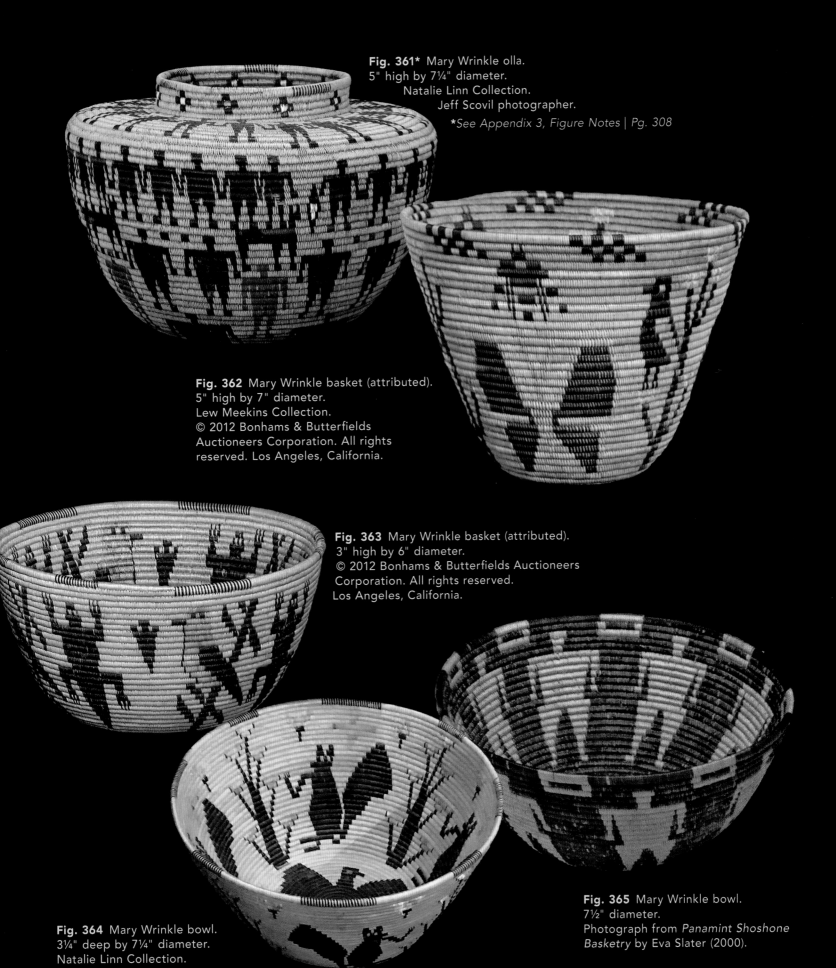

Fig. 361* Mary Wrinkle olla.
5" high by 7¼" diameter.
Natalie Linn Collection.
Jeff Scovil photographer.

See Appendix 3, Figure Notes | Pg. 308

Fig. 362 Mary Wrinkle basket (attributed).
5" high by 7" diameter.
Lew Meekins Collection.
© 2012 Bonhams & Butterfields
Auctioneers Corporation. All rights
reserved. Los Angeles, California.

Fig. 363 Mary Wrinkle basket (attributed).
3" high by 6" diameter.
© 2012 Bonhams & Butterfields Auctioneers
Corporation. All rights reserved.
Los Angeles, California.

Fig. 365 Mary Wrinkle bowl.
7½" diameter.
Photograph from *Panamint Shoshone
Basketry* by Eva Slater (2000).

Fig. 364 Mary Wrinkle bowl.
3¼" deep by 7¼" diameter.
Natalie Linn Collection.

Dolores Saneva Patencio

Cupeño | 1864–1931

Dolores Patencio, whose birth name was Saneva, was born in her native village known as Kupa (what is known today as Warner's Hot Springs) at the base of Hot Springs Mountain in northern San Diego County. When she was about 20 years old, she married Francisco Patencio in San Bernardino and then they moved back to Palm Springs, where Francisco was headman of the Agua Caliente Cahuilla.

She would become the best known of all the Cupeño weavers. Unlike Mary Wrinkle, where there are no known photographs, there are numerous vintage photographs that show Dolores weaving large basketry ollas or bowls. Two baskets, acquired from her granddaughter Sarah Torres, were made by Dolores before her marriage to Francisco around 1880; both use red juncus and are in the style of the Cupeño characterized by the bold use of dyed black juncus.

Fig. 367 Dolores Saneva Patencio bowl.
12" diameter.
Courtesy of the Agua Caliente Cultural Museum.
On loan from James Norris.
Catalogue number L20030020004.
All rights reserved.

Fig. 366 Dolores Saneva Patencio. This item is reproduced by permission of the Huntington Library, San Marino, California. Photograph number CL 276 100

Two magnificent large ollas now in the Palm Springs Art Museum are attributed to Dolores Saneva Patencio through photographic records (Figs. 371, 377). There is a flared bowl made by Dolores in the same museum (Fig. 378), as well as several other similar baskets, which may be her work. One documented basket made by Dolores Saneva Patencio resides in the Malki Museum on the Morongo Reservation near Banning, California, and another great olla is in the Autry Museum collection.

These few exceptional works of art show Dolores to have been a master basketmaker. The Riverside Museum commemorative volume on Southern Californian Native American basketry provided the biographical materials on Dolores Saneva Patencio (Moser 1993:75–76 and 78; also photographs of Riverside Museum Catalogue Numbers 124, 125, and 127 are identified as Dolores Saneva Patencio baskets).

Fig. 368 Dolores Saneva Patencio with olla shown in Fig. 369, early- to mid-1900s. Braun Research Library Collection. Autry Museum, Los Angeles. Item number P.1639.

Fig. 369 Dolores Saneva Patencio olla. 11½" high by 13" diameter. Braun Research Library Collection.

BASKET WEAVER, PALM SPRINGS, CAL.

BASKET WEAVER, PALM SPRINGS, CALIF.

Fig. 370 Dolores Saneva Patencio weaving olla shown in Fig. 371. Photograph courtesy University of Southern California. On behalf of the USC Special Collections.

Fig. 371 Dolores Saneva Patencio olla storage basket.
18" high by 22" diameter, ca. 1910.
Collection Palm Springs Art Museum, acquisition by exchange:
Gift of Winifred Little, Edwin D. Walker, and Mr. and Mrs. James H. Kelley.
Catalogue number A1-1988.
Sherrill & Associates photographer.

Fig. 372 Dolores Saneva Patencio. Photograph courtesy Palm Springs Art Museum. Catalogue number Patencio 004.

Fig. 373 Chief Francisco and Dolores Saneva Patencio. Braun Research Library Collection. Autry Museum, Los Angeles. Item number P.1729.

Fig. 374 Dolores Saneva Patencio. This item is reproduced by permission of the Huntington Library, San Marino, California.

Fig. 375 Dolores Saneva Patencio. Courtesy of the Agua Caliente Cultural Museum. Catalogue number 1992002001. All rights reserved.

Fig. 376 Dolores Saneva Patencio with Chief Francisco Patencio. She is holding unfinished basket shown in Fig. 377, ca. 1920. Photograph courtesy Palm Springs Art Museum. Catalogue number Patencio002.

Fig. 377 Dolores Saneva Patencio olla. 11" high by 16" diameter. Collection Palm Springs Art Museum. Gift of Nellie Coffman. Catalogue number A506-1974. Jeff Scovil photographer.

Fig. 378 Dolores Saneva Patencio bowl.
7¼" high by 15¾" diameter.
Collection Palm Springs Art Museum.
Gift of Nellie Coffman.
Catalogue number A580-1974.
Jeff Scovil photographer.

Fig. 379 Dolores Saneva Patencio. Courtesy of the Agua Caliente Cultural Museum. Catalogue number 2005045001. All rights reserved.

Fig. 380 Dolores Saneva Patencio with Francisco and Albert Patencio. Courtesy of the Agua Caliente Cultural Museum. Catalogue number 1991004041. All rights reserved.

Daisy Charlie
Mono Lake Paiute (Kuzedika) | 1890–1957

Daisy Charlie was born near Mono Lake, Mono County, California in 1890. Her mother was the famous weaver, Nellie Charlie (see pages 206–208) and her father was Young Charlie. Another famous weaver, Tina Charlie (see pages 15–23), was her aunt (Dean et al. 2004).

Daisy attended school around 1900 where she learned English. She was the first in her family to do so.

She married Ed Cluette, a Paiute man, and had two children, Rosie and Jessie. After Ed died, Daisy moved to Mono Mills on the southern shore of Mono Lake where she worked as a cook. There she was exposed to an emerging new style of basketry. She became a proficient weaver, commonly using butterflies and eagles in her designs. In 1912, she sold several baskets to well-known collector Ella Cain.

Around 1917, she and her daughters moved to Bishop, California, where she was employed doing domestic work and weaving baskets. Most of her baskets were collected by the families she worked for or by local collectors. As a result, her baskets were rarely made available to the wider collector market.

Daisy married Jack Mallory, a Paiute, around 1920, and moved to Round Valley, California, where Jack had a home and together they had six children. They moved to the Bishop Indian Reservation in 1939. Daisy continued throughout these periods to create fine baskets until her death in 1957 (Dean et al. 2004; 77–79).

The Ella Cain Collection was sold in 2005 by the Bonhams and Butterfields auction house in San Francisco. Interestingly, there was a note left in one of Daisy's baskets that Ella wrote saying Daisy was one of the finest weavers at that time (Marsha Blaver personal communication 2016). Two Daisy Charlie baskets collected by Ella Cain in 1912 were sold into the collector market and are now in the Stevia Thompson collection (Figs. 382 and 384).

Fig. 381 Daisy Charlie, 1917. Photograph courtesy Jesse Durant.

Fig. 382 Daisy Charlie degikup 3½" high by 6¾" diameter. Stevia Thompson Collection. Jeff Scovil photographer.

Fig. 383 Daisy Charlie with daughters. Rosie and Jessie ca. 1913. Photograph courtesy Jesse Durant.

Fig. 384 Daisy Charlie degikup 2½" high by 6" diameter. Stevia Thompson Collection. Gene Meieran photographer.

Maggie Mayo James
Washoe | 1870–1952

Maggie Mayo James was the daughter of Captain Pete Mayo. Her mother—who died after Maggie's birth—is unknown. Captain Pete later married Sarah Jim Mayo, one of the most influential Washoe weavers (see pages 68–72). Sarah's influence on Maggie's work is apparent, and she was among the first to adopt Sarah's style around 1912 (Cohodas 1981).

Maggie James' weaving career was long and very successful. She sold her works consistently to both Margaretta Dressler, a local rancher's wife, and to Mrs. George Pope of San Francisco, a collector. Maggie taught her art to her daughter and four granddaughters, all of whom became fine weavers.

Maggie James' basketry varied over her career and her work is well documented. Two early photographs of her with her baskets show both geometric and butterfly designs. A later photo (mid-1920s) shows Maggie selling her baskets, one of which is in the Lowie Museum (now known as the Phoebe Hearst Museum at the University of California, Berkeley). At least one basket has a Cohn label and it is now in the Smithsonian Institution in Washington, DC.

A number of other pieces are documented; at least six have written labels crafted by Margaretta Dressler identifying Maggie James as the maker of the basket. In 1979, Cohodas attributed 60 baskets to Maggie James, based on the documented examples (Cohodas 1981).

Maggie's weaving varied from fairly good to exceptional with over 40 stitches per inch. Figural images—eagles, flowers, butterflies, humans, arrows, horses, and trees— were commonly intermixed with geometric motifs. Other baskets were decorated with well-spaced and balanced geometric designs. Her earlier works were her finest; the quality of her baskets declined as she aged, and her weaving career ended around 1935. Maggie James is one of the influential Washoe weavers, and at her peak was among the best. Her works today are extremely desirable and very valuable.

Maggie's granddaughter—Margie James—carried on with her grandmother's tradition as a weaver, with many fine baskets to her credit.

Fig. 385 Maggie Mayo James degikup. 16" diameter.

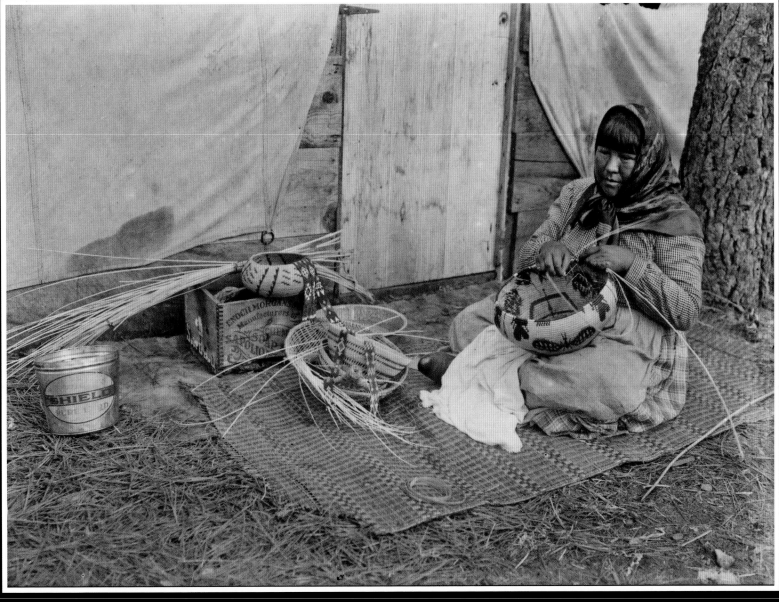

Fig. 386 Maggie Mayo James, ca. 1915. Braun Research Library Collection. Autry Museum, Los Angeles. Item number P.2173.

Fig. 387 Maggie Mayo James degikup.
10½" diameter.
Private collection.
Photograph courtesy Gene Quintana.
John Law photographer.

Fig. 388 Maggie Mayo James degikup.
5" high by 8" diameter.
Photograph courtesy Phoebe A. Hearst
Museum of Anthropology and the Regents
of the University of California.
Catalogue number 1-70647.

WASHOE INDIAN
LAKE TAHOE, CAL.

Fig. 389 Maggie Mayo James, ca. 1927. Her right hand is holding basket seen in Fig. 388. Photograph courtesy University of Nevada, Reno.
Catalogue number UNRS-P1984-22-9.

Fig. 390 Maggie Mayo James, ca. 1913. Basket seen in Fig. 391 is in her lap. Photograph courtesy National Anthropological Archives, Smithsonian Institution. Catalogue number NAA-79-1659.

Fig. 391 Maggie Mayo James degikup.
12½" high by 22½" diameter.
Southwest Museum of the American Indian Collection.
Autry Museum, Los Angeles.
Catalogue number 811.G.1637.

Fig. 392 Maggie Mayo James degikup.
5" high by 9" diameter.
Photograph courtesy Phoebe A. Hearst Museum of Anthropology
and the Regents of the University of California.
Catalogue number 70623.

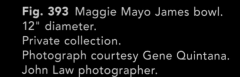

Fig. 393 Maggie Mayo James bowl.
12" diameter.
Private collection.
Photograph courtesy Gene Quintana.
John Law photographer.

Fig. 394 Maggie Mayo James degikup.
5" high by 7" diameter.
The Collection of Ken and Judy Siebel.
Gene Meieran photographer.

Fig. 395 Maggie Mayo James. Photograph courtesy Braun Research
Library, Autry National Center of the American West. Item number P2127.

Fig. 396 Maggie Mayo James degikup.
4½" high by 7½" diameter.
The Collection of Ken and Judy Siebel.
Gene Meieran photographer.

Fig. 397 Maggie Mayo James degikup.
8¾" diameter.
Photograph courtesy Gene Quintana.
John Law photographer.

Fig. 398 Maggie Mayo James degikup.
11" diameter.
Photograph courtesy Gene Quintana.
John Law photographer.

Fig. 399 Maggie Mayo James degikup.
9½" high by 19" diameter.
The Collection of Ken and Judy Siebel.
Gene Meieran photographer.

Lupe Alberras (Alberas, Alveras)
Desert Cahuilla | 1871–1954

Little is known about the life of Lupe (Guadalupe) Alberras, except that she lived in the Palm Springs area in the first part of the twentieth century.

Seven of her documented baskets are in the Palm Springs Art Museum including a unique, innovative depiction of a diamondback rattlesnake (Fig. 401) and two visually intriguing images of polychrome rain birds (also known as thunderbirds) that border on reverse-image patterns (Figs. 402 and 403). A third similar rain bird bowl (Fig. 400) can also be seen in another exhibit in the Agua Caliente Cultural Museum.

These rain bird bowls are both complex but yet artistically well balanced; her style is comparable to a few of the other highly talented Native Californian weavers.

There seem to be no known photographs of Lupe Alberras.

Fig. 400 Lupe Alberras bowl.
9½" diameter.
Collection of Agua Caliente Band of Cahuilla Indians.
Catalogue number L2007004001.
Photograph courtesy Jeff Scovil.

Fig. 401 Lupe Alberras bowl.
4½" deep by 16¼" diameter.
Collection Palm Springs Art Museum.
Gift of Cornelia B. White from the Marjorie Rose Dougan Collection.
Catalogue number A96-1974.
Jeff Scovil photographer.

Fig. 402 Lupe Alberras bowl.
5" deep by 17¾" diameter.
Collection Palm Springs Art Museum.
Gift of Cornelia B. White from the
Marjorie Rose Dougan Collection.
Catalogue number A80-1974.
Jeff Scovil photographer.

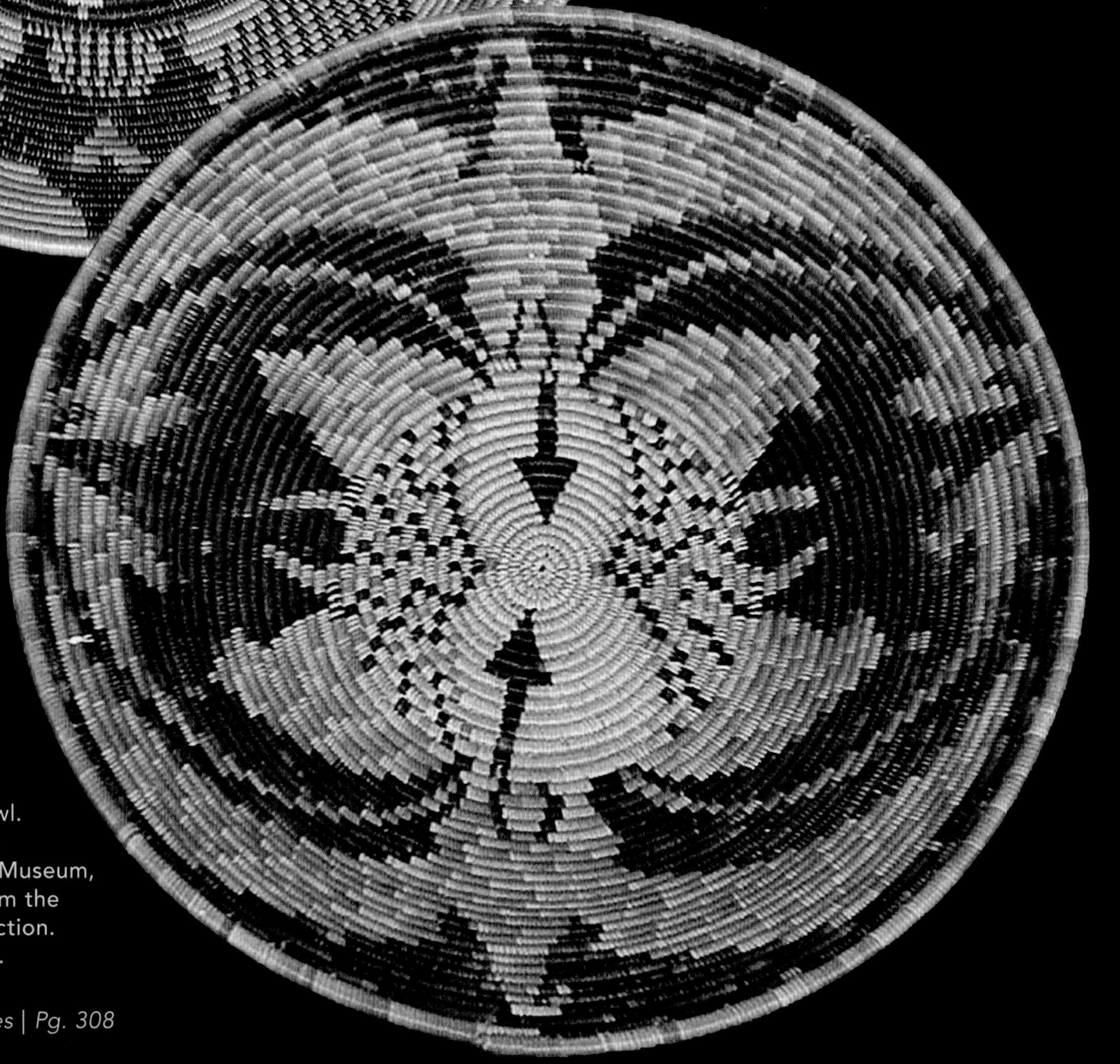

Fig. 403* Lupe Alberras bowl.
4½" deep by 16¼" diameter.
Collection Palm Springs Art Museum,
Gift of Cornelia B. White from the
Marjorie Rose Dougan Collection.
Catalogue number A95-1974.
Jeff Scovil photographer.
*See Appendix 3, Figure Notes | Pg. 308

Nellie Charlie

Mono Lake Paiute (Kuzedika) | 1867–1965

Nellie Charlie was born near Mono Lake on the eastern side of the Sierra Nevada in Mono County, California in 1867, as was her famous sister Tina Charlie. Her mother was Patsy Jim and her father Na-Ha or Pete Jim, a former headman. Her Paiute name was Pooseuna (Bates and Lee 1990:146–149).

Nellie married a Mono Lake Paiute man named Young Charlie. He was one of the many Mono Lake Paiutes who traveled from Mono Lake to the Yosemite and Hetch Hetchy areas and back. Young Charlie also married Nellie's sister Tina (see pages 15–23) and they all lived on a ranch along Rush Creek. Nellie and Young Charlie had six children including daughters Daisy, Lula, and Mildred, all of whom were weavers in their early years. Daisy continued with her work throughout her life and became a well-known weaver (Bates and Lee 1990:147). Nellie divorced Young Charlie in 1927 (Dean et al. 2004).

Nellie wove traditional single-rod, space-stitched, and twined baskets, as well as triple-rod baskets. In 1903, she sold baskets to C. Hart Merriam—a noted anthropologist, photographer, ethnographer, and collector. She appears in one of his photographs (Fig. 409). Nellie developed her own style when the "new style basketry" was spreading, and by the 1920s, she was known as a fine weaver. She competed regularly in the Yosemite Indian Field Days events (Bates and Lee 1990:147)

Fig. 404 Nellie Charlie with her baskets at Yosemite Indian Field Days, 1924. Braun Research Library Collection. Autry Museum, Los Angeles. Item number P.377.

By the 1940s, Nellie lived with her daughter Daisy (see page 197) in Bishop. In the 1950s, she moved to the Bishop Reservation with her granddaughter Jesse Durant. Her sister Tina Charlie also lived with them.

Fig. 405 Nellie Charlie degikup. 12" diameter, ca. 1940. Photograph courtesy Gene Quintana. John Law photographer.

My mother, Elma Hess Blaver, granddaughter of Nellie Jim Charlie, told me of stories about visiting her grandparents at their encampment at Rush Creek. She spoke of the ladies working together in a "circle of sage" (for protection from the sun and wind), preparing their willows and other basket making materials. She enjoyed her visits right up to the end of the day when "MooAh" would tuck her in at nightfall under a cozy rabbit blanket. "MooAh" always wore a headscarf and black sweater.

—Alan Blaver, Nellie Jim Charlie's great grandson

Fig. 406 Nellie Charlie, 1962. Photograph courtesy Alan Blaver.

Fig. 407 Nellie Charlie, ca. 1944. Photograph courtesy Bridgeport Museum. Mono County Historical Society.

Fig. 408 Nellie Charlie at her home in Bishop, California, ca. 1950. Photograph courtesy Elma Blaver.

Fig. 409 Nellie Charlie, 1903. Photograph courtesy Bancroft Library, University of California, Berkeley. C. Hart Merriam photograph.

Fig. 410 Nellie Charlie, 1925, Yosemite Indian Field Days. Photograph courtesy Yosemite Museum and Research Library. National Park Service Catalogue number YOSE 46106.

Mary Sampson
Yokuts | 1855–year of death unknown

Mary Sampson was born in the mountains east of Dunlap and Squaw Valley, California. She married Jack Sampson around 1910, and then moved to Dunlap, California (Bob Adams personal communication 2009).

While Mary wove in a traditional style, the quality of her work was truly exceptional. She was apparently overshadowed by contemporary weaver, Mary Topino (Mrs. Britches, see pages 238–252), as they both wove large friendship bowls. As a result, Mary Sampson is virtually unknown to many collectors and dealers today, which is unfortunate considering the quality of her work.

Fortunately, Bob Adams located a small photograph of her weaving a great friendship bowl, and many years later, he obtained that very bowl seen in the old faded photograph. This archival material was most helpful in documenting Mary Sampson as one of the finest of the great Yokuts artists. Another beautiful piece is in the Adams' photograph that accompanied the great friendship bowl.

The Overhouster family of Squaw Valley collected a few Mary Sampson bowls; in addition, a very fine lidded jar resides in a top-quality private collection. While small in number, these few documented pieces place Mary Sampson in the highest echelon of great California Indian basketry artists (Bob Adams personal communication 2009).

Fig. 411 Mary Sampson.
Photograph courtesy Alex Schwed.

Fig. 412 Mary Sampson jar with lid.

Fig. 413* Mary Sampson. Mary is holding partially completed basket shown in Fig. 414.
Photograph courtesy Alex Schwed.

*See Appendix 3, Figure Notes | Pg. 308

Fig. 414 Mary Sampson bowl.
12" deep by 25½" diameter.
Bob and Carol Adams Collection.
Todd Adams photographer.

Fig. 415 Mary Sampson bowl.
12" deep by 21" diameter.
Bob and Carol Adams Collection.
Todd Adams photographer.

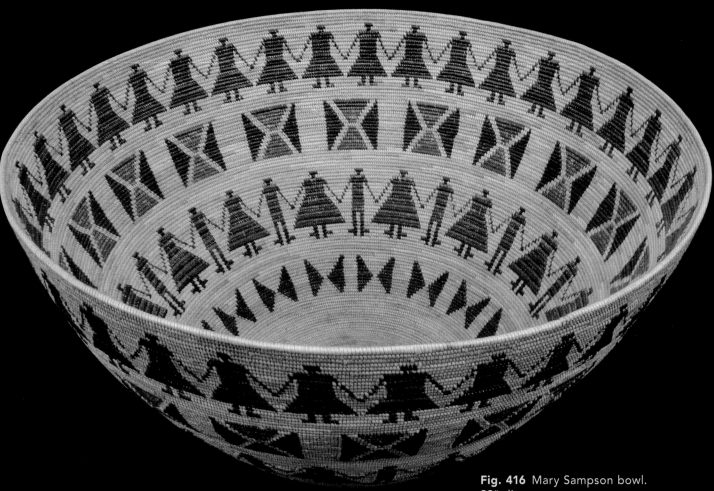

Fig. 416 Mary Sampson bowl.
23" diameter.
Alex Schwed Collection.
Todd Adams photograph.

Anna (Annie) Hughes

Panamint Shoshone (Timbisha) | Year of birth/death unknown

In the early 1900s, many Native Americans did not know their birthdates and often census takers and anthropologists guessed at a person's age and used that year as "fact." Information had to be gathered from many disparate sources and researching a person's background was difficult and uncertain. So it was for Anna Hughes.

For example, based on the Southern Nye County 1910 Census, Ash Meadows Charley, whose parents were Paiute, was 84 years old and "married" to an unnamed Shoshone woman, aged 65. There are six children of theirs listed: Annie, Paiute/Shoshone (P/S), age 32; John, P/S, age 31; Dan, P/S, age 27; Hannah, P/S, age 29; Winters, P/S, age 24; Hawley, P/S, age 19. Presumably, Annie Charlie was born in 1878.

Anna is believed to have married John Hughes in the early 1900s; their son Mike was born in 1904. From John's Enrollment Application under the Act of 1928, John was born in 1859 in Saline Valley, as were both his parents, all of whom were identified as Shoshone Indians.

Information from Mike's Enrollment Application has his mother as Annie Charlie, born in Ash Meadows, Nye County, Nevada. He said that his parents lived during the summer at Beatty and the winter in Death Valley and they had been doing so since their marriage. Mike also said that he usually remained with his maternal grandfather in Ash Valley. A daughter, Emily Bellas, was born in 1911 to John Hughes and Annie (Charley) Hughes; and lists her maternal grandfather as Ash Meadows Charley. Also, Bessie Shaw, a basketweaver whom Julian Steward, noted ethnographer and anthropologist, met in the Beatty area, said she (Annie) was the daughter of Mrs. John Hughes who also made baskets; presumably this was in reference to Annie Hughes (personal communication Greg Sarena and Bob Seng 2016).

While there are few baskets attributed to Anna Hughes, the quality of those pictured qualifies her as a masterpiece weaver.

Fig. 417 Anna Hughes holding basket shown in Fig. 418. Photograph courtesy of Steve Nelson, Greg Sarena, and Bob Seng.

Fig. 418 Anna Hughes bowl.
5¼" deep by 11½" diameter, ca. 1926.
Courtesy of Steve Nelson, Greg Sarena, and Bob Seng.
Arvin Carlson photographer.

Fig. 419 Anna Hughes bottleneck olla.
5¾" high by 7" diameter.
Courtesy Steve Nelson.
Arvin Carlson photographer.

Alice James Wilson

Mono Lake Paiute (Kuzedika) | 1899–1959

Alice James Wilson, sister of Lucy Parker Telles, daughter of Louisa Tom, and niece of Leanna Tom, obviously is a member of a prestigious family of basketweavers. She married a Chukchansi Yokuts—Freemont James—and had four children between 1916 and 1923. After she had separated from Freemont, she was remarried to Westley Wilson. They lived in Yosemite Valley where Westley worked first as a laborer for the Yosemite Park, and later as a custodian (Bates and Lee 1990). Alice also worked at the Sentinel Hotel in Yosemite Park.

Alice often entered the Yosemite Field Days, and many of the Field Days photographs show her with her sister and her aunt. She used many designs in her baskets—human figures, animals, and butterflies—perhaps inspired by her sister Lucy. She wove many beaded baskets, with geometric designs, as well as large baskets, one of which is seen in Figs. 422, 424, and 425. One of these baskets is also seen at the feet of Lucy Parker Telles in Fig. 490.

One basket image was used to create a famous Yosemite postcard, showing her son Norman seated in the basket (Fig. 420); however, the design of this particular basket has also been ascribed to Lucy Parker Telles. Indeed, many weavers have been photographed with baskets made by other weavers (e.g., the Alice Wilson basket in Lucy's photograph, mentioned earlier), as well as many Alice Wilson photos with baskets clearly made by weavers from other tribes.

Fig. 420 Photo of Norman James in degikup shown in Fig. 421, attributed to Alice James Wilson, 1926. Photograph courtesy Yosemite Museum and Research Library. National Park Service Catalogue number YOSE RL 014013.

Alice became a craft demonstrator during the late 1920s and early 1930s at the famous Ahwahnee Hotel in Yosemite Valley, and was reported to be very popular with the visiting tourists (Bates and Lee 1990). She was noted for her beadwork, not only in basketry but for sashes, gloves, and lapel pins.

Although not reaching the exalted weaver status of her sister Lucy or her aunt Leanna, Alice Wilson clearly was a major weaver during the period of the Florescence. She died in 1959 and is buried in Mariposa.

Fig. 421* Alice James Wilson degikup.
7" high by 12¼" diameter.
This basket is also seen at the feet of Lucy Parker Telles in Fig. 501.
Photograph courtesy Yosemite Museum and Research Library.
National Park Service Catalogue number 81044.
*See Appendix 3, Figure Notes | Pg. 309

Fig. 422 Alice James Wilson weaving degikup shown in Fig. 424. Lucy Parker Telles is to her right, behind her large basket. Photograph courtesy Yosemite Museum and Research Library. National Park Service Catalogue number YOSE 14134.

Fig. 423 Alice James Wilson at Yosemite Indian Field Days, 1929. Photograph courtesy Yosemite Museum and Research Library, National Park Service Catalogue number YOSE RL 2081.

Fig. 424* Alice James Wilson degikup. 20" diameter. This basket is also seen at the feet of Lucy Parker Telles in Fig. 490. Private collection. Photograph courtesy Ari Maslow.

*See Appendix 3, Figure Notes | Pg. 309

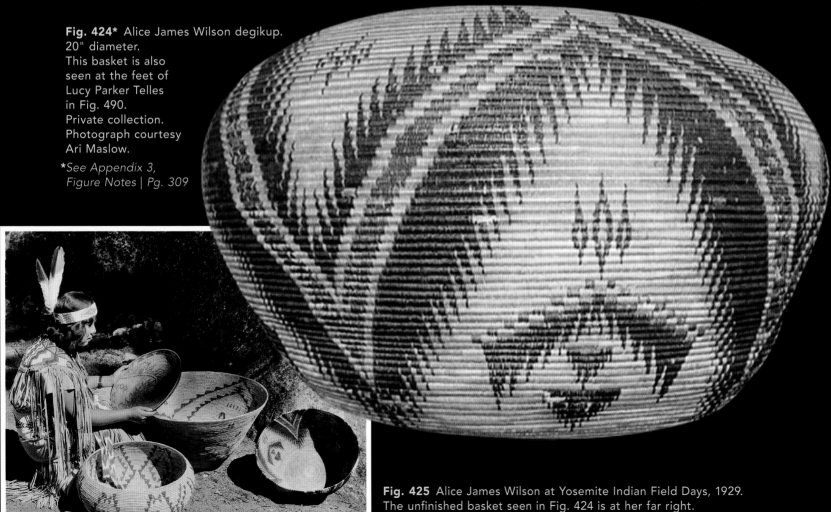

Fig. 425 Alice James Wilson at Yosemite Indian Field Days, 1929. The unfinished basket seen in Fig. 424 is at her far right. Photograph courtesy Yosemite Museum and Research Library. National Park Service Catalogue number YOSE RL 14103.

Rosa Burris Smith

Pomo | 1875–1929

Rosa Burris Smith was born in 1875 and grew up in the Pomo community of Habematolel near the shores of northern California's Clear Lake. Around 1894 she married Bill Smith from the Yokayo Rancheria, and they lived at Habematolel. Rosa and Bill had three children.

Rosa probably learned to weave from her mother Sally Burris, a well-known weaver. Rosa wove the boat basket shown in Fig. 427 around 1905, when her parents were living with her and her husband. Several other members of her family were also weavers.

As can be seen from the photograph (Fig. 428), Rosa's baskets are similar in design and style to her family's baskets. Rosa is the sister of Laura Burris Willum (see pages 170–171) suggesting that the weavers had influenced each other (McLendon 1998; Penn Museum 2018).

Rosa died of a gunshot wound while in her early fifties, around 1929.

Fig. 426 Rosa Burris Smith oval bowl.
7½" deep by 4½" wide by 11" long.
Photograph courtesy Penn Museum.
Image number 195213, Object NA8800.
Catalogue number NA 7871.

Fig. 428 Rosa Burris Smith with boat basket shown in Fig. 427, ca. 1905. Photograph courtesy Penn Museum. Catalogue number NA 7875, image 140385. H. C. Meredith photographer.

Fig. 427 Rosa Burris Smith boat bowl. 5¾" deep by 23½" wide by 15¾" long. Photograph courtesy Penn Museum. Image number 195213, Object NA8800. Catalogue number NA 7875.

Dolores Cassero Lubo was from the Cahuilla Reservation, and she was married to Pablino Lubo. Unfortunately, very little other information is available about her personal life.

Like her personal life, few photos of Dolores are available. This 1947 photograph (Fig. 429) shows Dolores with one of her baskets (Fig. 430). Eight more baskets made by Dolores are in the Palm Springs Art Museum. She was a fine weaver, commonly weaving flying eagle or rain bird (thunderbird) figures along with geometric patterns. Seen in Fig. 432 are the very skillful negative images of the dark eagles.

Fig. 429 Dolores Cassero Lubo, ca. 1947. Photograph courtesy Dee Alvarez.

Fig. 430 Dolores Cassero Lubo bowl. 4" deep by 17½" diameter. Gift of Cornelia B. White from the Marjorie Rose Dougan Collection. Catalogue number A504-1974. Photograph courtesy Palm Springs Art Museum.

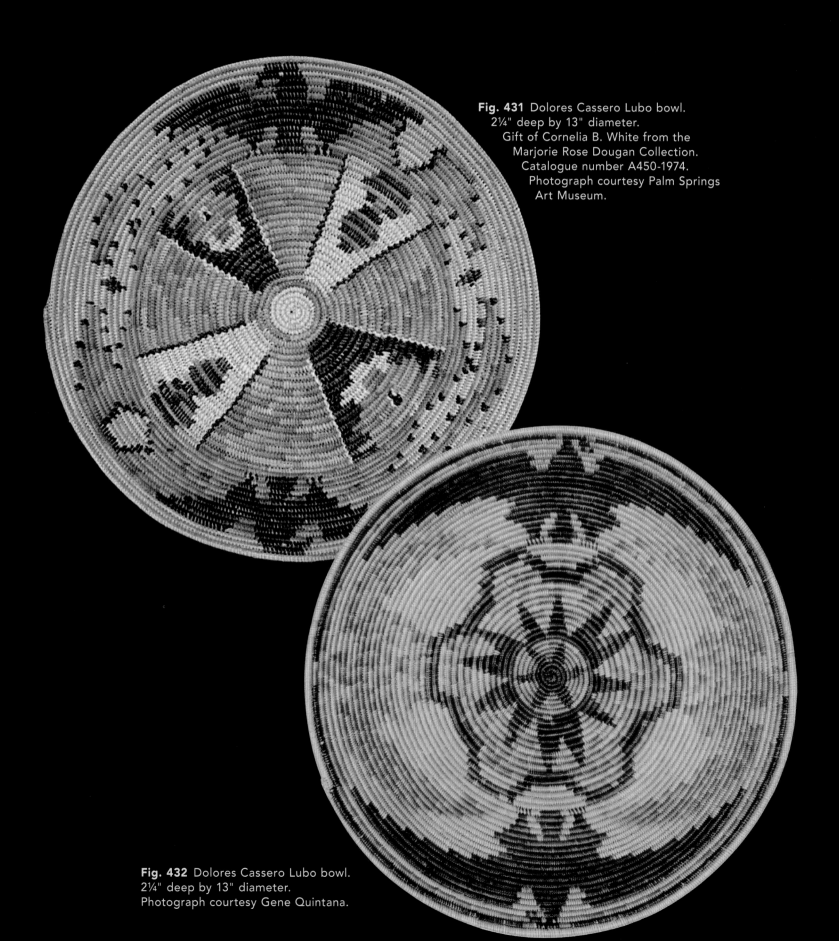

Fig. 431 Dolores Cassero Lubo bowl.
2¼" deep by 13" diameter.
Gift of Cornelia B. White from the
Marjorie Rose Dougan Collection.
Catalogue number A450-1974.
Photograph courtesy Palm Springs
Art Museum.

Fig. 432 Dolores Cassero Lubo bowl.
2¼" deep by 13" diameter.
Photograph courtesy Gene Quintana.

Lucinda Hancock

Nutunutu Yokuts | 1870–1932

Lucinda Hancock was born on the Kings River, just north of Tulare Lake and south of Fresno, California (Latta 1949:166). In 1929 she was one of the last two surviving Nutunutu Yokuts. She was the first wife of Mr. Ben Hancock, whose second wife, Minnie Hancock (see pages 162–166), was also an exceptional weaver. Ben Hancock married Minnie after the death of Lucinda, causing a great deal of confusion over the identity of "Mrs. Ben Hancock" (Bob Adams personal communication 2016).

Lucinda Hancock was one of the most innovative Yokuts weavers. She is best known for the seven large bottleneck ollas she made beginning around 1900. These pieces show an outside influence—most probably Apache—as they are like no other known Yokuts baskets. Until recently, only six of these baskets were known; the seventh, Fig. 449, only made its appearance shortly before this book was written! This design is not characteristic of the pre-contact basket forms recognized for the Yokuts, but fairly recently, another Yokuts weaver copied her design on a smaller olla, and the similarity in shape and design is obvious.

Lucinda also made two small rounded jars with a beautiful geometric design, and at least three large bowls with a more typical Yokuts pattern. At least two large bowls with a pattern similar to that of the large bottlenecks are also known. One of Lucinda's large bottlenecks sold at the Green sale in 1971 for $2,100, about half of the selling price for a large Dat So La Lee work sold at the same sale.

Fig. 433 Lucinda Hancock in 1902 holding the bowl shown in Fig. 434. Photograph courtesy Bob and Carol Adams. C. Hart Merriam photographer, October 1903.

Fig. 434 Lucinda Hancock bowl.
9½" deep by 16½" diameter, ca. 1902.
Photograph courtesy Department of
Anthropology Smithsonian Institution.
National Museum of American History.
Catalogue number E313220-0.

The seven large bottleneck pieces are unique and most top collectors consider them masterpieces. An interesting feature of these pieces are their varying shoulders: one being very rounded, one being almost flat, and the other five being angled from the rim to the neck. All seven have almost identical designs; one has to closely inspect each pattern to see the subtle differences.

Lucinda Hancock was a master at controlling shape, and her stitching was always tight and clean. While most Yokuts weavers stayed within the boundaries of traditional Yokuts style, Lucinda broke the barriers and created several masterpieces unlike any other baskets made in California Indian basketry art history.

Fig. 435 Lucinda Hancock with bottleneck olla shown in Fig. 438. Photograph courtesy Bob and Carol Adams.

Fig. 436 Lucinda Hancock with bottleneck olla shown in Fig. 438.

Fig. 437 Lucinda Hancock, ca. 1929, holding olla shown in Fig. 438. Photograph courtesy Yosemite Museum and Research Library. National Park Service Catalogue number YOSE RL 19404.

Fig. 438* Lucinda Hancock bottleneck olla.
19½" high by 23½" diameter, ca. 1929.
Wayne and Malee Thompson Collection.
Jeff Scovil photographer.

*See Appendix 3, Figure Notes | Pg. 309

Fig. 439 Lucinda Hancock weaving bottleneck olla shown in Fig. 438, ca. 1929. The Lucinda Hancock jar shown in Fig. 440 is also included in the photograph. Photograph courtesy Bob and Carol Adams.

Fig. 440 Lucinda Hancock jar. 7½" high by 11" diameter, ca. 1929. Todd Adams Collection. Jeff Scovil photographer.

Fig. 441 Lucinda Hancock bowl.
12" high by 25" diameter.
Wayne and Stevia Thompson Collection.
Jeff Scovil photographer.

Fig. 442* Lucinda Hancock bottleneck olla.
16" high by 21" diameter.
The Collection of Ken and Judy Siebel.
Photograph courtesy Sotheby's.

*See Appendix 3, Figure Notes | Pg. 309

Fig. 443 Lucinda Hancock bottleneck olla.
16" high by 20½" diameter.
Table Mountain Rancheria Yokuts Tribe Collection.
Jeff Scovil photographer.

Fig. 444* Lucinda Hancock bottleneck olla.
15¼" high by 20¼" diameter.
Photograph courtesy Sotheby's.

*See Appendix 3, Figure Notes | Pg. 309

Fig. 445 Lucinda Hancock with George Pierson.
Photograph courtesy Bob and Carol Adams.

Fig. 446 Lucinda Hancock. Woodblock print
created from a photograph taken at the
same time as Fig. 445. Photograph courtesy
Gene Meieran.

Fig. 447* Lucinda Hancock bowl.
8½" deep by 14" diameter.
© 2012 Bonhams & Butterfields Auctioneers.
Syd Bottomley Collection. All rights reserved.
See Appendix 3, Figure Notes | Pg. 309

Fig. 448 Basket collection, ca. 1926. Lucinda Hancock basket shown in Fig. 438 in front. Photograph courtesy Bob and Carol Adams.

Fig. 449* Lucinda Hancock bottleneck olla.
This basket, the seventh of the Lucinda
Hancock bottleneck ollas, was discovered
during writing of this book—it has never
before been published.
19" high by 23" diameter.
Todd Adams Collection.
Jeff Scovil photographer.

*See Appendix 3, Figure Notes | Pg. 309

Fig. 450 Lucinda Hancock bottleneck olla.
19" high by 25" diameter.
The Collection of Ken and Judy Siebel.
Gene Meieran photographer.

Fig. 451* Lucinda Hancock bottleneck olla.
23" high by 18" diameter.
Private collection.
Photograph courtesy Phil Cohen.
See Appendix 3, Figure Notes | Pg. 309

Maggie Painter
Chemehuevi | 1898–1963

Maggie Painter was born on the Colorado River. Although she was deaf at birth, she apparently attended school for a few years. Her mother taught her to weave from a very early age but died when Maggie was still young. Maggie married at about age 18.

By 1907, she was selling baskets to Mrs. Birdie Brown, who had begun collecting in 1905. Mrs. Brown eventually built one of the finest collections of Chemehuevi baskets ever assembled. In 1958, collector Jerry Collings met Maggie, and they became close friends. Before her death, Maggie taught Jerry the art of weaving, and he is today a master weaver. He wrote an article in 1975 for *American Indian Art* magazine about the Chemehuevi and discussed the works of Maggie Painter (Collings 1975).

Maggie was a master weaver who developed the butterfly design. Each weaver owned the designs she developed, and recognition of these was a commonly used technique by which one weaver identified the other's work. While many designs had little or no significance, serving only to enhance sales to non-Indian buyers, Maggie said the butterfly motif as used in her baskets symbolized spring: she typically made a butterfly basket during the spring.

Her favorite materials were juncus (to create a variegated effect) and bulrush root, and she often used the quill from the red-shafted flicker, a bird found along the Colorado River. She also wove figures of chuckwalla lizards into her baskets, and integrated birds with both geometric and floral designs (Collings 1975). A friend of Maggie's died from the bite of a rattlesnake, and so for much of her life she feared the consequences of using a snake design, but near the end of her life she did make one rattlesnake basket, telling Jerry Collings she was no longer afraid to do so.

Maggie Painter was a great artist, one of the most innovative of the great Chemehuevi weavers (personal communication Jerry Collings 2016).

Fig. 452 Maggie Painter. Photograph courtesy Alex Schwed.

Fig. 453* Maggie Painter tray. 14½" diameter, ca. 1963. Jerry and Heidi Collings Collection. Jerry Jacka photographer.

*See Appendix 3, Figure Notes | Pg. 309

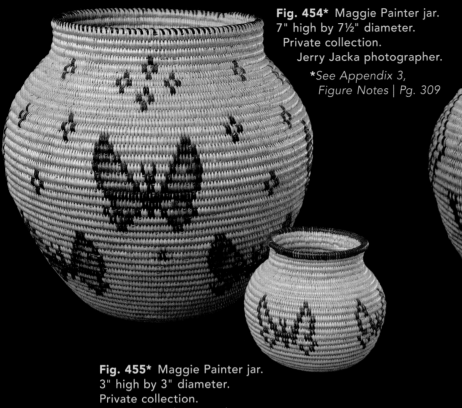

Fig. 454* Maggie Painter jar.
7" high by 7½" diameter.
Private collection.
Jerry Jacka photographer.

**See Appendix 3,
Figure Notes | Pg. 309*

Fig. 455* Maggie Painter jar.
3" high by 3" diameter.
Private collection.
Jerry Jacka photographer.

*See Appendix 3, Figure Notes | Pg. 309

Fig. 456 Maggie Painter jar.
6" high by 7" diameter.
Robert and Bunny Jochim Collection.
Jeff Scovil photographer.

Fig. 457 Maggie Painter jar.
7" high by 8" diameter.
Private collection.
Jerry Jacka photographer.

Fig. 458* Maggie Painter jar.
6" high by 6½" diameter.
The Collection of Ken and Judy Siebel.
Jerry Jacka photographer.

*See Appendix 3, Figure Notes | Pg. 309

Fig. 459 Maggie Painter.
Photograph courtesy Jerry Collings.

Mary Dick Topino (Tupino)
aka "Mrs. Britches"
Wukchumni Yokuts | 1863/68–1923

Mary Dick Topino (Mrs. Britches) was born in the 1860s and lived near the Kaweah River north of Porterville and southeast of Fresno, California. Her mother was Chah-Dah and her father was Chief Chappo of the Wukchumni Yokuts (Bob Adams personal communication 2009). Her Native Indian name was said to be akin to the word Tupanol (Bates and Lee 1990). Other information provides alternate designations including Kee-nay-what or Ha-nawut (Bates 1989).

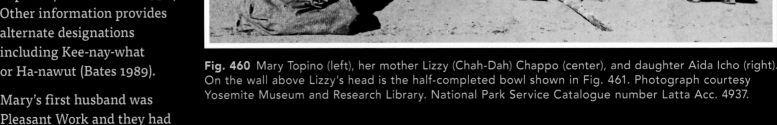

Fig. 460 Mary Topino (left), her mother Lizzy (Chah-Dah) Chappo (center), and daughter Aida Icho (right). On the wall above Lizzy's head is the half-completed bowl shown in Fig. 461. Photograph courtesy Yosemite Museum and Research Library. National Park Service Catalogue number Latta Acc. 4937.

Mary's first husband was Pleasant Work and they had one son (Dave) before Pleasant died. She then married Dick Yahnee and that union produced two daughters including Maggie (Aida). Dick Yahnee was killed in a fight. Mary, following Native traditions, married his brother, Jim Topino (aka Tawpnaw) (Bates and Lee 1990). Jim Topino was known as "Big Britches" because he often wore clothes given to him—especially trousers that were too big. Hence, Mary gained the nickname, Mrs. Britches (Bob Adams personal communication 2009). Jim and Mary had a dozen children; unfortunately all but two died in their youth. However, Mary's daughter Maggie (Aida) married Henry Icho and became a master weaver on her own (see pages 150–151).

Mary's baskets were made of traditional Yokuts materials in traditional shapes and designs, including bottleneck ollas, gambling trays, and bowls. Her large friendship and spring dance bowls (over 15 inches in diameter) are icons of basketry and other weavers made similar bowls often attributed to "Mrs. Britches." Frank Latta, collector and noted author on Yokuts culture, documented an oval friendship bowl in his collection as "Friendship, Britches, before 1900" (Bates and Lee 1990; Latta 1949).

An unfinished friendship bowl appears in a vintage photo of Mrs. Chappo, Mary Topino, and Aida Icho (Fig. 460). The same bowl appears in a later photo of Mary Topino and Aida Icho, Fig. 462, with the piece now finished along with another large friendship bowl, other bowls, ollas, and a gambling tray, Fig. 463. The finished bowl is now in the Bob and Carol Adams collection.

It has been suggested by knowledgeable scholars and collectors that the "Britches Baskets" were a family effort although there is no specific evidence to substantiate this claim.

Mary Topino is one of the finest artists in California basket history and her baskets are sought after and extremely collectable. While many are exhibited in museums and private collections, a few occasionally come up for sale or auction.

Fig. 461* Mary Topino bowl. This basket
is seen in both Fig. 460 and 462.
12" deep by 21" diameter.
Bob and Carol Adams Collection.
Todd Adams photographer.

*See Appendix 3, Figure Notes | Pg. 309

Fig. 462 Mary Topino with daughter, Aida Icho, with bowl shown in Fig. 461, gambling tray shown in Fig. 463, and bowl shown in Fig. 474. Photograph courtesy Bob and Carol Adams.

Fig. 463 Mary Topino gambling tray.
25½" diameter.
Private collection.
Jeff Scovil photographer.

Fig. 464 Mary Topino bowl.
9" high by 21¼" diameter.
Alan and Bronnie Blaugrund Collection.
Jeff Scovil photographer.

Fig. 465 Mary Topino bowl.
7¾" high by 16½" diameter.
Photograph courtesy Terry DeWald.
Jeff Scovil photographer.

Fig. 466 Mary Topino bowl.
8½" high by 21" diameter.
E. J. and Mimi Nusrala Collection.
Jeff Scovil photographer.

Fig. 467 Mary Topino bowl.
8" deep by 17½" diameter.
E. J. and Mimi Nusrala Collection.
Jeff Scovil photographer.

Fig. 468 Mary Topino bowl.
9¼" deep by 19½" diameter.
Natalie Linn Collection.
Justin Tunis photographer.

Fig. 469 Mary Topino bowl.
9½" deep by 21" diameter.
Lew Meekins Collection

Fig. 470 Mary Topino bowl.
9¼" deep by 18" diameter.
Eddie and Nadine Basha Collection.
Jeff Scovil photographer.

Fig. 471 Mary Topino bowl.
11¼" deep by 22½" diameter.
Private collection.
Jeff Scovil photographer.

Fig. 472 Mary Topino bowl.
10" deep by 21" diameter.
Photograph courtesy Charles and Valerie Diker Collection.

Fig. 473 Mary Topino bowl.
8½" deep by 17" diameter.
Private collection.
Ben Watkins photographer.

Fig. 474 Mary Topino bowl.
12½" deep by 23" diameter.
Private collection.
Ben Watkins photographer.

Lucy Parker Telles (Pa-ma-has)

Mono Lake Paiute (Kuzedika)/Miwok | 1885–1955

Lucy Parker Telles, universally acknowledged as one of the most prolific and best known of the masterpiece weavers, was born near Mono Lake, Mono County, California in 1885 (Bates and Lee 1990:172–179), although some sources place her birth earlier and her death a year later (*Yosemite Basketmakers* 2017). Her parents, Mack Bridgeport Tom and Louisa Sam Tom were of mixed heritage—Mono Lake Paiute and Miwok ancestry. Her grandmother, Suzie Sam, was Miwok and her grandfather, Captain Sam, was Paiute. They lived in both Yosemite Valley and the Mono Basin. Lucy's sister Alice Wilson (see pages 216–217) also became a master weaver.

Around 1900, Lucy married Jack Parker, a Paiute, and in 1902 they had one son, Lloyd. Jack Parker died after Lloyd was born and in 1914, Lucy then married John Telles, a Mexican-American, and they lived in Yosemite Valley for most of their lives. They had two children, Hazel and John Jr. During this period, Lucy worked part-time as a housekeeper.

As a young girl, Lucy learned to weave from her mother, making traditional, single-rod, and triple-rod baskets, some following the new style designs. In 1912 Lucy sold three of her fancy new-style baskets to Salter's Store in Yosemite. By the 1920s, Lucy was well known for these fancy baskets and became a regular contestant in the Yosemite Indian Field Days events, usually winning prizes. She participated as a winner in the last Indian Field Day in 1929.

Fig. 475 Lucy Parker Telles, ca. 1950. Photograph courtesy Helen Coates.

Lucy copied designs from crochet books, as well as using butterflies, and a serrated zigzag pattern. In 1929, she displayed a new style basket and in 1930 she began a basket that she was to spend four years completing (Fig. 477). This was to become the largest basket (20 x 40 inches or 50 x 100 cm) to ever be created in the Yosemite Region (Bates and Lee 1990:175). This basket was featured on postcards at Yosemite and later displayed at the Golden Gate Bridge Exposition in 1939. Lucy began to demonstrate basketmaking at the Yosemite Museum in the 1930s and continued to do so until her death in 1955.

Her technical skills and artistic talent rate her very high, even among the top masterpiece weavers of the Florescence. Her works are extremely collectable and in great demand by museums and collectors, bringing prices approaching the mid six figures.

It should be mentioned that Lucy Parker Telles' basketmaking legacy continued in the artistic talents of Julia Dominguez Parker (Miwok/Pomo). Julia married Telles' grandson, Ralph Parker. She learned to weave baskets from many of the famous weavers identified in this book including Carrie Bethel, Minnie Mike, Tina Charlie, and Alice Wilson. Julia Parker eventually became an employee of Yosemite National Park and worked as their in-residence basketry weaver for 68 years until her retirement in 2015.

Fig. 476* Lucy Parker Telles degikup.
4½" high by 10¼" diameter.
Private collection.
*See Appendix 3, Figure Notes | Pg. 309

Fig. 477* Lucy Parker Telles degikup.
20" high by 40" diameter, ca. 1930/1933.
Photograph courtesy Yosemite Museum and Research Library.
National Park Service Catalogue number YOSE 13761.
Gene Meieran photographer.
*See Appendix 3, Figure Notes | Pg. 309

Photo by Ellen St. Clair of.

Fig. 478* Lucy Parker Telles, ca. 1933. This basket, Fig. 477, took four years to weave. Photograph courtesy Yosemite Museum and Research Library. National Park Service Catalogue number YOSE 08694. Ellen St. Clair photographer.

See Appendix 3, Figure Notes | Pg. 309

Fig. 479 Lucy Parker Telles at Yosemite Indian Field Days, 1924. Baskets shown in Figs. 502 and 503 are in the picture. Braun Research Library Collection. Autry Museum, Los Angeles. Collection item P.376.

Fig. 480 Lucy Parker Telles with degikup shown in Fig. 477, ca. 1933. Photograph courtesy Yosemite Museum and Research Library. National Park Service Catalogue number YOSE 02051.

Fig. 481 Lucy Parker Telles weaving baskets by Yosemite Museum, 1935. Photograph courtesy Yosemite Museum and Research Library. National Park Service Catalogue number YOSE RL 4425.

Fig. 482 Lucy Parker Telles, left, with Carrie Bethel, Governor Friend Richardson, and Tina Charlie at Yosemite Indian Field Days, 1926. She is shown with the basket shown in Fig. 483. Braun Research Library Collection. Autry Museum, Los Angeles. Item number P.39688.

Fig. 483 Lucy Parker Telles degikup. 6½" high by 14" diameter, ca. 1926. Natalie Linn Collection. Jeff Scovil photographer.

Fig. 484* Lucy Parker Telles lidded degikup.
6¾" high by 11¼" diameter.
Natalie Linn Collection.
Gene Meieran photographer.
*See Appendix 3, Figure Notes | Pg. 309

Fig. 485* Lucy Parker Telles lidded degikup.
6¾" high by 11¾" diameter, ca. 1923.
Wayne and Stevia Thompson Collection.
Jeff Scovil photographer.
*See Appendix 3, Figure Notes | Pg. 309

Fig. 486 Lucy Parker Telles degikups shown in Figs. 484 and 485. Photographed on Lucy Parker Telles' front porch in 1923.
Photograph courtesy Yosemite Museum and Research Library. National Park Service Catalogue number YOSE RL-2052.

Fig. 487 Lucy Parker Telles. Photograph courtesy Yosemite Museum and Research Library. National Park Service Catalogue number YOSE 02052.

Fig. 488 Lucy Parker Telles. Photograph courtesy Yosemite Museum and Research Library. National Park Service Catalogue number YOSE 02063.

Fig. 489 Lucy Parker Telles. Photograph courtesy Yosemite Museum and Research Library. National Park Service Catalogue number YOSE RL14168. Ernest Amoroso photographer.

Fig. 490 Lucy Parker Telles with Anita Antone at the 1939 Golden Gate Bridge Exposition with olla shown in Fig. 491 and Alice Wilson degikup shown in Fig. 424. Photograph courtesy Helen Coates.

Fig. 491* Lucy Parker Telles olla. 15" high by 15" diameter, ca. 1939. Wayne and Stevia Thompson Collection. Gene Meieran photographer.

*See Appendix 3, Figure Notes | Pg. 309

Fig. 492 Lucy Parker Telles
lidded degikup.
10" high by 20" diameter.
Colorado Springs Art Center.
Gift of Phillip B. Stewart
Catalogue number TM5641.

*Lucy Telles my great grandmother
has inspired me when I was very
young to become a basketmaker
like her and to carry on the
Yosemite legacy of baskemaking.*

—Lucy Ann Parker, Granddaughter

Fig. 493 Alice Wilson, Louisa Tom, and Lucy Parker Telles. Catalog number RL 14009.
Courtesy of the National Park Service, Yosemite National Park.

Fig. 497 Lucy Parker Telles degikup.
9¼" high by 7¼" diameter.
Photograph courtesy California Academy of Sciences.

Fig. 498 Lucy Parker Telles degikup.
11¾" diameter.
National Anthropological Archive.
Smithsonian Institution.
Catalogue number 115307.

Fig. 499 Lucy Parker Telles lidded degikup.
7½" high by 11" diameter.
Robert and Bunny Jochim Collection.
Jeff Scovil photographer.

Fig. 500 Lucy Parker Telles degikup.
7½" high by 12¾" diameter, ca. 1925.
Donated by Mrs. Camilla Chandler Frost to the
Southwest Museum of the American Indian Collection.
Autry Museum, Los Angeles. Item # 2011.22.30.

Fig. 501 Lucy Parker Telles at Yosemite Indian Field Days, 1924. She is holding baskets shown in Figs. 502 and 503. Alice Wilson basket seen in Fig. 421 is at her feet. Braun Research Library Collection. Autry Museum, Los Angeles. Item number P.374.

Fig. 502* Lucy Parker Telles lidded degikup.
12" diameter.
Private collection.
Photograph courtesy Ari Maslow.
**See Appendix 3, Figure Notes |
Pg. 309*

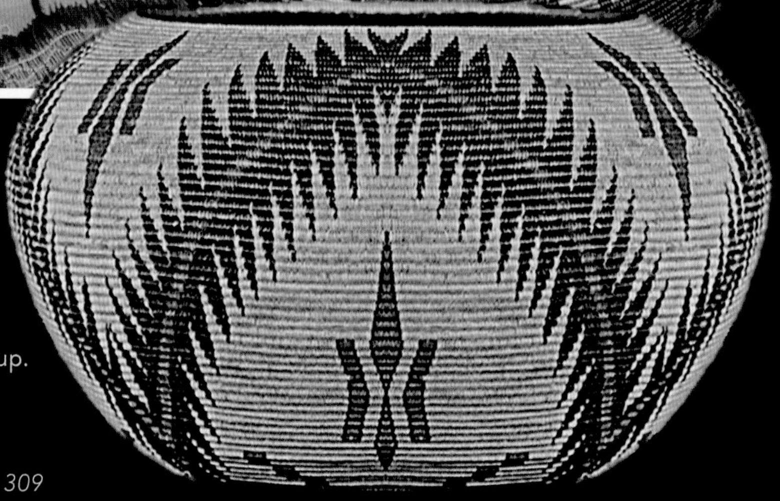

Fig. 503* Lucy Parker Telles degikup.
12" diameter.
Private collection.
Photograph courtesy Phil Cohen.
*See Appendix 3, Figure Notes | Pg. 309

Fig. 504 Lucy Parker Telles degikup.
5¾" high by 11¾" diameter, 1915–1920
Southwest Museum of the American Indian Collection.
Autry Museum, Los Angeles. Item # 2011.21.1.

Fig. 505 Lucy Parker Telles degikup
7½" high by 13" diameter, ca. 1916.
Photograph courtesy Yosemite Museum and Research Library.
National Park Service Catalogue number YOSE 38383.

Fig. 506 Lucy Parker Telles degikup.
8½" high by 11" diameter.
Photograph courtesy Yosemite Museum and Research Library.
National Park Service Catalogue number YOSE 66844.

Fig. 507 Lucy Parker Telles degikup.
6" high by 11" diameter, ca. 1920s.
Photograph courtesy Yosemite Museum and Research Library.
National Park Service Catalogue number YOSE 66823.

Fig. 508 Lucy Parker Telles lidded degikup.
6¼" high by 8½" high, ca. 1912.
Courtesy Museum of Indian Arts and Cultural Anthropology,
Santa Fe, New Mexico. Catalog number 14305.

Fig. 509 Lucy Parker Telles lidded degikup.
5¼" high by 8½" diameter.
Photograph courtesy Yosemite Museum and Research Library.
National Park Service Collection item 15918.

Fig. 510 Lucy Parker Telles bottleneck olla.
7" high by 18" diameter.
Photograph courtesy Yosemite Museum
and Research Library.
National Park Service Catalogue
number 66839.

Fig. 511 Lucy Parker Telles lidded jar.
5½" high by 9¼" diameter, ca. 1915.
Photograph courtesy Yosemite Museum and Research Library.
National Park Service Catalogue number YOSE 237671.

Fig. 512 Lucy Parker Telles on the left, behind her big basket. Alice Wilson is weaving a basket to her left. Photograph courtesy Yosemite Museum and Research Library. National Park Service Catalogue number YOSE 14134.

Fig. 514 Lucy Parker Telles bottleneck jar. 3" high by 6" diameter. Photograph courtesy Gene Quintana. John Law photographer.

Fig. 513 Lucy Parker Telles. Photograph courtesy Yosemite Museum and Research Library. National Park Service Catalogue number YOSE 2151.

Other Important Basketweavers

In this book, we focus first on highlighting 46 important weavers with photographs of their masterpiece baskets, accompanied by text and visual information in some detail.

This second section presents vintage images of 15 other well-known basketweavers, each with images of baskets they have created. For those interested in further information about these weavers, additional baskets along with some supplemental personal and tribal information can be found using various Internet search engines.

Finally, we follow with two additional sections highlighting 17 unidentified weavers, then 34 exceptional masterpiece baskets of unidentified weavers, most of which we were able to identify by their tribal affiliation. Unfortunately, being unable to identify the weavers of these works of art, we could not provide photos of their artisans. Any help in identifying the weavers and locating such pictures would be gratefully appreciated!

Salvadora Valenzuela

Cupeño | 1874–1953

Fig. 515 Salvadora Valenzuela, 1927–1936. Braun Research Library Collection. Autry Museum, Los Angeles. Item number P.949.

Fig. 516 Salvadora Valenzuela tray. 4" deep by 16" diameter. Natalie Linn Collection. Photograph courtesy Gene Quintana. John Law photographer.

Fig. 517 Salvadora Valenzuela, 1927–1936. Braun Research Library Collection. Autry Museum, Los Angeles. Item number P.943.

Fig. 518 Salvadora Valenzuela, ca. 1930. Braun Research Library Collection. Autry Museum, Los Angeles. Item number P.955.

Fig. 519 Salvadora Valenzuela at home, 1934. Braun Research Library Collection. Autry Museum, Los Angeles. Plate 948A.

Fig. 521 Maggie Howard degikup.
8½" diameter.
E. J. and Mimi Nusrala Collection.
Photograph courtesy Gene Quintana
John Law photographer.

Fig. 520 Maggie Howard with degikup shown in Fig. 521.
Photograph courtesy Yosemite Museum and Research Library.
National Park Service Catalogue number RL14183.

Fig. 522 Maggie Howard. Photograph courtesy Yosemite Museum and
Research Library. National Park Service Catalogue number YOSE RL 14181.

Fig. 523 Maggie Howard with degikup shown in
Fig. 521. Photograph courtesy Gene Quintana.

Lena Peconum
Maidu | ~1872

Fig. 525 Lena Peconum degikup. 2¾" high by 5¼" diameter. Natalie Linn Collection. Jeff Scovil photographer.

Fig. 524 Lena Peconum. This photo appears in *Roseberry* (1915) as Plate No. 1. Photograph courtesy Natalie Linn.

Mary Kea'a'ala Azbill
Maidu | 1864–1932

Fig. 526 Mary Kea'a'ala Azbill bowl. 14¾" deep by 8" diameter, ca. 1905. Photograph courtesy Brooklyn Museum.

Fig. 527 Mary Kea'a'ala Azbill. Photograph courtesy California State University, Chico, California.

Kate Meadows McKinney

Maidu | 1863–1954

Fig. 528 Kate Meadows McKinney tray, 1926.
12½" diameter.
Photograph courtesy Pat Kurtz.
David Bozsik photographer.

Fig. 529 Kate Meadows McKinney.
Photograph courtesy Pat Kurtz.

Fig. 530 Kate Meadows McKinney
with tray shown in Fig. 528, ca. 1940.
Photograph courtesy Pat Kurtz.

Rosie Brown August

Mono Lake Paiute (Kuzedika) | 1900–1984

Fig. 531 Rosie Brown August degikup.
6½" high by 12¼" diameter.
© 2012 Bonhams & Butterfields Auctioneers
Corporation. All Rights Reserved.
German Herrera photographer.

Fig. 532 Rosie Brown August, ca. 1944. Photograph courtesy
Bridgeport Museum. Mono County Historical Society.

Mamie Gregory

Panamint Shoshone (Timbisha) | 1867–1947

Fig. 533 Mamie Gregory
with bowl shown in Fig. 534.
Photograph courtesy
Bancroft Library. University
of California, Berkeley.
Catalogue number 1978.008
X/23u/P23no.1

Fig. 534 Mamie Gregory bowl.
8" high by 14¾" diameter.
Photograph courtesy Bowers Museum Collection,
Santa Ana, California.

Ramona Balenzuela
Diegueño (Kumeyaay/Ipai/Tipai) | 1850–1930

Fig. 535 Ramona Balenzuela, ca. 1930. She is holding the tray shown in Fig. 536. Photograph courtesy San Diego History Center. Catalogue number P87-1. Edward H. Davis photographer.

Fig. 536 Ramona Balenzuela tray, 1926.
3¾" high by 12" diameter.
Photograph courtesy Riverside Metropolitan Museum.
Funds from Riverside Metropolitan Museum Trust.
Chase Leland photographer. Catalogue number P87-1.

Sally Edd
Yokuts | 1870–1953

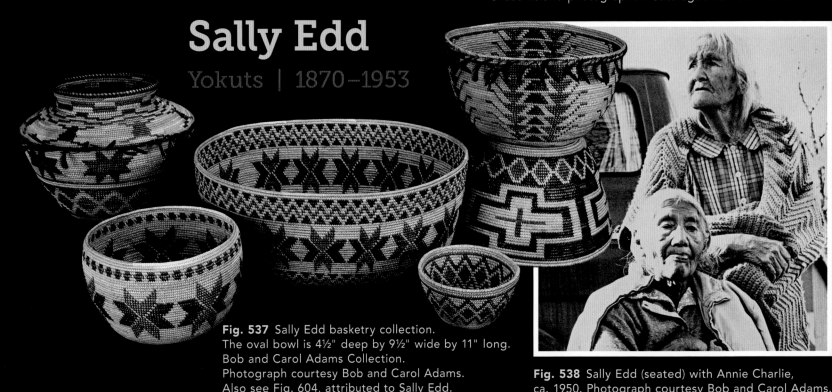

Fig. 537 Sally Edd basketry collection.
The oval bowl is 4½" deep by 9½" wide by 11" long.
Bob and Carol Adams Collection.
Photograph courtesy Bob and Carol Adams.
Also see Fig. 604, attributed to Sally Edd.

Fig. 538 Sally Edd (seated) with Annie Charlie,
ca. 1950. Photograph courtesy Bob and Carol Adams.

Lillie Frank James
Washoe | 1885–1948

Fig. 539 Lillie Frank James degikup.
6½" high by 10¾" diameter.
© 2012 Bonhams & Butterfields Auctioneers Corporation.
All Rights Reserved.

Fig. 540 Lillie Frank James degikup.
6¾" high by 10¾" diameter.
Natalie Linn Collection.
Jeff Scovil photographer.

Fig. 542 Lillie Frank James degikup.
6¾" high by 10¾" diameter.
Photograph courtesy
Donner Pass Museum.
California State Parks, Item #39-1-291.
Gene Meieran photograph.

Fig. 541 Lillie Frank James degikup.
4½" high by 6½" diameter.
Photograph courtesy Heard Museum,
Phoenix, Arizona.
Basket number 291BA.

Fig. 543 Lillie Frank James degikup.
3½" high by 7" diameter.
Photograph courtesy Donner Pass Museum.
California State Parks, Item # 339-1-294.
Gene Meieran photographer.

Juanna Sands
Cahuilla

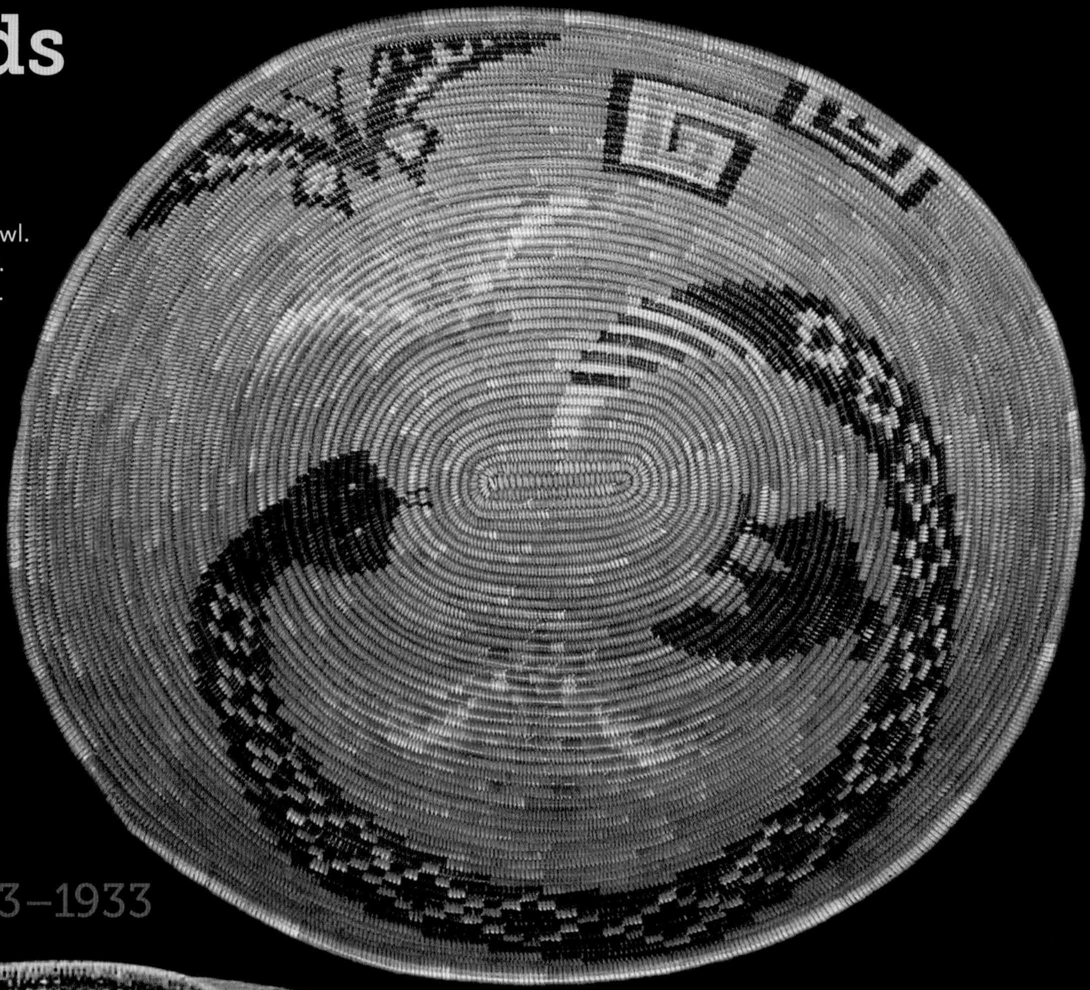

Fig. 544 Juanna Sands bowl.
6" deep by 15¾" diameter.
Jeff Greenstein Collection.
Jeff Scovil photographer.

Ellen Amos
Casson Yokuts | 1853–1933

Fig. 545 Ellen Amos olla.
7" high by 16½" diameter.
Photograph courtesy Gene Quintana.
John Law photographer.

Mrs. Elizabeth Graham
Chukchansi Yokuts | 1870–1930

Fig. 546 Mrs. Elizabeth Graham degikup.
6½" high by 12" diameter.
Photograph courtesy Department of Anthropology Smithsonian Institution.
Item number 96-20069, basket E 328051.

Amanda Wilson
Maidu | 1860–1946

Fig. 548 Amanda Wilson bowl.
14¼" diameter.
Brooklyn Museum.
Collection number 08-491-8680, purchased in 1908.

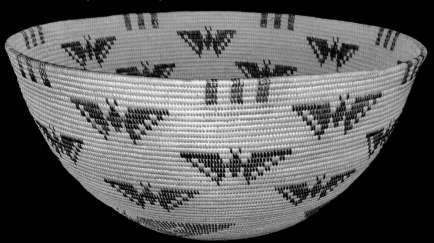

Fig. 547 Amanda Wilson and Granddaughter, 1940.
Braun Research Library Collection. Autry Museum, Los Angeles.
Item number P.364.

Rosenita Marcus Hicks
Kawaiisu (Nüwa)

Fig. 549* Rosenita Marcus Hicks "Butterfly Bowl."
5½" deep by 12" diameter, ca. 1910.
Photograph courtesy Gene Quintana.
John Law photographer.
*See Appendix 3, Figure Notes | Pg. 309

Fig. 550 Rosenita Marcus Hicks (on the right).
Photograph courtesy Gene Quintana.

Pomo Baskets

Pomo weavers have created some of the most beautiful feathered baskets, but have also pioneered in making some of the largest— as well as smallest—woven baskets.

Their skill is demonstrated by the extremes in size of the two baskets depicted on this page.

The large basket shown was woven by a group of Pomo weavers over the span of 10 years.

In contrast, a tiny half-inch-wide basket encircling a gem becomes an item of jewelry.

For a detailed account of the weaving of the large basket, see Craig Bates (1991) "The Big Pomo Basket."

Fig. 551* Pomo big basket; weaving began in 1910 and was completed in 1920. This basket was woven by many Pomo weavers, including Mrs. Martin Smith. Photograph courtesy Penn Museum. Catalogue number P122.

*See Appendix 3, Figure Notes | Pg. 309

Fig. 552* Man and boy with big Pomo basket, ca. 1940. Braun Research Library Collection. Autry Museum, Los Angeles. Item number P.771.

*See Appendix 3, Figure Notes | Pg. 309

Fig. 553* Jewel stick pin formed by a miniature coiled basket, about half of an inch in diameter, with a garnet center. Created by William Benson, circa 1905. Grace Hudson Museum, Ukiah, California. Gene Meieran photograph.

*See Appendix 3, Figure Notes | Pg. 309

Vintage Photos of Other Important Basketweavers

Fig. 554 Ina Jackson, Maidu.
Photograph courtesy Bob and Carol Adams.

Fig. 555 Ellen Snapp, Pomo. Photograph courtesy National Anthropological Archives, Smithsonian Institution Catalog number 76-4659. H. C. Meredith photograph, ca. 1905.

Fig. 556 Tillie Snooks, Washoe.
Photograph courtesy Marvin Cohodas.

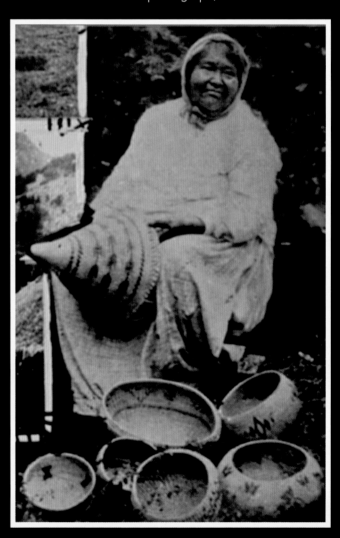

Fig. 557 Sally Snooks, Washoe. Photograph courtesy North Lake Tahoe Historical Society; Marion Steinbach Indian Basket Museum and Gatekeeper's Museum, Tahoe City, California.

Fig. 558 Barefoot Annie, Washoe. Photograph courtesy North Lake Tahoe Historical Society; Marion Steinbach Indian Basket Museum and Gatekeeper's Museum, Tahoe City, California.

Fig. 559* Linda Hancock (Mrs. Ben Hancock), Tachi Yokuts. Photograph courtesy Phoebe A. Hearst Museum of Anthropology and the Regents of the University of California. Catalogue number 15-23215. C. Hart Merriam photographer.

*See Appendix 3, Figure Notes | Pg. 309

Fig. 560 Esperanza Sobonish, Luiseño, ca. 1919. Photograph courtesy San Diego History Center. Edward H. Davis photographer.

Fig. 561 Polineria, Desert Cahuilla. Photograph private collection.

Fig. 562 Mary Sampson, Yokuts. (Mrs. Dick Sampson). Photograph courtesy Sanger Depot Museum, Sanger, California.

Fig. 563 Maria Antonia Subish, Luiseño. Photograph courtesy San Diego Historical Society. Edward H. Davis photographer.

Fig. 564 Maggie Bellas, Panamint, ca. 1920. Aurelia McLean photographer.

Fig. 565 Julia Davis, Choinimni Yokuts. Photograph courtesy Sanger Depot Museum, Sanger, California.

Fig. 566 Julia Davis, Choinimni Yokuts. Photograph courtesy Bob and Carol Adams.

Fig. 567 Merced Wellmas, Cupeño, 1895–1923. Braun Research Library Collection. Autry Museum, Los Angeles. Item number P.951. George Wharton James photographer.

Fig. 568 Josie Polecat Hawkins, Kathryn Marler, and Mollie Charley, Yokuts. Photograph courtesy Bob and Carol Adams.

Fig. 569 Gertrude Arenas, Cahuilla. Photograph courtesy Palm Springs Art Museum.

Fig. 570 Susie Wilson, Panamint. Photograph courtesy Eastern California Museum, Independence, California.

Fig. 571 Susie Wilson, Panamint, mid-1900s. Braun Research Library Collection. Autry Museum, Los Angeles. Item number P.2372.

Fig. 572 Joseppa Dick, Pomo. Photograph courtesy National Anthropological Archives, Smithsonian Institution. Image number 01507000.

Unidentified Basketweavers

Fig. 573 Unknown Desert Cahuilla weavers. Photograph courtesy San Diego History Center. Photograph number OP7854.

Fig. 574 Unknown Chemehuevi weaver. Photograph courtesy University of Southern California. Call number CHS 3503.

Fig. 575 Unknown weavers. Photograph courtesy Phoebe A. Hearst Museum of Anthropology and the Regents of the University of California. Object number 15-23501.

Fig. 576 Unknown Yokuts weavers. Photograph courtesy Sanger Depot Museum, Sanger, California.

Fig. 577 Unknown Washoe weaver. Photograph courtesy University of Nevada Research Center, Reno, Nevada. Photograph number P2710-0298.

Fig. 578 Unknown Yokuts weaver. Grace Nicholson photograph.

Fig. 579 Unknown Washoe weaver. Marion Steinbach Indian Basket Museum and Gatekeeper's Museum, Tahoe City, California. C. Hart Merriam is on the left.

Fig. 580 Unknown Yokuts basketweaver, 1895–1923. Braun Research Library Collection. Autry Museum, Los Angeles. Item P.564.

Fig. 581 Unknown Maidu weaver, ca. 1908. National Museum of the American Indian, Smithsonian Institution. Grace Nicholson photo. Image number P21032.

Fig. 582 Unknown Yokuts weaver. Photograph courtesy Phoebe A. Hearst Museum of Anthropology and the Regents of the University of California. Object number 15-23504.

Fig. 584* Unknown Yokuts and Mono Indians from Cold Springs Rancheria in Sycamore Valley, Fresno County, California with groups of baskets. Photograph courtesy Greg Sarena and Bob Seng.

See Appendix 3, Figure Notes | Pg. 309

Fig. 585 Unknown Cahuilla weaver. Photograph courtesy San Diego History Center. Item number SDHS 2001.30.21.

Fig. 586 Unknown Washoe weaver. Photograph courtesy Donner Museum, Donner Pass, California.

Fig. 587 Unknown Pomo weaver. Photograph courtesy Penn Museum. Image number 195213, Object NA8800. Catalogue

Fig. 588 Gabrieliño (Tongva/Kizh) woman, late 1800s to early 1900s. Braun Research Library Collection. Autry Museum, Los Angeles. Item number P.1563.

Fig. 589 Yokuts weavers, ca. 1905. Possibly Aida Icho with gambling tray. Photograph courtesy Bancroft Library. University of California, Berkeley.

Masterpiece Baskets by Unidentified Weavers

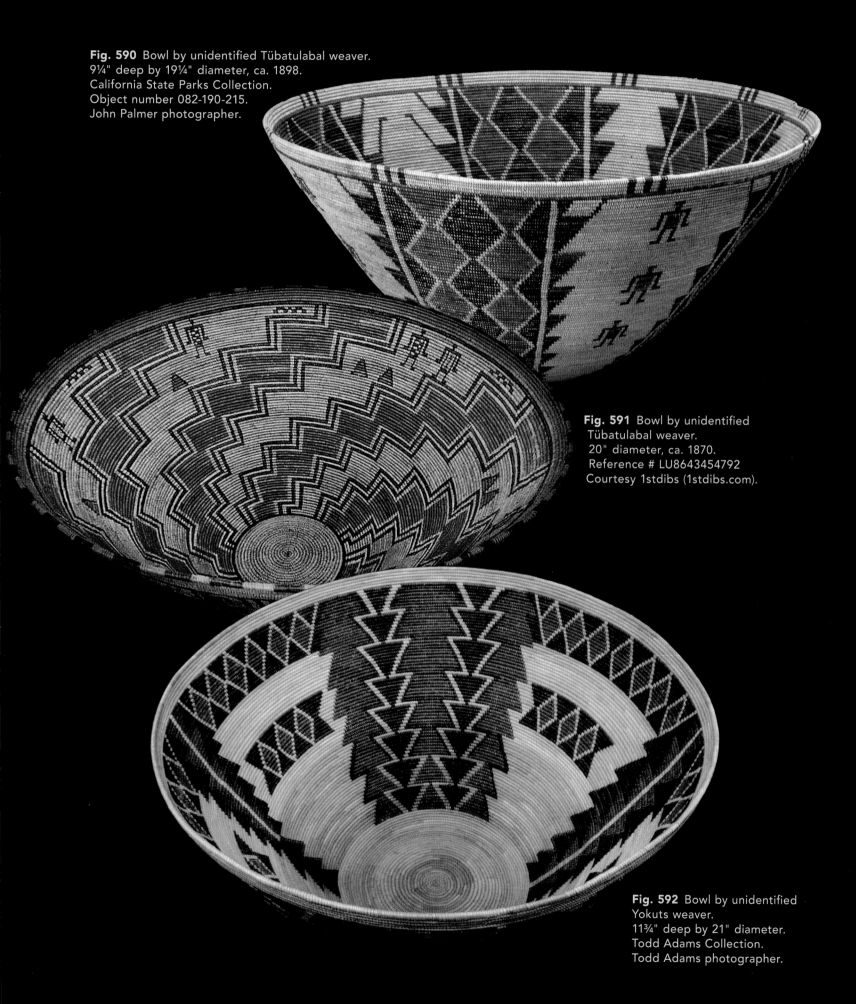

Fig. 590 Bowl by unidentified Tübatulabal weaver. 9¼" deep by 19¼" diameter, ca. 1898. California State Parks Collection. Object number 082-190-215. John Palmer photographer.

Fig. 591 Bowl by unidentified Tübatulabal weaver. 20" diameter, ca. 1870. Reference # LU8643454792 Courtesy 1stdibs (1stdibs.com).

Fig. 592 Bowl by unidentified Yokuts weaver. 11¾" deep by 21" diameter. Todd Adams Collection. Todd Adams photographer.

Fig. 593 Bowl by unidentified Kawaiisu weaver.
12" deep by 25" diameter.
Alex Schwed Collection.
Todd Adams photographer.

Fig. 594 Basket by unidentified
Kawaiisu weaver.
12" diameter.
Private collection.
Ben Watkins photographer.

Fig. 595 Basket by unidentified
Kawaiisu weaver.
5½" high by 7" diameter.
Private collection.
Ben Watkins photographer.

Fig. 596* Luiseño-style basket
from Pechanga-Pala.
16¾" diameter, ca. 1890s.
Harwood Hall Collection A8-95.
Photograph courtesy Riverside
Metropolitan Museum.
Chase Leland photographer.

**See Appendix 3,
Figure Notes | Pg. 309*

Fig. 597* Basket by unidentified Luiseño weaver.
3½" deep by 16" diameter, ca. 1890.
Harwood Hall Collection A8-100.
Photograph courtesy Riverside Metropolitan Museum.
Chase Leland photographer.

*See Appendix 3, Figure Notes | Pg. 309

Fig. 598 Basket by unidentified Luiseño weaver.
3¼" deep by 13¾" diameter, ca. 1910.
California State Parks Collection.
Object number 186-24.

Fig. 599 Basket by unidentified Cahuilla weaver.
2 ⅛" deep by 9 ⅝" diameter, ca. 1900.
Portland Art Museum object 91.95.74.

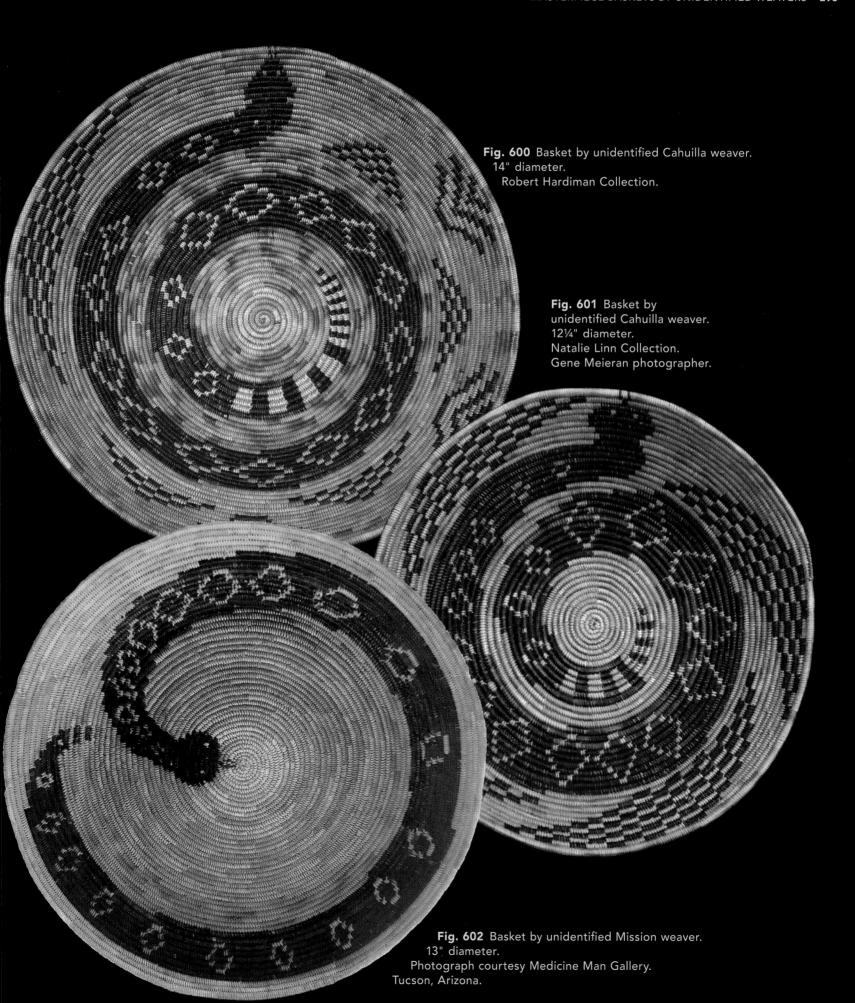

Fig. 600 Basket by unidentified Cahuilla weaver.
14" diameter.
Robert Hardiman Collection.

Fig. 601 Basket by
unidentified Cahuilla weaver.
12¼" diameter.
Natalie Linn Collection.
Gene Meieran photographer.

Fig. 602 Basket by unidentified Mission weaver.
13" diameter.
Photograph courtesy Medicine Man Gallery.
Tucson, Arizona.

Fig. 603 Basket by unidentified Yokuts weaver.
26½" diameter.
Photograph courtesy Bonhams.
Private collection.

Fig. 604 Basket by unidentified Washoe weaver.
5½" high by 8½" diameter.
Photograph courtesy Phoebe A. Hearst
Museum of Anthropology and the Regents
of the University of California.
Catalogue number 1-164412.

Fig. 605 Basket by unidentified
weaver, possibly Ellen Snapp, Pomo.
14" diameter.
Natalie Linn Collection.
Gene Meieran photographer.

Fig. 606 Basket by unidentified Yokuts weaver.
28" diameter, ca. 1900.
Photograph courtesy
Philbrook Museum of Art,
Tulsa, Oklahoma.

Fig. 607 Basket by unidentified Panamint weaver.
5½" high by 7¾" diameter, pre-1915.
Photograph courtesy Lauren Rogers Museum,
Laurel, Mississippi.

Fig. 608 Basket by
unidentified Kawaiisu
weaver.
9" high by 11¾" diameter.
Terry DeWald Collection.
Terry DeWald photographer.

Fig. 609 Yokuts gambling tray, 1910–1918.
14¼" diameter.
Collection of the Oakland Museum of California.
Bequest of Mary Louise Stong.
Ben Blackwell photographer.

Fig. 610 Luiseño-style gambling tray.
15" diameter.
Cornelius Earle Ramsey Collection A1-41.
Riverside Metropolitan Museum.
Chase Leland photographer.

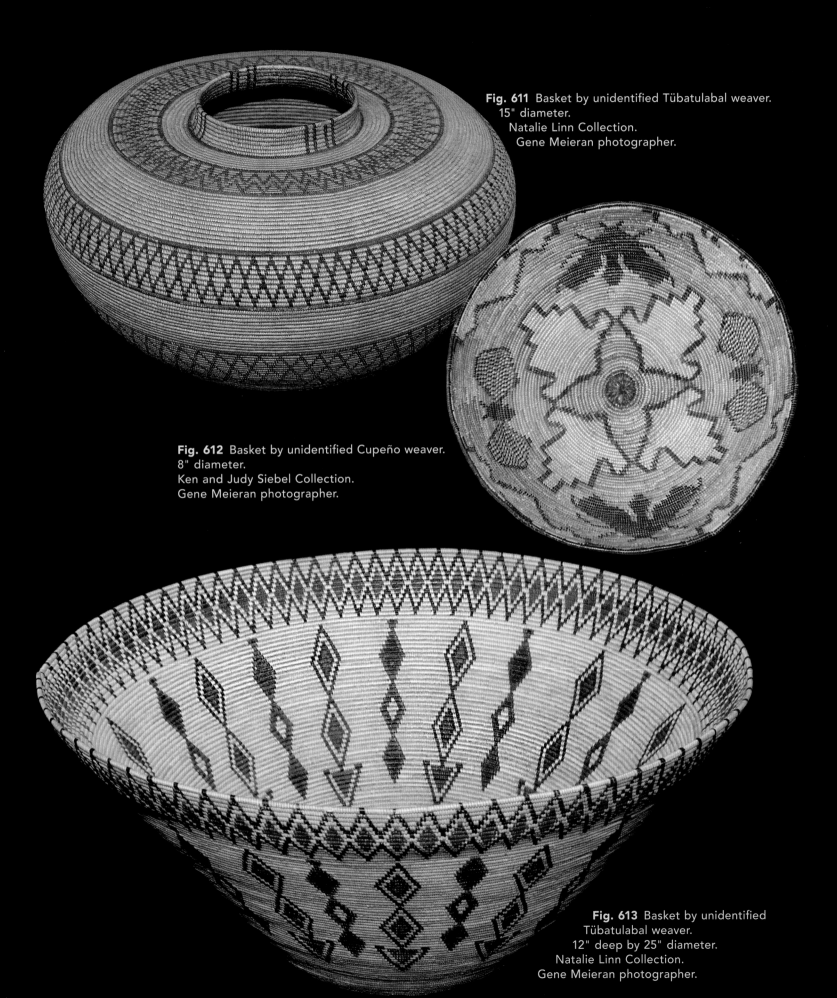

Fig. 611 Basket by unidentified Tübatulabal weaver.
15" diameter.
Natalie Linn Collection.
Gene Meieran photographer.

Fig. 612 Basket by unidentified Cupeño weaver.
8" diameter.
Ken and Judy Siebel Collection.
Gene Meieran photographer.

Fig. 613 Basket by unidentified
Tübatulabal weaver.
12" deep by 25" diameter.
Natalie Linn Collection.
Gene Meieran photographer.

Fig. 614 Basket by unidentified Pomo weaver.
4¾" high by 14½" diameter.
Private collection.
Ben Watkins photographer.

Fig. 615* "Apostolic Basket" made
by unidentified Kawaiisu weaver.
9" high by 14¾" diameter.
E. L. McLeod Memorial Collection.
Photograph courtesy Phoebe A. Hearst
Museum of Anthropology and the Regents
of the University of California.
Catalogue number 1-20934.

*See Appendix 3, Figure Notes | Pg. 309

Fig. 616 Basket by unidentified Panamint weaver.
7" high by 9¼" diameter, 1902.
Photograph courtesy Lauren Rogers Museum, Laurel, Mississippi.
Basket 23-133001.

Fig. 617 Basket by unidentified Chemehuevi weaver. 16" high by 15½" diameter. Ned Smith Collection.

Fig. 618 Basket by unidentified Washoe weaver. 10" high by 21" diameter. Photograph courtesy Phoebe A. Hearst Museum of Anthropology and the Regents of the University of California. Catalogue number 1-71459.

Fig. 619 Basket by unidentified
Chemehuevi weaver.
7½" high by 9½" diameter.
Terry DeWald Collection.
Terry DeWald photographer.

Fig. 620* Basket by unidentified Panamint weaver.
In January 2020 this basket was identified as being
made by Paiute weaver Mary Ann Howell.
4½" high by 6½" diameter.
Heard Museum, Phoenix, Arizona.
Basket 291-BA.
*See Appendix 3, Figure Notes | Pg. 309

Fig. 621 Basket by unidentified Maidu weaver.
8¼" high by 14½" diameter.
Elizabeth Cole Butler Collection.
Photograph courtesy Portland Art Museum.
Catalogue number 91.95.38.

Fig. 622 Miwok treasure basket.
3" high by 6" diameter.
Photograph courtesy Gene Quintana.
John Law photographer.

Fig. 623 Basket by unidentified Yokuts weaver, attributed to Mrs. Dick Francisco. 21" diameter. Syd Bottomley Collection.

Top view.

Side view.

Appendix 1
Basketweavers by Tribal Affiliation

Cahuilla
Gertrude Arenas | *Pg. 283*
Guadalupe Arenas | *Pgs. 167–169*
Bridgita Castro | *Pg. 159*
Casilda Saubel Chia | *Pg. 78*
Ramona Lubo | *Pgs. 101–106*
Dolores Cassero Lubo | *Pgs. 220–221*
Juanna Sands | *Pg. 276*
Unidentified weaver | *Pgs. 287–288, 294–295*

Desert Cahuilla
Lupe Alberras | *Pgs. 204–205*
Polineria | *Pg. 281*
Unidentified weaver | *Pg. 285*

Chemehuevi
Magdalena Augustine | *Pg. 143*
Mary Smith Hill | *Pg. 73*
Annie Laird | *Pgs. 154–155*
Maggie Painter | *Pgs. 236–237*
Mary Snyder | *Pgs. 172–177*
Unidentified weaver | *Pgs. 285, 301–302*

Chemehuevi/Paiute
Kitty Johnson | *Pgs. 107–111*

Cupeño
Dolores Saneva Patencio | *Pgs. 190–196*
Merced Wellmas | *Pg. 282*
Casilda Welmas | *Pgs. 148–149*
Salvadora Valenzuela | *Pg. 269*
Unidentified weaver | *Pg. 299*

Diegueño (Kumeyaay/Ipai/Tipai)
Ramona Balenzuela | *Pg. 274*

Gabrieliño (Tongva/Kizh)
Unidentified weaver | *Pg. 289*

Kawaiisu (Nüwa)
Rosenita Marcus Hicks | *Pg. 277*
Unidentified weaver | *Pgs. 292, 297, 300*

Luiseño
Esperanza Sobonish | *Pg. 281*
Maria Antonia Subish | *Pg. 282*
Unidentified weaver | *Pgs. 293, 298*

Maidu
Mary Kea'a'ala Azbill | *Pg. 271*
Ina Jackson | *Pg. 280*
Kate Meadows McKinney | *Pg. 272*
Lena Peconum | *Pg. 271*
Amanda Wilson | *Pg. 277*
Unidentified weaver | *Pg. 287*

Miwok
Unidentified weaver | *Pg. 302*

Mountain Maidu
Daisy Meadows Baker | *Pg. 88*
Salena Young Jackson | *Pgs. 24–34*
Rose Meadows Salem | *Pgs. 160–161*

Mono Lake Paiute (Kuzedika)
Rosie Brown August | *Pg. 273*
Carrie Bethel | *Pgs. 89–100*
Daisy Charlie | *Pg. 197*
Nellie Charlie | *Pgs. 206–208*
Tina Charlie | *Pgs. 15–23*
Maggie Howard | *Pg. 270*
Minnie Mike | *Pgs. 178–180*
Nellie Jameson Washington | *Pgs. 112–113*
Alice James Wilson | *Pgs. 216–217*

Mono Lake Paiute (Kuzedika)/Miwok
Lucy Parker Telles | *Pgs. 253–267*

Miwok/Mono Lake Paiute (Kuzedika)
Leanna Tom | *Pgs. 144–147*

Panamint Shoshone (Timbisha)
Maggie Bellas | *Pg. 282*
Mamie Gregory | *Pg. 273*
Isabel Hanson | *Pgs. 74–77*
Anna Hughes | *Pgs. 214–215*
Susie Wilson | *Pg. 283*
Mary Wrinkle | *Pgs. 188–189*
Unidentified weaver | *Pgs. 297, 300, 302*

Pomo
Mary Knight Benson | *Pgs. 79–83*
Joseppa Dick | *Pg. 283*
Rosa Burris Smith | *Pgs. 218–219*
Ellen Snapp | *Pg. 280*
Laura Burris Willum | *Pgs. 170–171*
Unidentified weaver | *Pgs. 288, 296, 300*

Tübatulabal
Unidentified weaver | *Pgs. 291, 299*

Washoe
Barefoot Annie | *Pg. 281*
Lena Frank Dick | *Pgs. 156–158*
Tootsie Dick | *Pgs. 181–183*
Lillie Frank James | *Pg. 275*
Maggie Mayo James | *Pgs. 198–203*
Sarah Jim Mayo | *Pgs. 68–72*
Lizzie Toby Peters | *Pgs. 152–153*
Scees Bryant Possack | *Pgs. 84–87*
Sally Snooks | *Pg. 280*
Tillie Snooks | *Pg. 280*
Unidentified weaver | *Pgs. 286, 288, 296, 301*

Southern Washoe
Louisa Keyser (Dat So La Lee) | *Pgs. 114–142*

Yokuts
Mollie Charley | *Pg. 283*
Sally Edd | *Pg. 274*
Josie Polecat Hawkins | *Pg. 283*
Kathryn Marler | *Pg. 283*
Mary Sampson (Mrs. Dick Sampson) | *Pg. 282*
Mary Sampson (Mrs. Jack Sampson) | *Pgs. 209–213*
Unidentified weaver | *Pgs. 286–289, 291, 296–298, 303*

Bancalache Yokuts
Mrs. Dick Francisco | *Pgs. 35–67*

Casson Yokuts
Ellen Amos | *Pg. 276*

Choinimni Yokuts
Julia Davis | *Pg. 282*

Chukchansi Yokuts
Mrs. Elizabeth Graham | *Pg. 276*

Nutunutu Yokuts
Lucinda Hancock | *Pgs. 222–235*

Tachi Yokuts
Linda Hancock | *Pg. 281*

Wukchumni Yokuts
Minnie Wilcox Hancock | *Pgs. 162–166*
Aida Icho (Wahnomkot) | *Pgs. 150–151*
Mary Topino | *Pgs. 238–252*

Yawelmani (Yowlumni) Yokuts
Sartonia Emeterio | *Pgs. 184–187*

Appendix 2
Endnotes

[1] The Indian Census, Tule Indian Reservation, for 1923 shows a "Mrs. Francisco" but gives no name or age for her. The 1930–1934 Censuses, however, list her as Louisa Francisco, wife, Pung-ko-lah-che tribe, born January 9, 1865.

[2] The identity of Louisa Olivier with Louisa Francisco is clearly indicated by a note on the 1926 Indian Census, which states that person no. 104 (in the alphabetical listing) — Luisa Loiver, widow, born 1869 — is the same person as no. 44, Louisa Francisco, wife of Dick Francisco. Her maiden name, before marrying Leymas Olivier, remains unknown because the Indian Census records, do not go back before 1885 when their first daughter was born. Leymas is listed as "Romaldo Lovien" on the 1890 Census and "Romund Loiver" on the 1895 Census, but appears thereafter as "Leymas" Olivier — possibly his Indian name.

[3] Louisa Olivier is listed as "widow" in 1914, 1915, and 1923 (when she first appears, unnamed, with Dick Francisco).

[4] She was the only Mary Knight in Mendocino County on the 1880 Federal Census; her brother Jimmie Knight (also shown on that census) appears to have lived next door to her as identified in the 1920 Federal Census. William and Mary both appear on the 1900, 1910, 1920, and 1930 Censuses in Ukiah, Mendocino County. Her Irish father was actually born aboard ship during the Atlantic crossing when his parents immigrated to America in 1828.

[5] The 1930 Federal Census shows both of them in Ukiah, listed as children of Pomo mothers and "mixed blood" fathers, though both of their fathers were actually white.

[6] The 1902 Indian Census, the earliest one in which she is recorded, gives her age as 35 (i.e. born in 1866/1867); this was surely just a guess, but being the earliest guess is probably closest to correct. Later census records indicate various birth dates as late as 1880. The 1910 Federal Census for the Cabazon Reservation at Indio gives her birthplace as "Needles, San Bernardino Co." and lists her occupation as "basketmaker." On the various census records her first name appears in a range of spellings including Magdalena, Molena, Monalena, Malena, Melena, Madelina, and Helena. The California Death Index listing for her gives the "Alvaldo" spelling for her maiden name, whereas the Indian Census records in 1924, 1926, and 1927 provide the name "Avalado" or "Avalada."

[7] The 1910 Federal Census also states that they were married, ca. 1900.

[8] Rodriguez appears on the 1902 Indian Census, but is gone by the 1910 Census when an unnamed baby is recorded, who was later named Roy Rodriguez, as shown on the 1933, 1936, and 1937 Indian Census. Roy is recorded on the California Death Index as born May 18, 1909 and died March 16, 1945 in Riverside County. Amelia appears, at age 10, on the 1902 Census and may have been married by the 1910 Census.

[9] California Death Index erroneously gives her birthplace as "Arizona." Needles is in California, but is on the border with Arizona.

[10] Beginning in 1769, the first of twenty-one Franciscan missions was established in California. The missions ranged from San Diego north to San Francisco and were a means for the Spanish to control the Indians. Previously these Indians had lived as hunter-gatherers, hunting with bows and arrows and harvesting key economic plants (seeds, nuts, berries, roots, bulbs, and corms). Under mission control, Natives were taught Catholicism, ranching, agriculture, and trades such as weaving, blacksmithing, hide tanning, and candle making. In 1834, thirteen years after Mexican independence from Spain, the missions were dissolved and their lands were turned into huge ranches intended for the initial settlers. The Indians became dependent on local ranchers and miners for employment. Today descendants of the "Mission"

Indians live on twenty-eight reservations principally in southern California.

[11] The 1910 Federal Census for the Colorado River Indian Reservation lists Anna Eddy as born in Arizona in 1872 or 1873 (both of her parents were also born in Arizona). It also identifies that her parents had been married for five years.

[12] Annie Laird also appears as Annie Eddie with her husband William Eddy on the Indian Census for the Colorado Indian Reservation in 1911, 1912, 1913, and 1914, but not in 1915, 1916, and 1917. William, by then, had passed away and she is listed as widowed. The 1920 Federal Census for the Colorado River Reservation listed "Mary Annie Laird," as the wife of George Laird. Annie Eddy Laird appears on the Indian Census for the years 1928–1934, 1937, and 1940.

[13] The 1931–1937 Indian Censuses give her name as Guadalupe Rice Arenas. The 1900 Tule River Indian Census shows her as Guadalupe Chevedore with her (maternal) grandparents—Maria and Joseph Rice—who apparently raised her and her younger sister Hypolite Chevedore. The Chevedore surname is a mystery, as it occurs nowhere else in the Indian or the general Federal Census.

[14] As was commonly the case with Native people of that era, she did not really know the precise year in which she had been born. The Indian Census for 1901–1904 gives her birth as 1875/1876, but in a different entry in the 1904 Census, her birth year is given as 1880/1881. In 1912, it is identified as 1883/1884; and in 1917–1918, it is specified as 1880. Finally, in the 1920–1934 Census, it is stated as 1881. In such a situation, it appears to us most likely that the dates provided in the earliest documents are the ones more likely to be correct.

[15] The 1930 United States Federal Census for Palm Springs, Riverside County, California, lists Lee Arenas, age 53 (b. 1876/1877), who was 24 years old when he married, ca. 1900. He is listed as a full-blooded Cahuilla, working as a fruit farmer. His wife, Guadalupe Arenas, age 47 (b. 1882/1883) was 18 when she married, ca. 1900, and is also listed as a full-blooded Cahuilla.

[16] They appear on the 1903 Indian Census Schedule living on the Tule River Reservation, and on the 1904–1937 Schedules, they are shown living in the Palm Springs area.

[17] U.S. Federal Census 1910 listed as Lee and Judlupe Areseo.

[18] 1900 Federal Census for Lake County.

[19] The 1937 Census Schedule for Palm Springs lists Lee and Guadalupe but a handwritten note appended states that she died March 26, 1937.

[20] 1880 Federal Census, Upper Lake Precinct.

[21] 1900 Federal Census for Lake County.

[22] 1900 Federal Census for Lake County.

[23] U.S. Federal Census, 1920 and 1930.

[24] She is listed as Sartonia (Sartonio) Emeterio (Emiterio) on the June 1890 and June 1900 Indian Census Schedules for the Tule River Reservation, living with her son Juan Emeterio and his family. In those records she gives her age as 101 and 102, respectively, indicating a birth year of 1797 or 1798. She also appears on the 1900 U.S. Federal Census, living with her son Juan; however, in that record she gives her name as Ramona Emeterio, age 106 (born in 1793/1794). Given that both of the 1900 Census records show a centenarian woman named Emeterio living with Juan Emeterio, it seems highly likely that Romano and Sartonia are the same person and that for unknown reasons she gave a different name and age to the federal census taker than she did for the Indian census.

[25] Her tribal affiliation is not mentioned in the records, but her grandson, Remac Emeterio (1881–1947), is identified in the census records as being of the Ya-will-min-ee or Wa-will-min-nee (aka Yowlumni) tribe. The Yawelmani (Yowlumni) are a Yokuts group that lived in the vicinity of Bakersfield, California. Some members of this tribe now live on the Tule River Reservation.

[26] See G. H. Phillips (2004), *Bringing Them Under Subjection: California's Tejon Indian Reservation and Beyond, 1852–1964*, University of Nebraska Press, pp. 25 and 123–124. The Indian leader named Emeterio (Francisco Emeterio, according to the genealogical records the Charmaine McDarmento Family Tree, Public member Tress, Ancestry.com) was born in 1799 in the village or Rancheria of Tubampet (Tulamniu) on Buena Vista Lake and was baptized at Mission San Fernando in 1804. There he was given the name of Emeterio (after St. Emeterio). Being the first and only person of that name in his tribe and being of approximately the same age as Sartonia, it is unlikely that she could have adopted his surname by any means other than marriage.

[27] The Federal Census states further that Mrs. Emeterio was a widow and had three children, only one of whom was still living.

[28] Mrs. Emeterio does not appear in the Federal Census (or anywhere) in the California Indian Census Schedules for the years 1891, 1892, 1898, 1900, 1901, 1903, or 1906, and thus clearly was living somewhere else for most of that time, though where she was remains unknown.

Appendix 3
Figure Notes

Fig. 2 This Tina Charlie degikup received a First Prize placement in the 1929 Yosemite Indian Field Days competition. This same basket was sold at Bonhams auction of the Ella Cain Collection in 2005, for the highest price (approximately $350,000) ever paid at that time at auction for a Native American basket. This basket is considered by many experts to be the finest basket made during the Florescence period.

Fig. 7 This Tina Charlie degikup sold at Bonhams auction of the Ella Cain Collection for over $200,000. Figs. 15/16, 17/18, 21/22, and 36/37 show four of the five known matched trays and bowls, or trays, and degikup sets made by Salena Jackson.

Fig. 29 One of two Salena Jackson baskets made in a "new style," similar to that of the Yosemite baskets.

Fig. 46 This basket was sold at Sotheby's auction in 2011 for approximately $375,000—the highest price paid to that date at auction for an American Indian basket.

Fig. 50 This is the largest known basket tray made by Mrs. Dick Francisco, and is one of the great "Cummings 10" baskets (which also includes the baskets seen in Figs. 39, 46, 48, 49, 60, 66, and 357). All these baskets are part of the Cummings Collection.

Fig. 59 All five baskets seen in this photograph are shown together for the first time in a full color image.

Fig. 67 This is probably the finest "reverse image" basket ever made during the Florescence. The red figures are two rows of butterflies but when the light areas are viewed, one can see a double flower image.

Fig. 87 "Missing" for a number of years, this Sarah Jim Mayo degikup appeared in the *Antiques Roadshow* in 2009 and was identified by Marvin Cohodas as being the one seen in a 1916 photo of Sarah along with her husband, Captain Pete Mayo. That 1916 photograph is shown here as Fig. 86. A second picture owned by Alex Schwed showing Sarah with this same basket is seen in Fig. 88.

Figs. 96–98 These pictures show the "President's basket" (presentation basket) made for President Woodrow Wilson by Sarah Jim Mayo. The current whereabouts of this basket is unknown. An excellent article about the missing presentation basket is provided by The *Reno Gazette-Journal*, written by Jenny Kane, and appearing in the January 6, 2016 edition of the *Journal*.

Fig. 107 The weaver in this photograph is believed to be Isabel Hanson because of the design of the baskets surrounding her (characteristic of Isabel Hanson) and the presence of the other individual who is believed to be her daughter who passed away in 1938.

Fig. 112 This Mary Knight Benson basket was made in the style of Louisa Keyser (Dat So La Lee) degikups.

Fig. 113 Craig Bates identified this large basket as a Diegueño/Kumeyaay storage vessel, not one woven by Mary.

Figs. 124, 125, and 132 Degikup baskets made by Scees Bryant Possack, in the style of those made by her sister-in-law, Dat So La Lee. The basket in Fig. 124 sold at the Sotheby's Green Sale in 1971 for $2,600.

Fig. 138 The "Dream Basket" of Carrie Bethel was purchased from James Schwabacher's heirs by Gene Quintana in 1987.

Fig. 140 This is one of Carrie Bethel's finest baskets, purchased from James Schwabacher's heirs by Gene Quintana in 1987. It was later sold for over $1,000,000.

Figs. 143, 148 These two baskets sold at the same time as the basket seen in Fig. 140; these two baskets are also valued in the seven-figure range!

Fig. 144 This is the last great basket made by Carrie Bethel in 1962, about 30 years after the end of the Florescence period.

Fig. 150 This basket won first place at the 1929 June Lake Field Days competition.

Fig. 151 This is Carrie Bethel's largest basket, completed in the 1930s after four years of work. It is on view at the Yosemite Museum.

Fig. 152 This basket was sold at Bonhams auction as part of the Ella Cain Collection in 2005 for about $225,000.

Fig. 160 This is the original "Star Basket" made by Ramona Lubo, for her husband Juan Diego, after he was murdered by a white man. This incident led to the writing of the book, *Ramona*, by Helen Hunt Jackson (1884); the story was recounted and forms the basis for the play of the same name performed annually in Hemet, California.

Fig. 172 This Kitty Johnson basket sold at Bonhams auction in 2001 for about $150,000 — at that time the highest price paid for a Native American basket at auction. It is the finest example of what has come to be known as the "Victorville Phenomena."

Fig. 175 The Palm Springs Art Museum was the recipient of the gift of the Mary Beal Collection, which contained a number of baskets by "Katie Johnson." While difficult to prove, we believe Katie Johnson and Kitty Johnson are the same person, with different spellings of the first name. The baskets attributed to Katie and Kitty look remarkably similar. The names in the figure captions reflect these alternatives, as supplied by the basket or the photographic image owner.

Fig. 180 This basket won second place at the 1929 June Lake Field Days competition and was sold by Bonhams during the Ella Cain Collection auction for about $90,000.

Fig. 181 This image of Dat So La Lee is Plate #530 in Volume 15 of Edward S. Curtis' 20-volume series *The North American Indian*. The series was published between 1907 and 1930. Other Curtis photographs are seen within this book, courtesy of a variety of credited sources.

Figs. 185, 195, 211, 212, 220, and 229 The baskets shown in these illustrations were sold at Sotheby's auction in 1971, for the then unheard-of prices ranging from $4,000 to $6,000. These baskets can now individually reach prices in the million-dollar range.

Fig. 198 A picture of this basket was used by the Cohns on their certificates of authenticity.

Fig. 199 This is an uncolored photograph of the basket bowl seen in Fig. 201. However, the old negative had coloring which seemed to serendipitously mimic the original bowl's color!

Fig. 204 This basket was started by Scees Bryant Possack but was completed by Dat So La Lee in 1918 after Scees perished in the great 1918 flu epidemic.

Fig. 207 This basket was purchased by Gottlieb Adam Steiner (1844–1916) in 1914 for $1,400.

Fig. 232 Color images of eight of the nine baskets seen in this famous picture of Dat So La Lee are shown on this page. The whereabouts of the ninth basket (fifth from right) is unknown.

Figs. 242 through 246 Part of a collection of smaller Dat So La Lee baskets, now in the Gene and Julie Quintana Collection. Many were recently on exhibit at the Gatekeeper's Museum in North Lake Tahoe, California.

Figs. 257, 258, 260, and 262 Leanna Tom's baskets that were entered in the Yosemite Indian Field Days competition in 1929.

Fig. 260 A similar photo taken at the same time is seen in Bates and Lee 1990, page 99, Fig. 190.

Fig. 267 Two views of this bowl are shown to illustrate its three-dimensional features. Many of the baskets shown in this book that appear as flat trays are actually bowls with considerable depth.

Fig. 300 This is an exceptional Minnie Hancock bottleneck with a count of 20 coils/inch and 40 stitches/inch.

Fig. 318 This is an exceptionally large and fine Pomo basket. The Pomo are one of the few California Indian cultures in which very large baskets are frequently encountered. See Figs. 551 and 552.

Figs. 320, 322, 324, 326, 331 and 332 Examples of Mary Snyder's rattlesnake baskets. In about 1896 she was the first Chemehuevi weaver to incorporate rattlesnakes in her basket designs and thus break the taboo against doing so. For many years she was the only Chemehuevi weaver to embellish her baskets with these rattlesnake figures.

Fig. 357 This is the largest known gambling tray and is valued in the high six figures.

Fig. 361 An exceptional bottleneck olla sold at Bonhams auction in 2012 for almost $50,000.

Fig. 403 A very fine reverse image tray. In Fig. 403, the most noticeable images are the black bird images seen on each side of the bowl; but if one looks carefully, one sees that the black images can also be used to outline the lighter tan images of eagles, on the top and bottom. Such reversal of contrast is a clever pattern technique often used by some weavers, and is referred to as "negative images," since, like in a photographic negative, the contrast is inverted from what one expects to see.

Fig. 413 This is one of the largest and finest Friendship Bowls made during the Florescence. It was woven by Mary Sampson, who seems to be virtually unknown to the basket collectors' market. "Friendship bowls" were so named after "friendship dances," where the bowl shows couples holding hands during a dance ceremony.

Fig. 421 This Alice Wilson basket was featured in Yosemite Museum postcards. It can also be seen at the feet of Lucy Parker Telles in Fig. 501. It has also been attributed as a basket made by Lucy Parker Telles.

Fig. 424 The only known color image of the large Alice Wilson degikup seen at the center-bottom of Fig. 490. Other pictures of the incomplete basket being woven by Alice Wilson are seen in Figs. 422 and 425.

Fig. 438 This is the finest of seven large bottleneck ollas made by Lucinda Hancock and is seen in several vintage photographs with her.

Fig. 442 This basket was sold at the Green Sale at Sotheby's in 1971 for $2,100—about half the price of what some of the Dat So La Lee baskets sold for at the same sale.

Fig. 444 This basket was sold at Sotheby's auction in 2011 for $275,000—then the third highest price paid at auction for a Native American basket.

Fig. 447 There is a strong resemblance between this basket and those of Sally Edd.

Fig. 449 This basket, the seventh of the Lucinda Hancock bottleneck ollas, was not known to the collectors' market until it surfaced in 2011. It has never before been published.

Fig. 451 The photograph of this olla was slightly photo-enhanced to add a small section missing in the original color photograph.

Fig. 453 This basket was woven by Maggie Painter near the end of her life. She told Jerry Collings that she was finally no longer afraid to make a basket with the image of a rattlesnake.

Figs. 454, 455, and 458 Made with butterfly images to symbolize springtime.

Fig. 461 This basket appears unfinished in Fig. 460 and is illustrated during a later stage after completion in Fig. 462.

Fig. 476 This is one of the first "fancy new style baskets" and was sold to Salter's Store in Yosemite in 1912.

Fig. 477, 478 This basket, finished in the 1930s, took four years to complete. It is the largest Yosemite basket and remains an important tourist attraction even now.

Figs. 484, 485 These baskets appear in a vintage photo in 1923, but were lost to the collectors' market until 2013, when they were found in a box packed in a closet. They were auctioned at Sotheby's in 2014.

Fig. 491 This is the only known olla of this shape made by Lucy Parker Telles; the basket is decorated with her characteristic diving hummingbirds.

Fig. 502 The only known picture of the lidded bowl held by Lucy Parker Telles in Fig. 501. A small section of the bottom of the bowl is missing in the photograph (hidden by the overlapping image).

Fig. 503 A small portion of the left side of the image of this basket was Photoshop restored.

Fig. 549 This bowl by Rosenita Marcus Hicks was featured in the book, *The Butterfly Basket*, by C. A. Waldman, 2014

Figs. 551–553 Show a very large Pomo basket made by a group of weavers; and a tiny basket, Fig. 553—about a half of an inch in diameter—was made by William Benson, husband of Mary Knight Benson. These baskets illustrate the range of style and size of baskets made by the Pomo tribe of northern California. Many wonderful Pomo baskets are on exhibit at the Grace Hudson Museum in Ukiah, California. An article by Craig Bates (Bates and Lee 1991) describes the big Pomo basket.

Fig. 559 The weaver is identified by the Hearst Museum and C. Hart Merriam as being Linda Hancock, but may actually be a photo of Lucinda Hancock.

Fig. 584 Craig Bates suggests this might have been a roadside stand selling baskets to tourists.

Fig. 596 This basket appears on the cover of the book *Rods, Bundles and Stitches: A Century of Southern California Indian Basketry,* edited by Paul A. Lopez and Christopher L. Moser. Riverside: Riverside Museum, 1981.

Fig. 597 This basket appears on the cover of Justin Farmer's (2004) book *Southern California Luiseño Basketry*. Its unknown maker was killed in a massive earthquake in 1899, in southern California.

Fig. 615 This Kawaiisu basket appears to be over 130 years old and is known as the "Apostolic Basket." See Maurice Zigmond's article on Kawaiisu basketry in *The Journal of California Anthropology* Volume 5, pg. 199 (1978). It is also is the subject of some discussion and is depicted in a color photograph on pages 87 and 88 in *The Handbook of the Kawaiisu* by Alan Garfinkel and Harold Williams, 2011, Wa-hi Sina'avi Publications, Bakersfield, California.

Fig. 620 During a recent (2019 to 2020) exhibit of baskets at the Heard Museum, Phoenix, this basket was attributed by John Kania as the work of Southern Paiute weaver Mary Ann Howell. Since this book was already in print layout, it was decided to simply add the weaver identification to the figure caption, rather than move the image to the known basketweaver section.

Appendix 4
References

Allen, Elsie
2013   *Pomo Basketmaking.* Naturegraph Publishers, Happy Camp, California.

Barrett, Samuel A.
1908   Pomo Indian Basketry. *University of California Publications in American Archaeology and Ethnology* 7(3):134–308. Berkeley, California.

Bates, Craig D.
1989   Letter to Sherry Brydon of the New York Historical Society from Craig Bates regarding the Thaw Collection pertaining to: The Yokuts Weaver known as "Mrs. Britches." Letter in possession of Alan Garfinkel.

Bates, Craig and Brian Bibby
1984   Maidu Weaver: Amanda Wilson. *American Indian Art Magazine* 9(3):38–43.

Bates, Craig D. and Martha J. Lee
1990   *Tradition and Innovation: A Basket History of the Indians of Yosemite—Mono Lake Area.* Yosemite Association, Yosemite National Park, California.
1991   The Big Pomo Basket. *American Indian Basketry* 3(3):12–14.

Bibby, Brian
1996   *The Fine Art of California Indian Basketry.* Crocker Art Museum, Sacramento, California and Heyday Books, Berkeley, California.
2004   *Precious Cargo: Childbirth and Cradle Baskets in California Indian Culture.* Heyday Books, Berkeley, California and Marin Museum of the American Indian, Novato, California.
2012   *Essential Art: Native Basketry from the California Indian Heritage Center.* Heyday Books, Berkeley, California.

Bibby, Brian and Dugan Aguilar
2005   *Deeper Than Gold: Indian Life in the Sierra Foothills.* Heyday Books, Berkeley, California.

Blomberg, Nancy J.
1987   A Historic Indian Community at Victorville, California. *Journal of California and Great Basin Anthropology* 9(1):35–45.

Cohodas, Marvin
1976   Dat So La Lee. *American Indian Art Magazine* 1(4):22–29.
1979a   *Degikup: Washoe Fancy Baskets 1895–1935.* The Fine Arts Gallery of the University of British Columbia, Vancouver, BC.
1979b   Lena Frank Dick, Washoe Basket Weaver. *American Indian Art Magazine* 4(4): 32–38.
1981   Sarah Mayo and Her Contemporaries: Representational Designs in Washoe Basketry. *American Indian Art Magazine* 6(4):52–59.
1984   The Breitholle Collection of Washoe Basketry. *American Indian Art Magazine* 9(4):38–46.
1986   Washoe Innovators and their Patrons. In *The Arts of the North American Indian: Native Traditions in Evolution* edited by Edwin L. Wade, pp. 203-219. Hudson Hills Press, New York.
1992   Louisa Keyser and the Cohns: Myth Making and Basket Making in the American West. In *The Early Years of Native American Art History* edited by Janet Catherine Berlo, pp. 88–119. University of Washington Press, Seattle, Washington.

Collings, Jerold
1975   The Yokuts Gambling Tray. *American Indian Art Magazine* 1(1):10–15.

Cook, Stephen W.
2005   *By Native Hands: Woven Treasures from the Lauren Rogers Museum of Art.* Lauren Rogers Museum of Art, Laurel, Mississippi.

Curtis, Edward S.
1907–1930   *The North American Indian: Being A Series of Volumes Picturing and Describing the Indians of the United States, and Alaska* edited by Fredrick W. Hodges, 20 volumes. Plimpton Press, Norwood, Massachusetts. (Reprinted: Johnson Reprint, New York, 1970.)

d'Azevedo, Warren L. (editor)
  1986   *Great Basin*. Handbook of North American Indians. Smithsonian Institution, Washington, D.C.

Dalrymple, Larry
  2000a   *Indian Basketmakers of the Southwest: The Living Art and Fine Traditions*. Museum of New Mexico Press, Santa Fe, New Mexico.

  2000b   *Indian Basketmakers of California and the Great Basin*. Museum of New Mexico Press, Santa Fe, New Mexico.

Dean, Sharon E., Peggy S. Ratcheson, Judith W. Finger, and Ellen F. Daus
  2004   *Weaving A Legacy: Indian Baskets and the People of Owens Valley, California*. University of Utah Press, Salt Lake City, Utah.

DeWald, Terry
  1979   *The Papago Indians and Their Basketry*. Privately printed, Tucson, Arizona.

Elsasser, Albert B.
  1978   Basketry. In *California*, volume editor, Robert F. Heizer, pp. 626–641. *Handbook of North American Indians*, Volume 8, William C. Sturtevant, general editor. Smithsonian Institution, Washington, DC.

Fane, Diane, Ira Jacknis, and Lise M. Breen
  1991   *Objects of Myth and Memory: American Indian Art at the Brooklyn Museum*. University of Washington Press and the Brooklyn Museum, Seattle, Washington.

Farmer, Justin
  2004   *Southern California Luiseño Indian Baskets: A Study of Seventy-six Luiseño Baskets in the Riverside Municipal Museum Collection*. Justin Farmer Foundation, Fullerton, California.

Fowler, Catherine S. and Lawrence E. Dawson
  1986   Ethnographic Basketry. In **Great Basin** edited by Warren L. d'Azevedo, pp. 435–465. *Handbook of North American Indians*, Volume 11, William C. Sturtevant, general editor. Smithsonian Institution, Washington, DC.

Garfinkel, Alan and Harold Williams
  2011   *Handbook of the Kawaiisu: A Sourcebook and Guide to the Primary Resources on the Native Peoples of the Far Southern Sierra Nevada, Tehachapi Mountains, and Southwestern Great Basin*. Wa-hi Sana'avi Publications, Bakersfield, California.

Heizer, Robert F. (editor)
  1978   *California*. Handbook of North American Indians, Volume 8. George C. Sturtevant, General Editor. Smithsonian Institution, Washington, D.C.

Hickson, Jane Green
  1967   Dat So La Lee: Queen of the Washoe Basketmakers. *Nevada State Museum Popular Series* Number 3, Carson City, Nevada.

Howard, Kathleen L. and Donna Pardue
  2000   *Inventing the Southwest: The Fred Harvey Company and Native American Art*. Northland Publishing, Flagstaff, Arizona.

Jackson, Helen M. (Hunt)
  1884   *Ramona*. Roberts Brothers, Boston.

James, George Wharton
  1901a   *Indian Basketry*. Privately printed by the author. Pasadena, California.

  1901b   Basket Makers of California and Their Work. *Sunset: A Magazine of the Border* 8:3–14.

Kane, Jenny
  2016   The Curious Case of Woodrow Wilson's Missing Washoe Basket. *Reno Gazette-Journal*, January 4, 2016.

Kania, John and Alan Blaugrund
  2014   *Antique Native American Basketry of Western North America: A Comprehensive Guide to Identification*. Marquand Books, Seattle, Washington.

Kroeber, Alfred L.
  1909   California Basketry and the Pomo. *American Anthropologist* 11(2):233–249.

  1925   Handbook of the Indians of California. *Bureau of American Ethnology Bulletin* 78. Washington, DC.

Kurtz, Pat Lindgren
  2010   *Our Precious Legacy: Mountain Maidu Baskets from the Meadows-Baker Families*. Maidu Museum and Historic Site, Roseville, California.

  2011   *Picking Willows: With Daisy and Lilly Baker, Maidu Basket Makers of Lake Almanor*. Universe Publishing, Bloomington, Indiana.

Latta, Frank F.
  1949   *Handbook of the Yokuts Indians*. Kern County Museum, Bakersfield, California.

Linn, Natalie
  1999   *The Artistry of American Indian Basketry*. MA Thesis, Portland State University and Reed College.

Lopez, Paul A. and Christopher L. Moser
  1981   *Rods, Bundles and Stitches: A Century of Southern California Indian Basketry*. Riverside Museum, Riverside, California.

McLendon, Sally
  1998   Pomo Basket Weavers in the University of Pennsylvania Museum Collections. *Expedition Magazine* 40 (1):34–47.

Mason, Otis Tufton
  1901   Aboriginal American Basketry: Studies in a Textile Art Without Machinery. In *Report of the United States National Museum, Smithsonian Institution for the Year 1902*, pp. 174–548. Washington DC. (Reprinted: Dover Publications, Mineola, New York, 2012).

Merrill, Ruth E.
1923   Plants Used in Basketry by the California Indians. *University of California Publications in Archaeology and Ethnology* 20(13):215–242.

Moser, Christopher L.
1993   *Native American Basketry of Southern California.* Riverside Museum Press, Riverside, California.

O'Neale, Lila M.
1932   Yurok-Karok Basket Weavers. *University of California Publications in Archaeology and Ethnology* 32(1):1–184.

Phillips, George Harwood
2004   *Bringing Them Under Subjection: California's Tejon Indian Reservation and Beyond, 1852–1964.* University of Nebraska Press, Lincoln, Nebraska.

Porter, Frank W., III
1998   *The Art of Native American Basketry: A Living Legacy.* Greenwood Press, Westport, Connecticut.

Quintana, Gene and Julie Quintana
2010   *The Dat So La Lee Miniatures: An Extraordinary Collection from the Emporium Company, 1900–1921.* Fong and Fong Printers and Lithographers, Sacramento, California.

Reno Gazette-Journal
1918   Obituary for Sarah Jim Mayo. January 6, 1918.

Robinson, Bert
1954   *The Basket Weavers of Arizona.* University of New Mexico Press, Albuquerque, New Mexico.

Roseberry, Viola M.
1915   *Illustrated History of Indian Baskets and Plates Made by California Indians and Other Tribes.* Privately printed. Reprinted by Leo K. Brown, 1970, Reedley, California.

Schaff, Gregory
2006   *American Indian Baskets I: 1,500 Artist Biographies.* American Indian Art Series. Center for Indigenous Arts and Cultures (CIAC Press), Santa Fe, New Mexico.

Shanks, Ralph and Lisa Woo Shanks
2006   *Indian Baskets of Central California: Art, Culture, and History Native American Basketry from San Francisco Bay and Monterey Bay North.* Costaño Books, Novato, California and Miwok Archeological Association of Marin.

2010   *California Indian Baskets: San Diego to Santa Barbara and Beyond to the San Joaquin Valley, Mountains and Deserts (Indian Baskets of California and Oregon, Vol. II).* Costaño Books, Novato, California and Miwok Archeological Association of Marin.

2015   *Indian Baskets of Northern California and Oregon.* Costaño Books, Novato, California and Miwok Archeological Association of Marin.

Shukla, Pravina
2000   Pomo Indian Basket Weavers: Their Baskets and the Art Market. *Museum Anthropology* 24(1):80–84.

Slater, Eva
2000   *Panamint Shoshone Basketry: An American Art Form.* Sagebrush Press, Morongo Valley, California.

Stacey, Joseph
1975   Special Edition American Indian Basketry. *Arizona Highways Magazine* 51(7).

Thompson, Wayne A.
2007   *Ikons, Classics and Contemporary Masterpieces of Mineralogy.* Mineralogical Record Inc., Tucson, Arizona.

Turnbaugh, Sarah Peabody and William A. Turnbaugh
1986   *Indian Baskets.* Schiffer Publishing Incorporated, West Chester, Pennsylvania.

2013   *American Indian Baskets: Building and Caring for a Collection.* Schiffer Publishing, Atglen, Pennsylvania.

2014   Discovering American Indian Baskets. *Journal of Antiques and Collectibles*, July 2014, Sturbridge, Massachusetts.

Waldman, Cynthia A.
2014   *The Butterfly Basket.* Privately printed by the author.

Weigle, Marta and Barbara A. Babcock
1966   *The Great Southwest of the Fred Harvey Company and the Santa Fe Railway.* University of Arizona Press, Tucson, Arizona

Wikipedia
2017   *Lucy Telles.* Listing in Wikipedia, The Free Encyclopedia. Accessed at https://en.wikipedia.org/wiki/Lucy_Telles on July 12, 2017.

Williams, Lucy Fowler, William S. Wierzbowski and Robert W. Preucel
2005   *Native American Voices on Identity, Art, and Culture: Objects of Everlasting Esteem.* University of Pennsylvania Museum of Archaeology and Anthropology, Philadelphia, Pennsylvania.

Wolfe, Anne M. and Kevin Starr
2015   *Tahoe: A Visual History.* Nevada Museum of Art, Reno, Nevada.

Yosemite Basketmakers
2017   *Yosemite Basketmakers: Miwok Paiute Tradition.* Accessed at http://www.kstrom.net/isk/art/basket/yosemite.html on July 12, 2017.

Zigmond, Maurice L.
1978   Kawaiisu Basketry. *Journal of California and Great Basin Anthropology* 5(2);199–215.

Appendix 5
Basket VIPs

Bob and Carol Adams

Fred "Bob" Adams was born in Sanger, California in 1939. He had a very successful career at Sears department store, where he worked his way up from stock boy in the shoe department, to Sears store manager—retiring in 1989 after 29 years. Bob's passion was, however, collecting Indian baskets. He became interested in Indian artifacts in 1954 from when his family owned a hotel in the Squaw Valley-Dunlap area. Bob wanted to learn more about Indian culture, and he met two prominent weavers—Sally Edd and Mary Sampson. He gained their trust and learned about their art and culture; Sally Edd even taught Bob how to weave a basket.

He soon met Leon Taylor, and through their shared knowledge, experience, and interests, a lifetime friendship emerged. Later, he met Jerry Collings and Terry DeWald, who became close friends and who had a profound influence on his life as fellow collectors—and, in the case of Jerry—an accomplished weaver in his own right. Sadly, Bob tragically passed away in mid 2011, even as he was actively working with the authors of this book—supplying photographs, information, encouragement, and support.

Bob had lived in Tucson, Arizona, with his wife of 48 years, Carol Adams. He had two children, Todd and Stacy, and three grandchildren, Jenna, Brennan, and Connor, who also live in the Tucson area. Todd has inherited his father's passion for collecting Indian baskets and has become an equally avid collector.

Natalie Linn

Many years ago, Natalie Linn bought an Indian basket for five dollars and proudly placed it on a shelf; she soon learned that it was not made by Native Americans and returned the ill-purchased piece. From that point on, Natalie decided to learn all she could about Native American basketry—never to be fooled again. But the more she learned, the more she wanted to teach about baskets and ultimately the more she yearned to buy more baskets. Like eating potato chips, Natalie could not stop with just one basket; she now has been a collector/dealer for close to 40 years and is still filled with a passion for these beautiful botanical sculptures.

Natalie received a BA from University of California at Berkeley and a Master of Arts MALS from Reed College in Portland, Oregon. Her 1990 Master's degree thesis was entitled *The Artistry of American Indian Basketry*. She currently serves as a basketry consultant and appraiser for the PBS series *Antique Roadshow* and has frequently appeared as a consultant on the television program *History Detectives*. Natalie has served as an appraiser and consultant for many major auction houses and art museums and taught an art history class at Portland State University. She is now an important dealer in fine Native American basketry.

Marvin Cohodas

Marvin Cohodas earned a PhD in Art History from Columbia University in 1974. His first full-time teaching appointment was at Arizona State University, teaching the indigenous arts of North America. Exposure to Native American basket-weaving left him passionate about learning to make coiled basketry himself.

At the same time, research led him to an interest in the Washoe artist Louisa Keyser (Dat So La Lee) and to using the abundant documentation left by her patron, Amy Cohn. This led to initial research with the Keyser basketry collections. While engaging in this research, Marvin determined that several baskets exhibited as Keyser's work could not have been woven by her.

This stimulated an exhibit of Washoe coiled basketry in the Fine Arts Gallery at the University of British Columbia in 1979. A secondary result of his research and study allowed Marvin to learn the skills of coiled basketry, and for many years he wove willow baskets in his spare time.

Cohodas also studied the twined basketry of Elizabeth and Louise Hickox from northwestern California, and in 1997 published a book on these two weavers that also examines in detail the "basketry craze" of the late nineteenth and early twentieth centuries. Marvin has been teaching at the University of British Columbia since 1976. Marvin is also author of the highly popular 1979 book, *Degikup: Washoe Fancy Baskets 1895–1935*, which is often quoted in this book.

William and Sarah Peabody Turnbaugh

Bill and Sarah Turnbaugh's interest in Native American baskets developed independently before merging into a lifelong research, partnership, and marriage. Bill's abiding enthusiasm for Indian craft arts was sparked in the early 1960s: while volunteering at a Pennsylvania museum, he found exceptional San Carlos Apache baskets donated a half century earlier. His interest rekindled a decade later when, as an anthropology grad student at Harvard, Bill encountered a fetching undergraduate, Sarah Peabody, assisting with basketry conservation at the university's anthropology museum. Sarah's introduction to basketry had come as a child during summers at her family's New Hampshire farm surrounded by baskets made by family members decades earlier. (Grandmother Peabody's lessons failed: Sarah is left-handed with a low pain threshold!)

Sarah is directly related to George Peabody, late philanthropist who founded both the Harvard and Yale Peabody museums.

Bill and Sarah's shared regard for Indian basketry nurtured their relationship, culminating in their 1974 marriage, and subsequent joint research and writing projects. After completing his Harvard PhD, Bill taught archaeology at the University of Rhode Island (URI) for 32 years. He continues research as professor emeritus. Sarah received her MS in textiles from URI, writing her thesis on Anasazi yucca ring baskets. She is a longtime curator of a small Rhode Island museum and adjunct assistant professor at URI.

Bill and Sarah frequently crisscross the United States by auto-mobile to research their books. Their first book, *Indian Baskets* (1986), was one of the few comprehensive surveys of the topic since Otis Tufton Mason's. Other co-authored basketry titles include *Basket Tales of the Grandmothers* (1999), *American Indian Baskets* (2013), and *Indian Basketry of the Northeastern Woodlands* (2014). They also co-wrote the popular *Indian Jewelry of the American Southwest* (1988) and other works.

Craig Bates

Ever since he was a five-year-old child, Craig Bates has continued to develop a strong interest in Indian history and ethnography, searching for evidence of Indian culture, artifacts, and history in his Pleasanton and Hayward, California, neighborhoods. He continued that interest through adulthood, where ethnography became his professional vocation. He wove his first basket at 18 years of age while in high school. Prior to his stroke in 2002, he had woven over 500 baskets and other Indian regalia. Craig was Curator of Ethnography at Yosemite National Park for over 30 years. He acquired most of his knowledge in traditional weaving from many elders throughout California.

Craig studied collections across the United States and Europe and authored more than 120 articles and books on Native culture. He has been an instructor for local tribal dances and was a development consultant for the National Museum of the American Indian, Washington, DC.

His son Carson, a Northern Miwok, shares his interest in Miwok culture and is actively making regalia and demonstrating other Native skills.

Many of Craig's creations are exhibited in museums and in private collections and are also in use by Natives. Craig is the recipient of numerous awards for his work on Indian ethnography during his tenure at Yosemite National Park. His book, *Tradition and Innovation: A Basket History of the Indians of the Yosemite-Mono Lake Area*, is widely used as a reference book on Indian basketry.

Todd Adams

Keeping the basket avocation in the family, Todd asks: "Where did my interest in Native American basketry come from? It could have been caused by location, beginning in the small town of Sanger, California in the shadows of the Sierra Nevada Mountains where the Yokuts people live. Or it could have been the cradleboard woven for me by Sally Edd before I was born, that I still own. But the truth is it came from my dad, Bob Adams."

Todd spent many years traveling with his father visiting the last of the Yokuts weavers and learning first-hand about their basketweaving ways. His father left him with a passion for baskets and the people who made them, and hooked him on the thrill of chasing down old collections. In the future, he hopes to keep hunting for the forgotten and lost collections to add to his own collection and to share with other collectors.

Gene Quintana

Gene Quintana, a native of Sacramento, California, has been a collector of American Indian baskets since 1980. He became interested in art at an early age, and fortunately was able to enjoy collecting works of art as a hobby even as he was building an automotive parts distributorship in 1963. He then discovered that he had acquired a very serious interest and love of Native American Indian art, particularly woven basketry from California and western Nevada.

After selling his business in 1993, he was able to devote more time to collecting, buying, and selling Native American baskets, and he acquired an extensive collection of antique California and Nevada baskets. Because of his growing expertise, he assisted with basket appraisals for individuals and museums, and he soon became known as the "Basket Man."

Gene currently advertises "Baskets for Sale" and "Baskets Wanted" on the Internet, displaying an incredibly diverse collection of baskets and other Western memorabilia. Gene has participated in the acquiring, exhibition of, and donation of several major and important collections, such as the display of Dat So La Lee baskets for the North Tahoe Historical Society at the Gatekeeper's Museum in Tahoe City, California.

In addition, he has contributed to displays in Yosemite National Park (1982–1995); "California Indian Basketry," Scottsdale Center for the Arts (1998); "Art of the Southwest," Crocker Art Museum, Sacramento, California (2006); "Fine Art of California Indian Basketry," Autry National Center, Los Angeles (2007), "Yosemite: Art of an American Icon."

Gene Quintana currently lives with his family in Carmichael, a suburb of Sacramento, but spends much of his time at his home in Lake Tahoe, California.

Terry DeWald

Terry DeWald has been a prominent lecturer, appraiser, and author in *American Indian Art* for more than 35 years and is the author of the book *The Papago Indians and Their Basketry*. He was exposed to this art form at an early age—his father was a journalist and photographer who covered the Southwest for *Time* and *Life* magazines and other national publications; and his mother's affiliation with and being a Founder of the docent guild at The Heard Museum. Terry earned degrees from the University of Arizona in history of the American West, anthropology, and Native American studies. After college he performed appraisal work for many museums including the Philbrook, the Heard Museum, the Autry/Southwest Museum, and the Arizona State Museum; and he has helped various tribes market their baskets.

Terry has also given numerous presentations including being a featured speaker at the Smithsonian and the National Park Service. He is a member of ATADA (Antique Tribal Art Dealer's Association) and is an advisor to many auction companies such as Bonham and Butterfield and Sotheby's.

As Terry puts it, "as one travels the globe from institution to institution, one witnesses the best ceramics, textiles, paintings, sculpture, jewelry...but arguably the finest universal basketry was produced here in the West by Native American weavers from the 1880s to the 1930s. These pieces stand as icons from a lifestyle that has passed."

Terry continues to find great pleasure in lecturing about, appraising, collecting, and dealing in these treasures. He strongly encourages the few remaining contemporary weavers to continue this tradition today.

Ralph Shanks and Lisa Woo Shanks

Ralph Shanks, a Western Abenaki, began collecting Native American baskets as a child, and this led him to his career as an anthropologist, with a primary interest focused on basketry of California. He has written highly acclaimed books on basketry, particularly a three-volume series *Indian Baskets of California and Oregon*.

He is currently a Research Associate at the University of California at Davis, where he teaches classes on analysis of Native American basketry, not only of California and Oregon but of the United States. He serves on graduate degree committees and has lectured widely both in the U.S. and Europe on his field of expertise. He is President of the Miwok Archeological Preserve of Marin County, California (MAPOM). As a result of his research and travels, he has worked extensively with Native American basketweavers and counts many as his personal friends.

Ralph's family has deep ties in both Oregon and California— his family migrated to the Willamette Valley in northern Oregon in the 1840s and another branch of the family arrived in California about the same time. He is a graduate of UC Berkeley and San Francisco State University.

Ralph's wife, Lisa Woo Shanks, a graduate of Humboldt State University, is also involved with basketry; she is the editor of Ralph's three volume series. Lisa is an Area Research Conservationist with the USDA Natural Resource Conservation Service.

John Kania

Growing up in Minnesota, John Kania became close to several Native American families and was invited to take part in Ojibwe and Winnebago activities. His interest in Native American culture grew to include items of material culture and various traditional crafts. Fresh out of the University of Minnesota with a degree in anthropology, John worked with urban teenage Native Americans in Minnesota and Canada, teaching them an awareness of their artistic heritage and instructing them in hands-on craft revival. Kania began studying at various museums and was especially fortunate to attend one of the few American Indian Basketry courses in the country at the time. He was initially employed in the Los Angeles area by a gallery where he was responsible for purchasing Native American baskets, and as a result he was introduced to a number of collectors, dealers, and researchers including Eva Slater, Natalie Linn, Bob Adams, and Craig Bates.

In August 1979, John participated in Don Bennett's Native American art show in Santa Fe, where he met Joe Ferrin, who later became his partner in the Kania-Ferrin Gallery, allowing John to be able to devote more time to travel and research.

Receiving encouragement from a number of people, he was invited to present at the Great Basin Anthropological Conference (GBAC) in 2004, after which he formally published two important articles on Chemehuevi basketry. Recently he presented a follow-up paper at the GBAC on the weavers of Victorville, California. Currently, John divides his time finishing a book on basketry identification for western North America and continues research on Chemehuevi/Paiute coiled basketry.

Sandra Horn

Sandra Horn's love of baskets was truly a love for art and for the recognition of great women in history; her passion for North American aboriginal baskets went back for over 40 years. Born and raised in Bakersfield, California, a region once occupied by the Yokuts tribe, she developed an early affinity for the finest of North American Native baskets.

Sandra achieved three academic certifications including a BA in Political Science, Secondary Teaching Credential in History and Social Studies, and a Masters in Special Education. She had worked with some of the most important private collections and museums in North America—from Stanford University, Favell Museum, Autry, and Southwest—as well as with Butterfields and Sotheby's auction houses. She had identified, appraised, and cataloged dozens of the most significant private collections in the United States.

Over the years she saw and dealt with thousands of baskets and had become well versed in tribal affiliation, origin, style, technique, and individual weavers and was known as a highly knowledgeable and regarded Indian arts dealer. Sandra passed away after Indian Market in 2013, but her passion lives on through her son, Ari Maslow, who has taken over Sandra's basket business.

Ari Maslow

Ari M. Maslow, son of renowned basket expert Sandra Horn, grew up surrounded by American Indian art. From an early age, Ari developed a great affinity for the Native American culture and art forms, and in particular basketry. Having toured museum archives, private collections, and American Indian art shows for over three decades, Ari grew in his own right to become an expert in California basketry.

Today, Ari carries the torch as a second-generation American Indian art advisor and dealer, introducing new generations to the art forms, while providing services to seasoned collectors and institutional art development.

Based in Mill Valley, California, Ari is steadfast in his commitment to environmental, cultural, and educational stewardship.

Jerold Collings

Fascination with western American Indians and their cultures began quite early in Jerry Collings' life. Because of a childhood health condition, he moved to a remote area on the Colorado River in the Mojave Desert. The nearest town—Parker, Arizona—had been built on a section of land surrounded by an Indian reservation, the Colorado River Indian Tribes. While he believed he never had seen a "real live Indian" prior to this time, he knew at once that he wanted to learn all that he could about these new acquaintances.

He took advantage of numerous opportunities to visit their homes—some of traditional construction—and others that were without electricity and modern conveniences. He was always welcome and the response to his endless questions was met politely and with patience. Jerry had the great fortune to meet and befriend several Chemehuevi basketweavers including Kate Fisher, Maggie Painter, and Bessie Waco. These elderly ladies treated him more like a favored grandson than a pesky, probing outsider. Jerry's early fascination turned into an obsession.

Jerry's education at California State University, Long Beach was followed with work as Assistant Director, and eventually, Museum Director with the Arizona State Park Service; and Project Director at the Gila River Indian Community. He has served on the Editorial Advisory Board of *American Indian Art Magazine* from 1975 to present, and has several publications about Indian basketry. Jerry lives on his ranch in New Mexico and continues to weave his own baskets.

Christopher L. Moser

When Christopher Moser came to Riverside, California in 1979, with an anthropology and archaeology background, this new curator of anthropology had little knowledge of Indian baskets—the core collection that had led to the museum's founding in 1924. However, the museum's collection of baskets from California had a dramatic impact on his future. During his nearly 24 years at the museum, he became a nationally known expert in California Indian baskets.

Chris received a Bachelors degree in Mesoamerican Anthropology from University of the Americas in Mexico City, and Masters and Doctoral degrees in Anthropology and Archaeology from UCLA. His knowledge of California basketry increased, according to Justin Farmer, during periodic discussions of basketweaving, where experts would discuss 50 to 100 baskets a session: materials used, design, provenance, and the weaver, if known. "We did this for months on end and Chris got more and more interested," according to Justin.

He wrote three books on Native American basketry, which became (for the basketweaving and collecting community) best sellers: these books detailed basketmaking in southern, central, and northern California.

His passion for keeping detailed records and his expertise in photography—an example of which is seen in this book— where the Riverside Museum exhibited both a photograph of Ramona Balenzuela as well as the basket she is holding in the photograph.

Chris turned detective at one point in his career after he discovered that someone had stolen 14 valuable baskets in the collection, replacing them with cheap ones. He published a "rogues' gallery" of photos and recovered two that were stolen.

Chris passed away January 20, 2003.

The Huntington Library, San Marino, California.

Grace Nicholson

Grace Nicholson was born in Philadelphia in December 1877 and moved to California in 1901 (the same year Fred Harvey passed away). She started purchasing Native American baskets and other art by the next year, for her shop and studio in Las Robles, California. She had a habit of paying high prices for specific pieces, thus acquiring the finest objects. She also paid weavers to produce unique forms and designs, supported Indian families, and was influential in encouraging other people to participate in tribal welfare. Grace passed away in 1948; prior to her death, her studio in Pasadena was deeded to the Pasadena Art Institute.

Grace spent much time travelling between various tribal areas—particularly those in central and northern California— and she created a photographic journal of many of her visits. Her photographic collection was donated to the Huntington Library in 1968. In addition, another collection of her works was donated by Florence Rand Lang to the Montclair Art Museum in New Jersey.

Several of her photographs appear in this book. Her extensive notes and correspondence continue to provide insight on tribal languages, customs, and art forms.

In recognition of her expertise, Grace was elected to the American Anthropological Association in 1904, for her contributions to the understanding of Native American cultures.

The Grace Nicholson building in Pasadena was renamed the Pacific Asia Museum, reflecting Grace's new focus on Asian arts and crafts. Its architecture reflects that which she saw in China during her visits.

Her influence on basketweaving carries on through her documents, correspondence, and photographs. She was a major contributor to the Florescence period.

Fred Harvey

Frederick Harvey was born in London in 1835, immigrated to the United States in 1850, and died in 1901. In his 51 years in the United States, he established himself as a restaurateur and leading advocate of tourism, primarily in the American Southwest. His Harvey House tourist stops took advantage of the expansion of the rail system and his involvement with railway companies. He recognized the poor quality of the existing meal and lodging services, and in 1876 he commenced a relationship with AT&SF Railroad leading to the first Harvey House Restaurant in Topeka, Kansas. This led to the opening of numerous Harvey Houses; by 1901 there were 47.

An avid collector and travelled businessman, he promoted local Native American artisans, where they purchased Native American arts and influenced how artists created and marketed their work. This time period is the period of the Florescence in basketweaving in which the production of utilitarian baskets was put aside and the focus became the creation of the masterpiece baskets that are illustrated in this book.

In 1997, the Heard Museum featured his role in influencing Southwest art. Timothy Luke at Virginia Polytechnic Institute stated "Hand-woven textiles once worn as clothing became Navajo blankets; household pottery was made smaller, lighter, more refined; massive silver jewelry once used to display wealth became more delicate, less heavy, more ornate; baskets were made more decoratively and much smaller—all of these changes responded to what tourists fancied, could carry, would put on their fireplace mantels back home."

"Fred Harvey has done more for all the Indian tribes in the Southwest than thousands of people who have written books, people in Congress, humanitarian committees, etc., because we have created a market for their goods." (from *The Great Southwest of the Fred Harvey Company and the Santa Fe Railway.* Weigle and Babcock, 1996: 67).

Brian Bibby

Brian Bibby is an independent scholar who has worked for over twenty-five years with elders of many of California's Native communities on song, dance, language, and artistic traditions. He has taught at a number of institutions and has served as a consultant and guest curator for cultural and folk art programs, including "The Fine Art of California Indian Basketweaving" at the Crocker Art Museum (1996). More recently, Brian curated the "Precious Cargo: Childbirth and Cradle Baskets in California Indian Culture" exhibition that originated at Novato's Marin Museum of the American Indian (2004) and the "American Masterpieces: Artistic Legacy of California Indian Basketry" exhibition at The California Museum (2009–2010). Brian has also published several scholarly works such as *Precious Cargo: Childbirth and Cradle Baskets in California Indian Culture* (2004) and co-authored many others such as *Deeper Than Gold: Indian Life in the Sierra Foothills* with Dugan Aguilar (2005).

His book (Bibby 2012) *Essential Art: Native Basketry from the California Indian Heritage Center* is "must" reading for anyone interested in Native American basketry. It contains highly important information on weaving materials, baskets, tribes, weavers, and culture.

Justin Farmer

Justin Farmer's maternal grandmother was unfortunately brought up to dislike Indians; as an example, even a piece of Indian art like a basket was unwelcome in her house. Hence, when Justin started collecting baskets in his middle age, this conflict alienated Justin from his family. But his activity brought him into contact with a cousin—Christina Beresford Osuna—on the Santa Ysabel Reservation. In the early 1970s, Christina was one of only three known California Indian weavers still able to make baskets in the traditional way. Under her tutelage, Justin learned much of Christina's basketry knowledge.

Over the next three decades, Justin conducted many classes, lectures, and demonstrations on southern California Indian basketry. He is quite religious in his adherence to the traditional methods and materials: he gathers his own materials, prepares them with traditional methods, and uses them in his traditional weaving techniques.

Justin eventually amassed a large collection of 215 Mission baskets and 1,000 pieces of primarily southern California artifacts, which he sold in 2002 to the Pechanga Band of Mission Indians, near Temecula. With proceeds from that sale Justin established The Justin Farmer Foundation, which offers grants to Indian students doing research on local Indian arts, artifacts, culture, or history.

In 2004, Justin authored and his foundation published *Southern California Luiseño Indian Baskets*, a book on the study of 76 Luiseño baskets in the Riverside Museum Collection. He has also authored and coauthored a number of other treatises on Indian basketry, religion, and deer hunting. Justin has served on the Board of Trustees of the Southwest Museum of the American Indian, The Autry Center, and is a member of or a consultant for virtually every museum with Indian collections in southern California.

Otis Tufton Mason

Otis Tufton Mason was born in Maine in 1838, and died in Washington, DC in 1908, just as the era of basketweaving known as the Florescence was beginning in California. In 1901, he published his two-volume work, *Indian Basketry*, which remains in print to this day (titled *American Indian Basketry*)—an exhaustive text on Native American basketweaving.

He graduated from Columbian College (now George Washington University) in 1861, and remained as principal of the college's preparatory school for 23 years. In 1872, he joined the Smithsonian Institution (then as the United States National Museum), working as a collaborator in ethnology.

Mason's interests began with the culture-history of the Eastern Mediterranean, but he abandoned his Oriental studies to focus on the peoples of America—a crucial event in his life. He became curator of the Department of Ethnology in the National Museum; for the next 25 years he curated, studied, and cataloged the ever-growing collections now coming to the Museum. His first years were devoted to the classification of this material, in setting forth the scope of ethnology, and in publishing the results of his studies. In 1879 he was one of the founders of the Anthropological Society of Washington. He was anthropological editor of the *American Naturalist* and the *Standard Dictionary*, and was a member of the United States Board on Geographic Names for 18 years.

Dr. Mason believed in stepwise evolution of cultures and that technology was a marker of a culture's stage of development. New technology (such as metals to replace plant material as the structural basis for utilitarian baskets) and the coming of the railroad and tourists to places not previously visited, resulted in the loss of much of the highest level talent of basketweaving as these influences changed the landscape of basketweaving. Mason's influence has lived on long after the Florescence vanished.

The Authors

Wayne Thompson

Considered an expert field collector for museum-quality minerals and also a recognized collector of Native American pottery, it is no surprise that Wayne Thompson is now receiving recognition for his work on the art of Native American basketry, circa 1900 to 1940. When his late wife Laura was in the hospital undergoing cancer treatments, Wayne turned his attention to masterpiece baskets made by Native Californians, which has resulted in the publication of this book that complements his earlier work on fine mineral specimens. (Pictured above, daughter Stevia, Wayne, wife Malee)

Gene Meieran

Known for his career in materials science and his passion for collecting mineral and crystal specimens, it did not take much to turn Gene's interest to collecting Native American pottery because of his wife's work as a ceramic artist. These interests coincided with those of Wayne and Laura Thompson, and Gene's computer expertise in dealing with images and his systematic organization skills complemented Wayne's in-depth knowledge of Native American basketry, leading to their collaboration on authoring this book.

Appendix 6
Museums and Cultural Centers Exhibiting Native American Baskets

Agua Caliente Cultural Museum
Palm Springs, CA
www.accmuseum.org

Art Institute of Chicago
Chicago, IL
www.artic.edu

Autry Museum of the American West
Los Angeles, CA
www.theautry.org

Baltimore Museum of Art
Baltimore, MD
www.artbma.org

Bowers Museum
Santa Ana, CA
www.bowers.org

Brooklyn Museum
Brooklyn, NY
www.brooklynmuseum.org

California Academy of Sciences
San Francisco, CA
www.calacademy.org

California State Parks
Sacramento, CA
www.parks.ca.gov

Carnegie Museums of Pittsburgh
Pittsburgh, PA
www.carnegiemuseums.org

de Young Museum
San Francisco, CA
www.deyoung.famsf.org

Douglas County Historical Society
Gardnerville, NV
www.historicnv.org

Emigrant Trail Museum
Truckee, CA
www.parks.ca.gov/?page_id=503

Fenimore Art Museum
Cooperstown, NY
www.fenimoreartmuseum.org

The Field Museum of Natural History
Chicago, IL
www.fieldmuseum.org

Gatekeeper's Museum
Tahoe City, CA
www.northtahoemuseums.org

Grace Hudson Museum
Ukiah, CA
www.gracehudsonmuseum.org

The Hamilton Museum
Anza, CA
www.hamiltonmuseum.org

Heard Museum
Phoenix, AZ
www.heard.org

Maidu Museum & Historical Site
Roseville, CA
www.roseville.ca.us/indianmuseum

Malki Museum
Banning, CA
www.malkimuseum.org

Museum of Indian Arts & Culture
Santa Fe, NM
www.indianartsandculture.org

Museum of Ventura County
Ventura, CA
www.venturamuseum.org

National Museum of the
American Indian
Washington, DC
www.americanindian.si.edu

Natural History Museum,
Los Angeles County
Los Angeles, CA
www.nhm.org

Nevada Historical Society
Reno, NV
www.nvhistoricalsociety.org

Nevada State Museum
Carson City, NV
www.carsonnvmuseum.org

Oakland Museum of California
Oakland, CA
www.museumca.org

Palm Springs Art Museum
Palm Springs, CA
www.psmuseum.org

Yale Peabody Museum
of Natural History
New Haven, CT
www.peabody.yale.edu

Penn Museum
Philadelphia, PA
www.penn.museum.org

Philbrook Museum of Art
Tulsa, OK
www.philbrook.org

Phoebe A. Hearst Museum
of Anthropology
Berkeley, CA
www.hearstmuseum.berkeley.edu

Pomona College Museum of Art
Claremont, CA
www.pomona.edu/museum

Portland Art Museum
Portland, OR
www.portlandartmuseum.org

Ramona Pioneer Historical Society/
Guy B. Woodward Museum
Ramona, CA
www.facebook.com/
GuyBWoodwardMuseum

Riverside Metropolitan Museum
Riverside, CA
www.riversideca.gov/museum

Rogers Historical Museum
Rogers, AR
www.rogershistoricalmuseum.org

Sanger Depot Museum
Sanger, CA
www.sangerdepotmuseum.com

Smithsonian Museum
Washington, DC
www.si.edu

Table Mountain Yokuts
Rancheria, CA
en.wikipedia.org/wiki/Table_
Mountain_Rancheria

Turtle Bay Exploration Park
Redding, CA
www.turtlebay.org

Yosemite Museum
Yosemite Valley, CA
www.nps.gov/yose

Appendix 7
Contributors to the Book

Patty Tuck
Agua Caliente Cultural Center

Dawn Wellman
Agua Caliente Cultural Museum

Jon Fletcher
Agua Caliente Cultural Museum

Lisa Deitz
Anthropology Museum at
University of California, Davis

Robert Bettinger
Anthropology Museum at
University of California, Davis

Lynn Mason
Antiques Roadshow

Marilyn Kim
Autry Museum of the American West

Kim Walters
Autry Museum of the American West

James Eason
Bancroft Library,
University of California, Berkeley

Lorna Kirwan
Bancroft Library,
University of California, Berkeley

Jim Hass
Bonhams and Butterfields

Julie Lee
Bowers Museum

Peter Keller
Bowers Museum

Ruth Janson
Brooklyn Museum

Susan Zeller
Brooklyn Museum

Ileana D. Maestas
California Indian Heritage Center

Chad Dressler
California State Parks

Natalie Davenport
California State Parks

Katie Metraux
California State Parks archives

George Thompson
California State University, Chico

Deborah Harding
Carnegie Museum of Natural History,
Pittsburgh

Sandy Olsen
Carnegie Museum of Natural History,
Pittsburgh

Ellen Martin
Carson Valley Museum,
Douglas County, Nevada

Dace Taub
Doheny Memorial Library,
University of Southern California

Donald Ellis
Donald Ellis Gallery

Jon Klusmire
Eastern California Museum

Roberta Harlan
Eastern California Museum

Linda Cano
Fresno Art Museum

Donnice Finnemore
Gatekeeper's Museum,
North Lake Tahoe Historical Society

Marguerite Sprague
Gatekeeper's Museum,
North Lake Tahoe Historical Society

Sarah Schaefer
Gatekeeper's Museum,
North Lake Tahoe Historical Society

Marvin Shenck
Grace Hudson Museum

Sherrie Smith-Ferri
Grace Hudson Museum

Diana Pardue
Heard Museum

Delia E. Sullivan
Heritage Auctions

Tommie Rodgers
Lauren Rogers Museum

Patricia Kurtz*
Maidu Museum & Historic Site

Rick Adams
Maidu Museum & Historic Site

Nathalie Colin
Malki Museum

Mark Sublette
Medicine Man Gallery

Kent Stoddard
Mono County Historical Society

Gina Rappaport
National Anthropological Archives,
Smithsonian Institution

Lou Sancari*
National Museum of the American
Indian,
Smithsonian Institution

Mary Ahenakew
National Museum of the American
Indian,
Smithsonian Institution

Patricia L. Nietfeld
National Museum of the American
Indian,
Smithsonian Institution

KT Hajeian
Natural History Museum,
Los Angeles County

Margaret Ann Hardin
Natural History Museum,
Los Angeles County

Lee Brumbaugh
Nevada Historical Society

Sheryln L. Hayes-Zorn
Nevada Historical Society

Sue Ann Monteleone
Nevada State Museum

Eugene Hattori
Nevada State Museum

Christina Ely
New York State Historical Association

John Hart
New York State Historical Association

Kathy Clewell
Palm Springs Art Museum

Darcy Marlow
Philbrook Museum of Art

Kathleen Howe
Pomona College Museum of Art

Steve Comba
Pomona College Museum of Art

Brenda Focht
Riverside Metropolitan Museum

Carol Meyers
San Diego Historical Society

Christine Travers
San Diego Historical Society

Bob Bosserman*
Sanger Depot Museum

Zoe Taubman
Sotheby's

Jerice Barrios
The Field Museum of Natural History

Hidonee Spoonhunter
The Fowler Museum at
University of California, Los Angeles

Erin Chase
The Huntington Library

Suzanne Oatey
The Huntington Library

Julia Pennington
Turtle Bay Exploration Park

Marvin Cohodas
University of British Columbia

Kim Roberts
University of Nevada Research Services

Donnelyn Curtis
University of Nevada, Reno

Briony Jones
University of New Mexico Press

Amy Ellsworth
University of Pennsylvania Museum
of Anthropology

Maureen Goldsmith
University of Pennsylvania Museum
of Anthropology

Rachelle Balinas Smith
University of Southern California
Library

Roger Colten
Yale Peabody Museum of Natural
History

Barbara L. Beroza
Yosemite National Park

Mary Gentry
Yosemite National Park

Alan and Bronnie Blaugrund
Collector

Alex Schwed
Collector

Bob* and Carol Adams
Collector

Bob Seng
Collector

Charles and Valerie Diker
Collector

David Salk
Collector

E. J. and Mimi Nusrala
Collector

Eddie* and Nadine Basha
Collector

Greg and Cathy Sarena
Collector

Janis and Dennis Lyon
Collector

Jeff Greenstein
Collector

Jim Merbs
Collector

Ken and Judy Siebel
Collector

Lew Meekins
Collector

Marc and Pam Rudick
Collector

Ned Smith
Collector

Ralph Shanks and Lisa Woo Shanks
Collector

Robert and Bunny Jochim
Collector

Robert and Claire Hardiman
Collector

Steve Nelson
Collector

Stevia Thompson
Collector

Syd Bottomley
Collector

Todd Adams
Collector

Ari Maslow
Dealer

Gene Quintana
Dealer

Jerry and Heidi Collings
Dealer

John Kania
Dealer

Natalie Linn
Dealer

Sandra Horn*
Dealer

Terry DeWald
Dealer

Arvin Carlson
Photographer

David Bozsik
Photographer

Jeff Scovil
Photographer

Jim Yoakum
Photographer

Lucile Day
Photographer

Alan D. Blaver, Jr.
Nellie Jim Charlie's great grandson

Chad and Tonia Dressler
Acquaintance

Frederick Dressler
Acquaintance

Helen Coates
Acquaintance

Jesse Durant
Nellie Charlie's granddaughter

John Hill
Mary Smith Hill's grandson

Louie G. Andrews
Relative

Milton Dressler
Acquaintance

Jerry Andrews
Minnie Mike's grandson /
Carrie Bethel's nephew

deceased

Special Acknowledgments

During the ten plus years of writing this book, many people and institutions were awesomely generous in giving us permission to use their vintage photographs of Native American weavers and their masterpiece baskets to illustrate this Age of Florescence in basketweaving. We have listed in Appendix 7 all of these donors, without whom this book would not be possible.

There were a few people, however, whose contributions to this book were so outstanding that they deserve special mention. In addition to providing us with pictures, these generous individuals also introduced us to other sources, offered valuable advice on various sections of the book, enlisted respected colleagues to help us, provided critical review of much of the text, helped correct factual errors, and otherwise created a community that greatly enhanced the quality of both the text and images found throughout the book.

Basket dealers Natalie Linn, Gene Quintana, John Kania, and Terry DeWald generously allowed us to photograph many wonderful baskets and also gave us access of their original photographs. Jeff Scovil travelled extensively to museums to photograph baskets of which there were no existing high quality photographs.

Several museums went out of their way to give us access to important pictures: in particular, the Autry Museum, the Nevada State Museum, and the Nevada Historical Society. The Palm Springs Art Museum, as well as the Agua Caliente Cultural Museum, and the Yosemite Museum, not only provided a large quantity of basket images, but allowed us to photograph their baskets for which high-resolution color photographs were not available.

Other institutions that provided us with significant help were the Phoebe Hearst Museum of Anthropology, the University of Pennsylvania Museum of Anthropology, the University of California Bancroft Library, and the Huntington Library that not only gave us the pictures we requested but offered us alternative photographs of which we were not aware. California

Parks were enormously cooperative, through the various California museums, particularly the Gatekeeper's Museum in North Lake Tahoe and the Donner Park Museum in Truckee.

Several basket collectors allowed us access to their private collections; while some requested privacy, others were quite generous in allowing us to use their names: Ken and Judy Siebel, Todd Adams, Greg Sarena, Charles Diker, and Alex Schwed let us use images of their baskets and even photograph baskets from their collections which were previously unpublished. Alex and Todd were particularly helpful in terms of providing us basket images, vintage photographs, and very important information about details of weavers, which we used extensively throughout the book. In addition, Todd Adams contributed to the funding of the book.

Several Indian tribes participated above and beyond the call of duty including Agua Caliente; Pat Kurtz helped us with the Maidu; Sherri Smith-Ferri who not only helped with images, but reviewed parts of the book, represented the Grace Hudson Museum and the Pomos; and Barbara Beroza from the Yosemite Museum, who helped enormously particularly with the great Mono Lake Paiute baskets.

Other basket experts who reviewed sections of the book and suggested invaluable corrections and edits, making enormous contributions to book quality. These include William and Sarah Turnbaugh, Craig Bates, Sheila Deeg, Ralph Shanks, Marvin Cohodas, and Gene Hattori. Without these folks' contributions, there would not be such a book.

High praise goes to our team—Alan Garfinkel, editor; Lorna Johnson, project manager; Debi Young, Sunbelt Publication's production manager; and Kathleen Wise, our book designer— experts in their fields who have spent countless hours in making this book an exceptional and definitive work as befitting the weavers and baskets featured within.

Wayne Thompson
Gene Meieran

Index

Lucinda Hancock | Yokuts | 1929